HIGHWIRE

HIGHWIRE

From the Backroads to the Beltway—

John Brummett

The Education of Bill Clinton

HYPERION

New York

To Shalah
and to the
memory of
J. T.
Brummett

Library of Congress Cataloging-in-Publication Data

Brummett, John.
    Highwire : from the backwoods to the beltway—the education of
Bill Clinton / by John Brummett.
        p.   cm.
    ISBN 0-7868-8123-2
    1. Clinton, Bill, 1946–   . 2. United States—Politics and
government—1993   I. Title.
    E886.B78   1994
    973.929'092—dc20   94-16089
                                                       CIP

FIRST PAPERBACK EDITION

10 9 8 7 6 5 4 3 2

Acknowledgments

Jimmy Breslin, a legend in journalism, invited me to be his house guest during the New York primary in the spring of 1992. He insisted that Bill Clinton would be the next president of the United States and that I, having spent nearly fifteen years chronicling Clinton's career, should not leave New York City without meeting a literary agent. I thank him for his hospitality, insight, encouragement, and friendship.

President Clinton found time for me twice during the first fifteen months of his presidency, for which I am deeply grateful.

Thomas F. (Mack) McLarty III, the former White House chief of staff, cooperated with me in this project. Numerous other administration sources also were helpful at times, among them Bruce Lindsey, George Stephanopoulos, James Carville, Paul Begala, Mark Gearan, Bill Burton of McLarty's staff, Greg Simon of Vice President Al Gore's staff, and Skip Rutherford, a Little Rock political operative and a consultant to the Democratic National Committee. The United States senators from Arkansas, Dale Bumpers and David Pryor, both Democrats, provided valuable insights. Betsey Wright, the longtime chief of staff to Clinton when he was governor of Arkansas, and Al From, the president of the Democratic Leadership Council, lent their worthy perspectives. All of those sources are quoted directly except on those occasions when they, along with scores of others, provided views and information that I accepted and assimilated on a background basis. I am indebted to all of them for their time and expertise.

David Black proved to be not only an agent but also an advocate, adviser, and friend. He told me I was fortunate to have Pat Mulcahy as my editor, and he was right. I thank them both.

During my year in Washington I continued to write columns for two Arkansas newspapers: the *Arkansas Democrat-Gazette,* a daily, and the *Arkansas Times,* a weekly. I thank the editors of both for their encouragement and patience.

William Green, my good friend from Little Rock, and a freelance journalist, lent a hand to make the move to Washington much smoother than it would have been otherwise. I am forever grateful.

Numerous seasoned Washington journalists were helpful, and quite pleasant, I must say.

Contents

Author's Note

This book chronicles the first seventeen months of Bill Clinton's presidency. Its focus is the first year, 1993, but final reporting and revisions came in June 1994.

The book's hardcover publication date was November 8, 1994. That happened to be the very date Republicans swept the mid-term elections to take control of the U. S. Senate and the U. S. House of Representatives. Newt Gingrich became Speaker of the House and Clinton was left to grapple yet again with the rejection he fears most, and struggle yet again to find himself as a man and a president.

While the book only indicates that Clinton's health care reform plan would die an ugly death, rather than report that it in fact happened, and while it only quotes the president's frustration regarding Haiti, rather than report his later action there, the story remains vibrant: Who is this man of great talent and glaring weakness and where might those two works-in-progress—his character and his presidency—take him and the country in 1996 and maybe beyond?

Clinton's affinity for conciliation carries new significance in the context of his typical attempt to do two things at once: distinguish himself from the Gingrich Republicans while finding a way to work with them lest he crash head-first into a countervailing public mood and lose his beloved political viability. His lamentation in the Epilogue about the decline of civil discourse in the country, labeled by some as whining, could not have foreseen the domestic terrorism in April 1995 in Oklahoma City and the ensuing furor about hate and talk radio. But those events took his measure as a man, a leader, and a president, and his views bear reading in light of them.

Through it all, even still, there are the presidential parallels with Clinton's career in Arkansas.

His time in Arkansas was marked by devastating early voter rejection and a stirring comeback. It was beset by the concerns of associates and even friends who found his finessing of truth and reliance on political expediency to be exasperating, though they admired and often adored him.

Clinton won again and again in Arkansas on the basis of reasonable progress, compelling personality, tireless campaigning, a savvy blend of modernism and populism, and the relative weakness or political ineptness of his Republican opponents.

Could that be the very prescription for him in 1996? In America today, there is no more relevant question.

HIGHWIRE

INTRODUCTION

A Real-Life

Psychodrama

Bill Clinton burst into cackling laughter one day in 1982 as he related what a friend had told him a day or two before: "Bill, there's just something about you that pisses people off."

Clinton found it funny. I thought it an utterly obvious political observation. He reacted with mostly egoistic self-entertainment, but it seemed that a bit of introspection would have been appropriate as well.

But then this was the fellow of whom the acerbic U.S. Senator Dale Bumpers of Arkansas once said, "He's the only guy I know who'll walk up to you and say, 'Hi. How am I doin'?' " This was the man who in 1988 drank the water from the glass that other leading Democrats in Arkansas had passed along the head table toward Lloyd Bentsen, who was speaking in Hot Springs, Arkansas, as the Democratic nominee for vice president. Bentsen needed to clear his throat, as everyone in the convention center except Clinton had sensed. Then there was the time Clinton took his family to Disney World. As he stood in line, he spotted a family whose attire promoted the University of Arkansas Razorbacks, his favorite team. Presuming the family members were from Arkansas, as they were, he went back to engage in the appropriate gubernatorial behavior and speak to them. He departed by telling them, "Thank you for coming," as if he were Walt Disney himself.

Certainly there was something about Bill Clinton that people found irksome. In fact, there were many things.

There was the egoism. There was an adulthood spent as a consummate politician in an era in which politicians were held in steadily declining regard. There was his meteoric youthful rise, first to the governorship and, in 1993, to the presidency, causing envy among those—especially fellow baby boomers who couldn't imagine or accept one of their own as president—who thought he had achieved too much too soon too easily. There was the seeming hypocrisy, singing in the choir of a televised church service in Little Rock while rumors abounded of marital infidelity. There was his tendency to chop the truth into little pieces that he would mete out only as required and in an attempt to avoid the whole truth. There was the ease with which he would make promises he wouldn't or couldn't keep. There was the fact that he had avoided the draft and Vietnam in the late 1960s. There was the basic liberalism of his heart and heritage in an era in which liberalism went out of fashion. There was his attempt to cloak that liberalism, creating an appearance of double-speak, expediency, and of standing for nothing except himself and his political fortunes.

But then there was his ability; he was the best politician of his era and a man of dizzying brainpower and awesome policy command. There was his disarming charm; he was almost impossible to dislike in a personal meeting. There was his mind-boggling accomplishment; he rose from the middle class and a backwater culture to become a Rhodes Scholar, a governor by thirty-two, and a president by forty-six.

In 1992 as he emerged as the presumptive Democratic presidential nominee, I was interviewed at length by Judy Woodruff, then with the MacNeil/Lehrer NewsHour, for a three-part biography of Clinton. I spent much of the interview explaining and criticizing Clinton's seemingly incurable tendency toward verbal finesse and political expediency. But I'll never forget the last question Woodruff asked; it disarmed my personal attack and forced me to consider Clinton simply as a public servant.

"Is Arkansas better off as a result of his administration?" she asked.

"Uh, yeah," I said.

The Hillary Rodham Clinton view, one that could not be discounted solely on the basis of its arrogance, was that people were irked by her husband because they were unhappy and dissatisfied with themselves. Though she could be as critical of her husband as anyone, she believed that widespread animosity toward him sprang from obsessive jealousy. Her instinct to react to criticism by attacking the motives or character of critics would become evident in Washington, D.C., in 1993.

For all those reasons, not to mention more substantive ones of political philosophy, America did not know quite what to make of this young man from Arkansas as he became President of the United States in January 1993. What unfolded in his first presidential year was a true-life psychodrama with Bill Clinton at centerstage, playing the role of a man Americans had elected without quite knowing or trusting him.

In the spring of 1979, only seven years after he had worked as a youthful war protester for George McGovern's kamikaze presidential campaign in Texas, Clinton was a tall, bushy-haired political prodigy and the thirty-two-year-old first-term governor of an underdeveloped and widely disregarded Southern state. He was the youngest governor in America, having won big the preceding November.

Senator Bumpers brought to Little Rock his first-term Democratic friend and colleague in the Senate, Colorado's Gary Hart, to address the annual banquet of the Arkansas affiliate of the National Conference of Christians and Jews. Hart, who had managed the national McGovern campaign and knew of Clinton, spent the night at the Arkansas Governor's Mansion with the young political phenom about whom Democratic insiders nationally already whispered such words and phrases as "smart," "attractive," and "the future of the Democratic Party."

On the flight back to Washington the next day, Bumpers asked Hart, "So, what did you think of our young governor?" Hart, as perceptive then as he would prove indiscreet later, replied: "I think the people elected him, but that they reserved judgment."

Clinton's youthful energy, good looks, ingratiating personal appeal, empathetic speaking style, and impeccable academic credentials had impressed the people of this small, rural, poor state. Because of the image damage caused by stereotypes of comedians and satirists like Bob Burns and H. L. Mencken, not to mention the televised spectacle of the Little Rock Central High School desegregation crisis of 1957, Arkansas voters had been favoring since the mid-1960s politicians of progressivism and good appearance who would be worthy ambassadors for a better image of the state. Bumpers, Clinton, and Senator David Pryor, all uncannily personable Democrats of mitigated liberalism, were the best examples.

By "mitigated" liberalism, I mean that these talented politicians offset and even veiled their liberalism with extraordinary personal touches and deft electoral skill. Their prominence made Arkansas seem the most liberal of the Southern states, when, more precisely, it simply was the most image-conscious, a small state where the intimacy between voters and politicians bestowed an advantage on gifted politicians. Arkansas had long been known for the production of national political talent; the generation preceding the one of Clinton, Bumpers, and Pryor had produced John McClellan, J. William Fulbright, and Wilbur Mills—powerful congressional committee chairmen. "It must be something in the water down here," Clinton once told me.

Eighteen months after Gary Hart's overnight stay at the Arkansas Governor's Mansion, Clinton became the nation's youngest ex-governor, defeated by a Republican political neophyte in a state that still relied on two-year gubernatorial terms. The people had finally made the judgment that Hart believed they had initially reserved. The young governor had proved too liberal, too transparently ambitious for a national political career, and, as they liked to put it, generally "too big for his britches." They determined that they had bestowed too much too soon on this boy, who had shown up late for virtually every public appearance, kept powerful businessmen waiting in his gubernatorial reception room, flown into a rage when a newspaper reported his driving at an excessive speed, and surrounded himself with self-indulgent aides who seemed to amuse themselves by taking on every entrenched interest in a state where the entrenched interests were inordinately strong. This inordinate power stemmed from the gap between the rich, who numbered a few thousand, and the poor, who numbered a quarter million, that being the number of people in Arkansas whose incomes were so insignificant that they were not required to pay federal income taxes.

The entrenched interests included the Arkansas Medical Society, which resented Clinton's rural health program and advocacy of increased roles for nurse practitioners; the timber industry, which resented Clinton's emphasis on curbing the practice of clear cutting; and the utility companies, which resented Clinton's advocacy of conservation over plant construction.

The day after his defeat, Clinton assembled teary-eyed friends and staff members at the Governor's Mansion and told them that those kinds of things happened in America. The Ronald Reagan landslide victory of the night before was a cyclical development, he said. In time, he predicted, the American people would turn back to a Democrat.

That time would be 1992, and then it would be all of America, even the world, that would consider Bill Clinton of Arkansas.

The people of the United States had turned against George Bush, for whom they had never felt a great affection, having elected him president in 1988 to something tantamount to Ronald Reagan's third term. They had done so partly because the Democratic challenger, Michael Dukakis, proved to be a dreadfully inept campaigner who couldn't or wouldn't deflect Republican attacks on his social liberalism.

The people had lost confidence in America's economic security. With the Cold War over, they placed less emphasis on the need for foreign policy expertise and maturity. H. Ross Perot interested them with his broadside attacks on the political establishment, which they held in near contempt, but he seemed a bit meteoric for sober consideration as President of the United States.

Along came Bill Clinton of Arkansas, now forty-six, plumper and gray, but fresh and appealing still. "A rising star for three decades," Senator Sam Nunn of Georgia once said of him, quite accurately.

Clinton presented himself nicely as a new kind of Democrat, an ideological synthesis who preached responsibility to black audiences and imposed the death penalty, and as the symbol of a new generation. So the American people elected him, though only by a minority, and reserved judgment.

That wasn't the only parallel.

After regaining the governorship of Arkansas in 1982, Clinton held it for a decade through a time of transition. The state was gradually and painfully transformed from a predominately agricultural economy with a smattering of low-wage, unskilled manufacturing jobs in shoes and textiles to a state dominated by agribusiness, primarily poultry. The shoe and textile industries were lost to cheap foreign labor and eventually replaced by retailing giants such as Wal-Mart and Dillard's, trucking, communications, and data processing. That had the effect of enriching the rich areas—central and northwestern Arkansas—while isolating the intense poverty of the Mississippi River Delta region, where agriculture had waned and the population was predominately black.

America in 1993 was in a state of transition. With the Cold War over, the defense establishment was reduced in size and scope, costing high-paying jobs and necessitating a basic restructuring of the economy that caused inordinate damage to the state of California. Major corporations got leaner, frightening Americans who always had believed in the lifetime job security provided by the likes of IBM and Sears. The nation adapted to the new dynamics of an economy based on service, technology, and information. It also adapted to international economics, which meant it had both to cooperate and compete with other nations and alliances of nations. It had to do all of that while trying to head off a trend toward oppressive public debt that, if not reversed, would either bankrupt the country, render it resourceless to compete in the world, or, at least, force the government to devote so much of its budget to debt that it would become dangerously constrained.

In other words, the American people had elected by a minority a young president about whom they had reserved judgment, deeming him an appealing but essentially unknown quantity, while assigning him the awesome task of leading the country through the perils of changing times.

Therein lies the prescription for a thrill-a-minute walk along a highwire.

This is a book about that new president and his volatile first year in the White House—an uncertain man for an uncertain time, you could say—that is drawn on fifteen years in Arkansas spent chronicling, analyzing, praising, and criticizing the personal and political style and substance of the compelling public figure who became America's forty-second president. The book will examine both policy and politics, but emphasize politics for two reasons: the author's incurable preoccupation, and his belief that the key to any successful presidency is its marketability to the pivotal and decisive American middle class, both white collar and blue collar, and mostly white. Does it find the right images and themes to connect with people who don't follow policy or politics closely because jobs and child rearing leave little time for anything else? The book also will lean heavily toward analyzing Bill Clinton personally because, after all, that is the central storyline. Who is this man they call "Slick Willie"?

In Arkansas, we knew Clinton as a man who made mistakes and learned from them, who took risks and added drama to legislative sessions with down-to-the-wire proposals that he advocated in hallway lobbying sessions with buttonholed legislators. He could be reckless, indiscreet, self-indulgent, dissembling, and disorganized in his personal and professional life and associations, tended to lose interest in programs after he'd managed to get them enacted, and combined seductive personal charm, boundless energy, ego, a burning desire for success and acceptance, and an extraordinary mind into a style of high-octane salesmanship and accomplishment that people tended to love or hate, to embrace or resent bitterly.

I had watched Bill Clinton so closely for so long that I had both embraced and resented, depending on the issue and whether his good or bad side emerged. Bill Clinton is a man of awesome talent and troubling personal weakness; his life and his public service are neck-and-neck contests to see if the awesome talent or personal weakness will win in the end. I think the talent will win; I think it edged ahead in 1993, despite the best efforts of critics and partisan opponents to destroy him by pounding his Achilles heel—his personal character.

Back in Arkansas in 1987, Clinton had told me, "There are things about this job you can only learn by doing it." He meant the governorship, but as it turned out, the point applied on an exponential basis to the American presidency.

CHAPTER 1

Unveto Man

I n the spring and early summer of 1987, Governor Bill Clinton of Arkansas, an ambitious young man holding the preeminent elective office in a rural state where ambition connotes haughtiness, was the subject of improbable speculation. Would he seek the Democratic presidential nomination the next year?

He was flitting hither and yon, speaking about national issues, enjoying the appearance of his name as a potential presidential contender in occasional articles in the national press, and insisting that his leadership roles in the National Governors Association and the Education Commission of the States necessitated such engagements as luncheon speeches to the National Press Club in Washington, D.C.

In perhaps the most cosmopolitan action ever taken by a governor of Arkansas, Clinton had announced in a hotel lobby in Boston, where he was to deliver a speech, that he would soon convene a special session of the Arkansas legislature for emergency spending measures. On the whole, Arkansas people were sufficiently provincial that they resented a frequent-flying governor. Announcing a major Arkansas news story from Boston signaled to many of them that their suspicions were correct: Clinton didn't care about them; he'd tend to their interests parenthetically. For all his political savvy, Clinton occasionally displayed boyish obliviousness and bad judgment, leaving his friends and advisers to ask, "Bill, why in the world?"

I couldn't see it—Clinton's running for president. His calling card would be that he was of a new breed of consensus-building, problem-solving governors who transcended traditional ideology and modernized government as they coped with the Reagan administration's passing of the buck from the federal government to the states. That was the take of David Broder of *The Washington Post,* the Sinatra of political journalists, who went regularly to governors' conferences through the 1980s and thought he had located a national trend among these technocratic progressives from America's statehouses.

Broder had told people that he thought Clinton might be the smartest and most impressive of the gubernatorial bunch, but *Newsweek* magazine had just polled all the governors to get them to rank their colleagues. Clinton was in the top five. Michael Dukakis of Massachusetts, already a declared candidate for the Democratic presidential nomination, led the pack, aided in no small measure by a booming state economy. Massachusetts was considerably larger and richer than Arkansas.

In the classic sense, Arkansas seemed one of the last states from which one could seriously contend for the presidency. It had only a little more than 2 million people, a mere six electoral votes, and a longstanding reputation for backwardness that seemed to give everyone in the state except Clinton an inferiority complex. Clinton's state budget was $3 billion, less than the budget of many major cities. Any number of mayors would have had larger bases and greater name identification.

What lured Clinton was the new-fangled Southern regional primary, cooked up by the Southern Legislative Conference, an alliance of white and conservative Southern Democrats with the intention of catapulting a Southern moderate past the unelectably liberal likes of George McGovern and Walter Mondale. Clinton could challenge Senator Al Gore of neighboring Tennessee as the Democrats' best "Bubba," i.e., regular guy or good ol' boy.

Gore was as much a product of St. Albans School for Boys in Washington, D.C., as Tennessee, and stiff as a board in public, with a tendency to shout inexplicably during speeches. (Privately, he could be quite charming, and his public performance would be much improved by 1993.) The soulful, earthy Clinton, possessed of an extraordinary talent for relating to all kinds of people, might have been onto something. He was Eastern establishment himself, educated at Georgetown, Oxford, and Yale, but he'd spent his adulthood honing the skills of Southern populism he'd been exposed to as a bright child growing up in a state where the politicians were crafty and powerful—John L. McClellan, J. William Fulbright, Wilbur D. Mills, and Orval Faubus.

In background and style, as in philosophy and policy, Clinton was a self-styled synthesis.

In July 1987 Clinton would decide to run for president. He would rent a ballroom at Little Rock's biggest hotel. Advance people would build the platforms for the press. Friends would be invited from all over the country. He had an idea for a 30-minute national television program to be videotaped at Little Rock Central High School, the site in 1957 of America's first angry, violent, and televised resistance to racial integration. His appearance there would be a symbol of progress and of the New South that he represented.

Well, not quite, in the end. At noon the day before the formal announcement, Clinton strolled down to the kitchen at the Governor's Mansion in Little Rock, looked at the assembled political operatives before him, surveyed his chicken salad, and declared, "I'm not running."

He happened to suffer from the Achilles heel *du jour*. He had the "Gary Hart problem." Unspecified extramarital activities on his part were commonly accepted truths among political insiders in Arkansas, and 1988 would not be the year to ante up a checkered private life in the presidential poker game. We in the Arkansas media had generally eschewed investigations, stakeouts, and direct questions about all of that. No Arkansas-based supermarket tabloid existed to break the ice for us; no right-wing periodicals devoted to his destruction were published on the state level, and state troopers assigned to the governor's security detail weren't yet offering lurid details based on circumstantial evidence in hopes of book contracts. I thought that an article about Clinton's marital infidelity might have been relevant for public consumption only as a psychoanalytical illustration of what I already knew, which was that Clinton had a tendency toward personal indiscretion and recklessness, a problem being loyal, and an insatiable need for ego gratification and approval.

It also seemed that Clinton had a problem making up his mind, as the nation would discover in 1993.

In the winter and spring of 1987, amid speculation about whether he would seek the presidency in 1988, Clinton appeared twice on a weekly news commentary program on the Arkansas Educational Television Network. Each time I sat on the panel of journalists questioning him. It seemed to me that if I had even the remotest ability as a questioner, I could break through Clinton's genius for finesse, evasion, and lawyer-speak to get him to say something modestly definitive about running for president. He didn't want to tell the simple truth, that he was gearing up to run, for two reasons: He is a chronic avoider of the simple truth, preferring to obfuscate or to dice the truth into little pieces; and he wasn't sure the people of Arkansas were ready to tolerate the ambition they had found so distasteful seven years before.

If successful in my attempts, I figured I'd lay into him the way the press was supposed to question those who presumed themselves to be worthy of the presidency.

In the first appearance, in February, I told him that Nancy Reagan's simplistic and failed anti-drug campaign carried a little motto that would suit my purpose. If he was not thinking of running for president in 1988, would he please "just say no."

"Well, I don't think running for president or abusing drugs is the same sort of sin requiring the same sort of answer," he replied.

I was sufficiently staggered that I only managed to regain my footing by changing the subject.

In late April, Clinton returned to the television program. In the interim, Senator Dale Bumpers of Arkansas had declared that he would not seek the Democratic presidential nomination. Clinton, freed of the prospect of being the second-favorite son of his home state, had acknowledged by now that, yes, he was actively considering the race.

So I forged ahead.

Wasn't it incumbent on anyone contemplating offering himself for the presidency to search his soul on the question of whether he was up to the job?

Of course, Clinton responded.

Well, then, what about that time he showed himself so indecisive that he used a coat hanger to "unveto" a bill?

"You've written about that a hundred times," he said.

The count was actually six.

"You ought to get a doctor's degree in Bill Clinton criticism," he continued.

Clinton admitted that he'd made a mistake. He said everybody makes mistakes: the important thing was that he'd corrected it, and learned from it.

I yielded the floor to another panelist, then the taping ended and I went back to the office. About an hour later, Clinton called. He'd chatted with reporters after the taping and they had convinced him that he had mishandled my questioning, letting me appear to get under his skin. He said he wanted to apologize.

I told him no apology was necessary, that I thought the exchange was fun, and then I hung up the phone to turn to my keyboard to write a column for the morning edition saying that Clinton was so indecisive that he couldn't even make up his mind whether to be mad at me.

Other leading Arkansas politicians told me they could not imagine baring their souls to a newspaperman that way. Senator David Pryor explained that his press philosophy was to cut one's losses and never risk compounding trouble by engaging a reporter about an article the reporter had written. It's like emitting an aura of fear to a biting dog. But Clinton thought he could undo everything if only he could get your ear.

Speaking of undoing everything, here is the story of the "unveto," for what may indeed now be nearing the hundredth time, counting speeches, interviews, and dinner-party chitchat.

It was the winter of 1985, a time of tight budgeting and slow economic growth for Arkansas, midway through Clinton's decade of dominance of the state's politics. The governor was signing tax-break bills left and right for just about whatever business and industry said they needed to keep Arkansas competitive with other states, many of which were also eroding their tax bases and abandoning any semblance of tax fairness to save or recruit jobs.

The public colleges in Arkansas—and private ones, too—proposed legislation that would grant tax credits to persons making financial donations to colleges and universities. They went to Clinton, who was wishy-washy. He liked the idea (he liked almost anything that might help the quality of education and smacked of a public-private partnership), but he couldn't commit because he didn't know if he could afford a tax credit. How many people would take advantage of it? What would be the drain on the treasury? He didn't know. It worried him.

But Clinton told the college presidents, many of his friends, to give the bill their best shot in the legislature. He wouldn't stand in their way, nor would he try to work with them on a preemptive compromise. An income deduction rather than an outright tax credit seemed quite appropriate, but neither the college presidents nor Clinton was inclined to engage in bargaining. The governor would pass the buck for now. He was focused on other things.

He'd been elected in 1978 at the tender age of thirty-two, but had been voted out in two years partly because he'd tried to do too much. The "Comeback Kid" came back for the first time in 1982, shamelessly asking voters for a "second chance," seeking Baptist-styled redemption, determined this time not "to lead without listening," and to limit his agenda, something a governor could do far more easily than a president.

Fund-raising officials at the state's colleges were champing at the bit. Their solicitations would be direct: Send us money and take it right off your taxes.

Naturally, the bill passed. The mostly irresponsible Arkansas legislature never met a tax break it didn't like. Clinton had five days to take action, either sign the bill, veto it, or let it become law without his signature.

He pondered. He fretted. He agonized. He stalled. What to do? It sounded a bit like a treasured "new Democrat" concept to him, eschewing the traditional tax-and-spend solution to help higher education through citizen participation in public causes. But his budget advisers said there was no way to estimate the drain on the treasury; this one could be enormous. In fact, so many tax breaks had been granted that the fiscal analysts had begun to wonder how in the world to estimate the state budget. Clinton wanted to spend more on schools to get Arkansas teachers out of forty-ninth or fiftieth place in salary rankings—because they were underpaid and because it did not behoove a presidential prospect to govern a place that had the lowest-paid teachers in America. As always, he needed money. An incurable government enthusiast, which is what Clinton is, always needs money.

After normal working hours on the fifth and final day for consideration, Clinton made his painful decision, and the right one: veto. He stamped "disapproval" on the bill, affixed his signature below the stamp, dictated a letter explaining his reasoning, and dispatched an aide to the third floor of the state Capitol to place the veto in the office of the House clerk so that it would be filed in a supposedly timely way. The aide, finding everyone gone for the day and the clerk's door locked, slid the bill under the door.

That night, back at the Governor's Mansion, Clinton courteously telephoned one of the college presidents to give him the bad news. They talked a while, after which Clinton called for a state police trooper. He instructed the trooper to go to the state Capitol and get the bill out of the House clerk's office and bring it back to him.

The trooper found the door to the clerk's office locked, but he could see the bill on the floor through the glass inside the door's oak frame. He found a cloakroom from which he retrieved a wire coat hanger that he retwisted and used to slide the bill out from under the door.

Back at the Governor's Mansion, Clinton took a pen and blotted out the prefix, "dis-" on the "disapproved" stamp, effectively "unvetoing" the bill and making it law.

I found out about all of that some months later. It made for a nice page-one article, since at that point Clinton had called a special legislative session, one of the emergencies being the need to repeal the overly generous tax credit for donations to colleges and universities.

I found out even later that the college president with whom Clinton had spoken that night had prevailed on him to let the bill become law as a matter of personal honor and fairness: Since Clinton hadn't said at the outset that he would veto the bill, doing so would be a kind of double-cross. Clinton couldn't say no.

I remembered those stories—the little flap on public television and the coat-hanger "unveto"—many times during 1993:

- In early February, when Clinton decided to name Kimba Wood Attorney General, almost.

- In May, when Clinton reversed himself on his first difficult foreign policy issue, Bosnia, declaring an air war one week and undeclaring it the next.

- In early June, when he decided to abandon his nomination for federal civil rights attorney, Lani Guinier, a black lawyer and old law school acquaintance who had written in esoteric law journal articles that in designing political districts for representation, minorities ought to be given something beyond the constitutionally guaranteed one-man, one-vote right. Then he was so moved by her stirring personal defense on ABC's "Nightline" that he reconsidered. Finally, he abandoned her, leaving her and her supporters feeling betrayed, and himself damaged.

- Later in June, when Brit Hume of ABC News suggested in a question to the president that Clinton had gone through "zigs and zags" to nominate Ruth Bader Ginsburg to the United States Supreme Court, and Clinton, left misty-eyed by Ginsburg's just-completed tribute to her mother, petulantly snapped.

- In October, when senator after senator rose to decry the foreign policy vacillation of the president. Inattention and confusion had led to the loss of eighteen American lives on an unclear assignment in Somalia. A ship carrying a few hundred lightly armed American troops turned back on Clinton's orders when it was met by a mob of thugs in Haiti.

- Whenever I read in a newspaper that Clinton would soon make a specific appointment or take a specific action. I knew that unless the matter had advanced past the point of last-minute retrieval, it was no sure thing.

Bill Clinton, the first of his generation to lead the country—lauded appropriately for his original thinking, policy command, political acumen, persuasive charm, and an uncanny ability to connect with all kinds of people—was indeed likable, warm, remarkably intelligent, earnest, and well meaning. But he also was indecisive, too easily swayed by the last person with whom he'd spoken, too eager to please, surprisingly thin-skinned, overly optimistic to the point of seeming naivete, and, altogether, a soft touch.

Some will ask how I can possibly suggest a lack of toughness on the part of a man who endured all that Clinton endured to win the presidency, and then, once elected, tackled all that Clinton chose to tackle.

The answer is that I can do so easily. Clinton is admirably resilient as a candidate for office; he is obsessed with achieving the personal validation that he gets by winning elections. It is true that the search for personal validation drives nearly everyone, especially politicians. But Clinton was conspicuous in that regard. His adulthood has been spent seeking and holding office; that's basically all he has ever done. His boyish exuberance about victory and the smell of victory could be breathtakingly obsessive. In November 1990, he won reelection as governor of Arkansas handily. As he neared the podium to deliver his victory speech, he saw an old friend and exclaimed, "Did you see the Cuomo and Bradley races?" The point was that while Clinton was winning handily that night, Mario Cuomo and Bill Bradley, probably Clinton's chief rivals for leadership of the Democrats nationally, were squeaking by, appearing vulnerable. Those national implications gave Clinton a shot of adrenaline and preoccupied him at the very moment he claimed victory to a four-year gubernatorial term he had promised to serve in full, though the job of governor had begun to bore him as early as 1987.

Campaign resilience does not necessarily translate into resolve or toughness once in office. Seeking office and holding it require different qualities. Getting elected requires promise, vision, salesmanship, and message control; good governing requires strategically sound implementation, service after the sale, and wise attention to problems as they arise unexpectedly even if they are not on one's message-control agenda. The resolve to win sustains Clinton the candidate, but over the years in Arkansas, the resolve to win sometimes led him once in office to pursue expedient courses.

Clinton is more talented in the art of campaign politics than anyone I have ever seen. No one combines as extensively the abilities to strategize and perform. But he is not as good in the strategic planning required by the politics of governing. The optimism that he can win elections sustains him as a candidate; the optimism that he can succeed once in office causes him to neglect to develop a strategy of alternatives if and when things go wrong, as in Washington they inevitably will. The optimism and will to win of the candidate breed great promises. The optimism and will to please of the officeholder breed oversold initiatives.

As for Clinton's ambitious agenda as president, it was just that: ambitious. There was no toughness in aiming for the moon and the stars. The tough thing would be getting there.

Over the years I have concluded that Clinton's overriding personal foible might not be indecisiveness, precisely, for he'd made plenty of decisions. Instead, it might be a need to oblige, placate, and gain approval. This tremendous desire to be liked stems from Clinton's lack of a solid center. Other than politics, his life's work and quest, there is nothing that keeps him settled and serene. Politics is hardly a settling calling; by its very definition it puts careers on the line every two, or four, or six years.

Consider that Clinton never knew his father. Apparently he never knew all of his half brothers and half sisters, either. He borrowed his name from a stepfather who was an alcoholic. His marriage had been rocky because, though he insisted and surely believed that his wife was the most extraordinary woman he'd known, he had sought pleasures and relationships outside it. For most of his adult life, he had no home of his own, living instead in the finest public housing—the Governor's Mansion of Arkansas—which he vacated after twelve years only to step up to the White House. He had no presidential retreat, no place to go that was regular and comfortable and his own. He claimed the Southern Baptist religion and sang for a while in the choir of his Little Rock church that televised its services, but the Southern Baptist Convention, now largely an adjunct of the Republican Party, essentially condemned his presidential candidacy as an affront to the Lord.

In 1993, America had a vigorous and accomplished young president who for all his admirable talents and achievements was a bit lost in the world. His younger half brother, Roger, had turned to rock music and drugs; politics was Bill's stage, and his narcotic. One brother went to prison, the other to the White House. "I'm afraid Roger is wasting his life," Clinton told me one day in the early 1980s. "But I guess he thinks maybe I'm wasting mine."

So, yes, it was important to this new president that you like him. He went into politics in the first place so that you could prove to him that you liked him by giving him your vote. He didn't need big money or business success; his sense of worth came on election nights as returns poured in. He was like Sally Field accepting an Oscar: "You like me. You really like me."

On June 18, 1993, I went to see Bill Clinton in the Oval Office, where he greeted me with such warmth that you would have thought I was his long-lost brother. (Ten days later, *The Washington Post* disclosed that he apparently had a previously undiscovered half brother in California, a man who might have been the son of his late father by another brief marriage. Clinton's father, William Blythe, was a traveling salesman and a marrying man who must have combined the charm and recklessness so evident in his son. Betsey Wright, researching Blythe during the campaign, discovered four marriages at least.)

Clinton greets everyone warmly; it is his natural instinct and his method of operation. Fred Barnes, the conservative columnist, was ushered in to see Clinton about this same time; he subsequently wrote that Clinton surely was one of the most charming men God ever created, winning notice in the "Clinton Suck-Up Watch" of his own publication, *The New Republic*.

Without solicitation that day, Clinton offered to sit down with me "at least two or three more times between now and the end of the year. I'll be more than happy to do that for your book." Someone who hadn't known Clinton well would have taken him seriously and banked on two or three more sessions, contentiously insisting on them as no less a matter than the value of the president's word. But I looked at George Stephanopoulos, who was sitting with us, and sensed that he was thinking precisely what I was thinking: I was lucky to get one meeting and would be luckier still to get one other, which, as it turned out, was what I was formally offered a couple of days later by Thomas F. "Mack" McLarty III, the chief of staff.

"You understand the president," McLarty said by way of dismissing Clinton's unsolicited offer of frequent meetings. Yes, I understood. At that moment, in his desire to please, Clinton had meant what he had said. But he forgot about it as soon as the moment passed.

Clinton cries out for a bad cop. Left to his own devices, he'd have personal obligations pending to a number of people approximating the population of the United States—which, at the end of his campaign, he essentially had. He'd have good intentions regarding every obligation.

Back in Arkansas, in 1974, in Clinton's first political campaign, a losing bid for Congress at age twenty-seven, a lawyer and contemporary named Steve Clark drove his car. In time, Clinton would be elected governor and Clark attorney general. In 1990, Clark tired of waiting for Clinton to vacate the governor's office and declared his candidacy for the Democratic nomination (Clinton would announce his candidacy for reelection later). In short order, the *Arkansas Gazette* uncovered quite a scandal. For years Clark had been padding his expense account handsomely by claiming to have had dinner with nearly everyone who was anyone in Arkansas. Scores upon scores of these "phantom diners" denied having had dinner with Clark on the date specified, or ever having had dinner with him at all. Instead, Clark was treating girlfriends to fine French cuisine, champagne, and after-dinner liqueur, and leaving a paper trail of fraud. Clark dropped out of the governor's race and eventually was convicted of felony theft. He fled Arkansas—still owing the state money, according to the new attorney general—and found work with a home health care company in Georgia. In the summer of 1993, he was in Washington jogging on the Mall one morning when Clinton, on his daily three-mile run, spotted him and invited him to jog along. Then Clinton encouraged him to make a jogging date the next time he was in town, which Clark did. A picture of that second morning run appeared on the Associated Press national wire. Many people back in Arkansas were outraged that the President of the United States would cavort with a felon who had declared himself a political opponent. But Clinton was a soft touch for an old friend, readily forgiving, sometimes oblivious to the political overtones of personal associations.

*   *   *

My "doctor's degree in Bill Clinton criticism" was quite something to possess on January 20, 1993, when Clinton became the forty-second President of the United States.

On that sunny day, the spirit of hope and celebration was contagious. Democrats were back in the White House after twelve years of the Reaganites' favoritism of the rich; opposition to abortion rights; nomination of conservative idealogues to the United States Supreme Court; questioning the patriotism of those who disagree with them; and of contempt for the idea that the federal government ought to try actively to help people. The Religious Right had been dealt a blow and wasn't taking it well. Some members of the Southern Baptist Convention wanted to censure Clinton's Immanuel Baptist Church in Little Rock for not giving him the boot because of his pro-choice view on abortion and his support of gay rights.

The source of the hope and celebration was a man I liked and whose talents and aims I admired, but whose personal strength and resolve I worried about. Had I not known him well, I would have joined in the revelry without hesitation.

As it was, I settled on the sentiment expressed by Senator Bumpers of Arkansas, a widely admired liberal who twice contemplated running for president himself, and who had served as something of a mentor to Clinton in the early 1980s. He told me, "My colleagues in the Congress come up to me and ask, 'Isn't this guy just another Carter?' And I say, 'All you need to know is that he's light-years better than what we've had for twelve years.' "

Bumpers was a deficit hawk nonpareil, a progressive Democrat on social policy, but a rabid advocate of abandoning the super-conducting super-collider research project, the NASA space station, new nuclear submarine missile systems, and a large chunk of the $30 billion Intelligence budget to reduce the federal budget deficit. The deficit will be the ruination of our future and our children, he believed. "Bill Clinton," he told me, "is not the last best hope for this country, but maybe the last hope."

Could it be? Or should I have mentioned that Bumpers can be a tad hyperbolic?

But the point was arguable. After a dozen years of the profligate borrow-and-spend government of Reagan and Bush, the country was on a path toward bankruptcy, lost economic dominance in the world, lingering unemployment as the economy grew choppily without creating jobs, crumbled cities, greater racial and social divisiveness and resentment, and rampaging gun-related and drug-related violence on streets, in schools, and in homes. Bumpers's point was that if Clinton failed at least to reverse that path, if his presidency failed, then the country might revert to Republican supply-side presidencies and squander a precious opportunity, if not the last one, to get things right before the deterioration—financial, social, and cultural—reached a dangerous or even irreparable state.

At the least, it seemed that whether Clinton succeeded as president would determine the nation's long-term course in the transitional era he had inherited. Would we reform our profligate spending habits? Reorder the federal budget? Come up with new ideas for burdensome problems such as health care and welfare? Find a way to better educate and train our people for the new international economy? Advance the cause of racial progress not through entitlements or quotas resented by the middle class, but through mutual responsibility? Essentially, the question was whether America would attack the twenty-first century with the government activism of Democrats or the hands-off, market-oriented philosophy of Republicans. It would depend on Clinton's performance.

I'd first met this "last hope," by my best recollection, in the old Heights Theater in Little Rock around midnight on a Saturday night in 1976. A movie documentary based on Willie Nelson's annual Fourth of July picnic and concert was about to be shown. I engaged Clinton in conversation about the progressive country music scene of Austin, which Clinton knew well from his time spent there during the McGovern campaign. I was twenty-two; he was twenty-nine. Never before had I talked to a prominent politician about the sounds and implications of a modern musical trend. Never before had I encountered a prominent politician at a midnight movie. Like so many others, I felt a generational bond.

I'd covered this "last hope" regularly since 1980, occasionally before that. Essentially, I'd covered him most of our adult lives, first as a young reporter for the *Arkansas Gazette* assigned to the Arkansas State Capitol and to Clinton's campaigns; then, beginning in 1986, as a political columnist devoting probably a third of my 1,800 or so columns to the state's leading political figure.

I'd been arguably one of Clinton's two best friends in the Arkansas press in the early 1980s when he got beat at the age of thirty-four after a stormy two-year term of arrogance and activism, then when he came back two years later pleading for a second chance as a reinvented listener, coalition builder, and moderate. By the late 1980s, as a columnist spouting opinions, I'd been all over the map—praising, supporting, criticizing, even ridiculing. Once, after a roast of a highway commissioner during which both of us had taken our turns as hopeful comedians, a woman walked up to us and said, "I can't figure you two out." Clinton replied, "It's love-hate."

That was Hillary Rodham Clinton's diagnosis, I suspect. It was not unusual for Hillary's thoughts on personal matters to come out of Bill's mouth. Months later, Clinton sent me a note saying, "Hillary understands far better than I what makes people like you tick." His deference to her better judgment about people would explain the proliferation of her friends, associates, and soulmates in the high echelon of the Clinton administration. Her assessment of me, he later explained, was that I adored him, wanted his attention, and, because of personal admiration, held him to a higher standard than I would apply to other politicians. It was egocentric excuse making and it was contradicted by another line in Clinton's note: "I think you prefer to write without contact. That's too bad." Clinton always prefers contact; he believes he can persuade intellectually and seduce interpersonally, and often he can.

If I thought Hillary was right, I'd admit it. But she showed a basic lack of understanding of the press. I was writing six political columns a week. Clinton was the most compelling political figure in a provincial state where the governor was the primary newsmaker. In an effort to avoid leaving seventeen column inches of white space in the newspaper, I often wrote about him. I defy anyone to write several hundred columns about any person and fill all of them with praise. That's especially hard to do when the subject has a profound tendency toward over-promise and disingenuousness.

For example: He said in his gubernatorial campaign in 1990 that he was not planning to raise taxes. It was an interesting choice of words, and perhaps accurate. Conceivably, he was planning at the time only to get reelected. Presumably, the planning for the sales tax increase he engineered in 1991 did not begin until after he was reelected. Had he ever used marijuana? "Not as an adult in Arkansas," he once said. "I have not broken the drug laws of my country," he said another time. "I'm glad I'm not running for president so I don't have to answer that question," he told me in 1987, after the last-minute bail-out on his presidential bid. If the voters of Arkansas gave him another term in 1990, would he promise to serve the full term and not interrupt it to seek the presidency in 1992? "Absolutely," he said. No waffle or trickery there. Instead, it was a promise to be wiggled out of, an assignment for which he has a nice touch.

As the country, even the world, was to find in 1993, Clinton's best side is the big portrait. There one could see a deficit-reduction plan in place, Reaganomics revised if not reversed, the United States Supreme Court improved, free trade advanced, and the problems of health care at least identified and attacked. But the daily snapshots could be most unattractive: hedging, retreat, reversal, premature compromise, and petulance. When you write six columns a week committed to topicality, you are a walking Polaroid Instamatic. You are a prisoner of what is called "process" rather than a student of what is called "product." In other words, you chronicle and comment on the often-messy process that Clinton follows toward a final product that is perhaps meritorious on balance, but seems less so because of his feints, false starts, broken promises, and hasty retreats along the way. Clinton always looks worst when compared to his own promise or promises.

This book will endeavor to analyze both the "process" and "product" of Clinton's first year as president. The former is unattractive; the latter not bad for the country. Both are relevant. It always has been so with Clinton. His political career is an action-adventure story, a series of tight spots he gets into because of mistakes, too many promises, and dissembling, then gets out of because of personal skills and the fact that the product of his governing is usually acceptable or defensible, even admirable sometimes.

Even on the "unveto," his instinct was correct. So was his eventual action, admitting a mistake and repealing the ill-conceived law. But between instinct and resolution was a tale of comic angst and un-certainty.

Nearly every person to whom I've related the story has been chilled or burdened by it in the context of a foreign policy crisis. Harry Truman said one must make a decision and never look back. Bill Clinton is a self-styled synthesis of many modern presidents: part JFK as a char-ismatic pragmatist and generational symbol of youthful vigor, part LBJ as a gregarious left-leaning Southerner of voracious personal appetites with politics and government in his veins, part FDR as a synthesizing activist with an ambitious agenda, even part Ronald Reagan as an occasionally effective communicator and advocate of positive spin and message control. But there is no plain-speaking, give-'em-hell, don't-look-back Harry Truman in him. The idea of Clinton at the national helm during anything resembling the Cuban missile crisis was best not even contemplated.

Thank God, then, that the Cold War was over. Thank God, one supposes, that we were entering that transitional era in which nearly everyone, not just the new president, pondered and agonized over the world's ambiguities and when, where, and how to flex America's military muscle. The world was troubled and dangerous in entirely different ways now. There were matters to be debated, and the new president's fertile mind would be the forum.

It wouldn't be pretty, and not only in regard to the gut-wrenching dilemma of Bosnia, about which Clinton preached a sermon of moral intervention and practiced confusion and uncertainty, false start and indecision; or to the tragic confusion of Somalia; or to the on-and-off flirtations with U.N. multi-national policing; or to the humiliating retreat of an American ship as it ran from thugs in Haiti. One day between his election and inauguration Clinton suggested in an interview that America should keep an open mind toward Saddam Hussein, saying all Baptists believed in deathbed conversions. The next day he denied having said it and implicitly attacked Tom Friedman, the respected veteran reporter for *The New York Times* who had quoted him precisely. Friedman could be forgiven if he began covering the Clinton White House with a measure of uncertainty about the honesty of its new occupant.

Clinton's greatest foreign policy moment was one for which he was masterfully suited, requiring a rare combination of obliviousness and warmth. Israel and the Palestine Liberation Organization (PLO), after years of bloodshed over inherent differences that had often seemed insurmountable, found it in their mutual best interest to enter into an agreement to work on co-existence. All Clinton had to do was offer the South Lawn of the White House for the actual signing of the agreement, deliver an appropriate speech, and, in a breathtakingly historic moment, encourage Israeli Prime Minister Yitzhak Rabin and the PLO leader Yasser Arafat to shake hands. Fifteen years earlier, another Democratic president, Jimmy Carter, had personally brokered an accord between Egypt and Israel. But the dynamics of the world had changed; America no longer needed the Cold War chess player or the Mideast micromanager. On foreign policy, Bill Clinton is a man for his time.

*   *   *

My relationship with Clinton is not "love-hate." Probably it's best described as affectionate skepticism. That is a common relationship between journalists and the politicians they cover for a long time and come to know well. More than one New York writer told me during the campaign in 1992 that when I talked to them about Clinton, they could hear themselves talking about Mario Cuomo, a person I admired from 1,300 miles away. The writers who swooned over Clinton in the Democratic primary of 1992 were doing so from 1,000-plus miles away, based on a superficial acquaintance. They'd see the snapshots soon enough.

Or maybe this explains it best: In 1990 back in Little Rock, the governor's photographer snapped a picture as I interviewed Clinton, who was pulling on his socks. His office sent me a print with this note inscribed by Clinton: "I'm still trying to keep you from knocking my socks off." Another print was enclosed with a request that I sign it for him. I wrote, "We could do worse for a governor."

I moved to Washington in January 1993 to pursue this project. The idea was that my lengthy acquaintance with the new president would give me a head start examining and explaining his first year, which was projected as defining and pivotal by most political watchers, and as the most important since FDR's first year by a few others, old-style liberals and Reagan-haters who believed that the reversal or revision of Reaganomics and the general undoing of the Reagan legacy would save the country.

Fortunately for these purposes, if not for the country, history repeated itself, rather eerily in fact. I'd seen the play before, but on a smaller stage, with a lesser-known cast.

The protagonist is boyishly likable and exuberant. "No one could have loved this job more," he said in a somber concession speech after his defeat for reelection as governor of Arkansas in 1980. The same surely could be said of the presidency.

In this drama from Arkansas, the protagonist gets off to a bad start on the job, appearing too much a liberal for the tastes of the mainstream, surrounded by a staff of arrogant youths, overextended with an unfocused, too-ambitious, fix-all-that's-broken agenda, victimized by his indecisiveness, boyish indiscretions, naive optimism, and mistakes of judgment; then, always adaptable and reactive, he sets out to slide to the political center, recruit experienced advisers, and reinvent himself while the pundits ponder whether he's a liberal or a moderate, an old Democrat or a new Democrat, a man of principle or a man of mush, and search diligently to discover his soul. Arkansas or Washington: take your pick.

Mack McLarty, the White House chief of staff from Arkansas, agreed with me when I called Clinton a "third-option guy" who, when presented with two alternatives, will almost always insist that he can cook up a third alternative that's a mix of the two and better. I had always called that indecisiveness; McLarty said it was extraordinary intelligence, though he acknowledged that it tended at times to generate too much superfluous intellectual byplay and too many delayed decisions.

Clinton is a synthesizer of policy and political philosophies who believes that his main drawback is that it is not possible for him to sit down with everyone in America and explain at length the nuances. "I'm a fairly superficial thinker; Bill Clinton gives me a headache," Senator Bumpers, the president's friend and one-time mentor, told me. Bumpers said there might be more intellectual men in public life — Senator Daniel Patrick Moynihan of New York and Senator Paul Sarbanes of Maryland earned his mention—but that the only person he knew who was in Clinton's league for profound political and policy analysis was Gary Hart.

Nuance and lengthy analysis aside, Clinton in his soul is a fairly conventional liberal Democrat except on the issue of the death penalty, in which he genuinely believes. Some called him an eighties-style liberal, to be distinguished from a sixties-style liberal. The difference? A sixties-style liberal could not get past the basic rightness of the social movements of his era; an eighties-style liberal would compromise because times had changed. Civil rights, Vietnam, and a war on poverty were matters of life and death; reducing the deficit and revamping America for the global economy are matters of prioritizing, numbers-crunching, and trade summits.

If you administered a five-question philosophical litmus test to Clinton and, say, Walter Mondale, you'd get pretty much the same answers. The differences would be that Clinton's answers would be longer, more professorial, better adapted to modern political dynamics, and more conciliatory to those who might disagree. If one of the questions was about flag burning, Clinton might say we shouldn't outlaw flag burning as an expression, which is free under the Constitution, but that maybe we could figure out how to ban it on some other basis. I'm not kidding about that. He asserted precisely that in Arkansas.

Here's another example: As a presidential candidate, Mondale announced he would raise taxes if elected. Clinton announced that he would cut taxes on the middle class if elected. Upon election, Clinton did what Mondale promised he would have done but never got the chance to do. Thus the basic difference between Clinton and a traditional liberal is that Clinton is a better mental and verbal gymnast, or at least a more willing one, and therefore electable. He was well trained in Arkansas, where traditional liberalism is tolerated more than in other Southern states, but not as generally embraced as in, say, Minnesota. Clinton will be as liberal as good politics will permit; when the poll numbers turn sour, he'll pick a fight with Jesse Jackson or hire David Gergen or bring up welfare reform or engage in what is called "counter-scheduling," which, by my simple definition, is picking a fight with a friendly audience to send a broader message to people who don't care for the politics of that audience. The best example: Attacking rapper Sister Souljah in a speech to Jesse Jackson's Rainbow Coalition. Another: Telling the AFL-CIO Convention why he believed in the North American Free Trade Agreement.

Most of my criticisms of Clinton over the years had been based on his attempts to be all things to all people through mental and verbal gymnastics. But you could make the argument—and many of the president's friends did—that in the 1990s, with America suburbanized, cynical, and politically inactive, with old-style liberalism passé and the Great Society an apparent failure, only a mental and verbal gymnast—an adroit and pragmatic synthesizer of polarized views—could win the presidency as a more-or-less traditional Democrat at heart to have the slightest chance to rearrange the tax burden, spend more on human needs, reform welfare in a humane and measured way, put a little money into the inner cities, restore sensitivity to civil rights in federal judgeship nominations, and fashion an acceptably activist government.

Consider the explanation in 1992 offered by Harold Ickes, a leading liberal political operative in New York City who for personal reasons twice turned down a chance to be Clinton's deputy chief of staff, before accepting the job at the start of Year Two: he supported Clinton's bid for the Democratic presidential nomination because he said he was tired of losing the presidency. The country had suffered immeasurably as a result of the policies of those to whom the liberals had lost. Now Ickes was resigned to overlooking or disregarding Clinton's support of the death penalty and his backing of the Persian Gulf War because, by God, the real virtue was electoral victory.

When true believers had urged "Let Reagan be Reagan," what they meant was that they wanted to untether Reagan's pure ideology, the right-wing simpleness. When Clintonites urged "Let Clinton be Clinton," what they meant was that they wanted traditional liberals to cut Clinton slack when, in the face of political reality, he espoused an impure ideology. In 1993 it also came to mean that they wanted self-professed "new Democrats," such as members of the Democratic Leadership Council (DLC), to cut Clinton slack when, in the face of political reality, he appeased the liberal wing of the party with an economic stimulus bill, an appointment, or a health care proposal that tried to negotiate between managed competition and a system of single-payer national health insurance.

A continuing conflict in our play is that while the protagonist tries to blend his natural inclinations into his synthesizer, he is beset by natural constituencies and old friends who believe and allege that he has betrayed them, and himself. Back in Arkansas, some of his harshest critics were liberals—of which the state literally had dozens—who bitterly complained that Clinton had betrayed them because of a yellow streak down the middle of his back. "I told you so," they said when Clinton abandoned Guinier.

Nothing incurred the wrath of Bill and Hillary more. How easy it was, they thought, for self-proclaimed liberals to wear principle and political impracticality on their sleeves while the right wing took over America. The Clintons saw themselves as more noble than that, as front-liners in the real world, seeking and winning office, participating in the political process while the self-righteous sat around at cocktail parties and regaled one another with their chic lamentations, essentially as political dropouts.

Meanwhile, the underlying storyline of our drama is that the protagonist is trying to do the right thing, or a scaled-down version of it, risking a measure of boldness blended with a measure of pragmatism. He raised taxes for better schools in Arkansas, seldom enjoying a legislative session in which "Clinton Tax Bill" wasn't practically a standing headline in the Arkansas press; as president, he raised taxes in a fair and progressive way to reverse or at least revise the plunge toward oppressive debt and the anti-government legacy of the Reagan Revolution. Meanwhile, he assigned his smart and efficiently organizing wife to the awesome but vital task of reforming health care in America, much as he'd assigned her to rewrite the public school standards in Arkansas, leading a good ol' boy in the state legislature to declare publicly, "We've elected the wrong Clinton."

The protagonist is as resilient as Rocky Balboa. Having covered Clinton for more than a decade, I'd written his political obituary three times: after his defeat for reelection as governor in 1980; after his dreadful speech to the Democratic National Convention in 1988 in Atlanta; and after Gennifer Flowers and the draft double-whammied him during the New Hampshire primary of 1992. I came to Washington convinced not to write it prematurely a fourth time, though the temptations were immense.

The main character is a work-in-progress. The Arkansas version had taken Clinton through most of his adulthood, from age twenty-seven, when he burst on the scene, to age forty-six, when he went to the big show, through a learning curve and personal ups and downs. Now all of America would see much the same thing.

"He'll figure it out. He always does," Betsey Wright, his longtime chief of staff and protector in Arkansas, told me in May 1993 when everything seemed to go wrong. "It's not as if he hasn't been through this before. But it may get uglier before he does."

Yes, a little Arkansas drama had opened to standing-room-only on Pennsylvania Avenue.

CHAPTER 2

Gay Nineties?

A small speaker's bureau in Washington had tracked me down. Everyone wanted to know about this new president. Would I be interested in flying out to California in mid-January to tell a group of mostly conservative businesspeople about Bill Clinton? Why, yes, I could do that. I had a great little story about an "unveto."

So, on the seventh day of America's new presidency, I expounded in sunny, 70-degree San Diego on the assigned topic, "Is Bill Clinton really a new Democrat?"

That was one of four burning questions that would decide the fate of Clinton's presidency: Would he prove somehow different from the stereotyped Democrat that the white middle class, both blue and white collar, had rejected in the 1980s?

This kind of Democrat was an anachronistic adherent of failed Great Society programs, whose stewardship of the economy would be anti-business, entailing higher taxes and bigger and more wasteful government, and causing something onerous, be it inflation, recession, unemployment, high interest rates, or all or parts of the above.

The middle class, for these purposes, meant people with incomes between $20,000 and $75,000 a year, give or take, according to most demographic groupings. A "new Democrat" was one less traditionally liberal on socioeconomic issues than, say, Ted Kennedy or Walter Mondale or George Mitchell, though perhaps no less activist. Stanley Greenberg, the pollster for Clinton, insisted that the middle class hadn't soured on government programs, only on government programs that didn't work and therefore squandered tax dollars.

A "new Democrat" was not necessarily the same as a moderate-to-conservative Democrat, as Al From, president of the Democratic Leadership Council, which Clinton had chaired for two years, explained: "An old Democrat loves FDR's programs. A new Democrat loves the fact that FDR *had* programs." Conceivably Bill Clinton would be a "new Democrat" and a government activist and social engineer all at the same time, a point that would be lost in early 1993 in Washington.

E. J. Dionne, Jr., the "new Democrat" guru, author, and columnist for *The Washington Post,* had described the movement's philosophy as one of government that would be "activist, but not intrusive." That is, a "new Democrat" wanted government to design and implement programs that would be designed to help people while staying as much out of their lives as possible. Self-professed "new Democrats" at the Democratic Leadership Council used "opportunity" and "responsibility" as their watchwords: That is, the government would provide you opportunity if you would take responsibility for yourself and your community.

The second question was whether Clinton had enough credibility as a president and a man to lead. He was a 43 percent president. That's a smaller proportion than Michael Dukakis had garnered in 1988 (though Clinton got a larger actual vote). Clinton wanted so desperately to win that he had promised the moon. Already, during his transition period, he had signaled retreat on a half dozen fronts and exposed greenness on foreign policy. He tended to oversell himself and his programs through a combination of delightful optimism and the incurable disingenuousness of a man who had never done anything except be a politician. He had campaigned as an outsider but was in fact a longtime political insider, a twenty-year networker whose Rolodex contained much of the membership list for the Democratic establishment. In an era in which politics-as-usual elicited resentment, this consummate career politician didn't need to be seen as a politician-as-usual.

The other questions were whether he could get anything accomplished in Washington—end "gridlock"—and, as always, whether the country would enjoy peace and prosperity, which is the common and ultimate denominator among questions pertaining to the ultimate success of presidencies.

I sought to explain to the businesspeople that indeed Clinton was a new kind of Democrat, if only because the time and the political climate required it. One could not think otherwise, knowing that Clinton had devoted much of his adult life to figuring out how to revive the Democratic Party as a presidential contender—how to slide from sixties–seventies liberalism into a new synthesis of attitudes and theories that would appeal to working-class and ethnic whites in the industrial Midwest ("Springsteen voters," he once called them), suburbanites, and Southern white males. Some had called them Reagan Democrats.

I told the audience about Clinton's voter-induced evolution in Arkansas from overambitious activist to a smartly paced pragmatist. I talked about his internal synthesizer, taking old theories and new ones to split the difference and fashion incremental progress. I mentioned his acquiescence to a business-friendly tax structure in Arkansas, one replete with tax breaks, credits, deductions, and exemptions. The regulatory structure was also business-friendly; the state's Pollution Control and Ecology Commission was dubbed by critics the "Pollution Permission Commission," and Clinton, emphasizing growth over conservation, did little to try to change it. I asserted that even if he was an old-style philosophical liberal deep in his soul—as I suspected he was when he pillowed his head at night—he read political attitudes too well and loved winning elections too much to behave as one. To that extent, he might be more palatable to businesspeople because of his willingness not to be philosophically pure or true to himself.

Beyond that, he might actually have a few worthy new ideas in his arsenal of synthesized "new Democrat" solutions. A system of managed health care competition, welfare reform, and a fresh attitude toward America's role in international economics were well worth a try.

Do not fear, I advised them: Clinton is a free trader. He was the first person I'd ever heard talk about the global economy as the wave of the future. It would require "working hard and working smart," not isolationism or protectionism, he'd always said. I recalled those speeches somewhat vaguely; they were easy to sleep through in the mid-1980s back in Arkansas.

But don't forget, I said, that Clinton is averse to conflict and a ready compromiser who tries hardest to please those who disagree with him or seem to lack respect for him. Confronted with a choice—oblige or not oblige—he'll try to oblige nearly every time. Eventually you'll come to like him more than you now think you will like him, I predicted. You may like him more than I like him. You may like him more than labor, blacks, and elitist liberals will like him.

The businesspeople might have been less than persuaded, and not only because Clinton appeared already—by that seventh day—to have backed down on the issue some of them asserted to be singularly most vital to fiscal reform and most revealing about his status as a new kind of Democrat: a presidential line-item veto. Clinton had advocated it as a candidate as a vital method for effecting a presidential check and balance against incurably profligate congressional spending.

Over their pre-dinner cocktails, several of these businesspeople lamented that they'd had such hope that Clinton could make the line-item veto his version of what China was to Richard Nixon. In other words, it was something he could get done as a Democrat that a Republican would never have been trusted to do—just as Nixon, respected on foreign policy, could take the dramatic, somewhat liberal action of opening diplomatic doors to China when no Democrat would have been ceded the credibility to do it. But Senator Robert Byrd of West Virginia, the tough and traditional chairman of the Senate Appropriations Committee, had put a stop to the line-item veto very quickly. He could personally insert programs into the appropriations bills. He didn't want a president who could personally take them out. Clinton chose not to fight him.

Since the advent of his second incarnation as governor of Arkansas, the new president had always picked his fights carefully and infrequently, even grudgingly, and almost always pragmatically. When he decided against an early battle with the king of appropriations over a line-item veto, it was tactical. People argued about whether it was common sense or tail-tucking retreat. It was both; in smart politics, as in war, well-chosen retreat is a matter of common sense. Maybe you don't fight for a line-item veto because you want to pass a budget. But this was an argument that would rage in coming months: Would Clinton make tactical retreats based on common sense until he'd been routed and lost a war? Would he synthesize too finely and die of self-inflicted pragmatism, overrun by his own concessions in his hallowed middle ground?

But the businesspeople were less than persuaded for a larger reason, or at least because of a larger distraction. The dinner conversation that evening centered on the lead story on the evening news: Clinton, right out of the box, with the sounds of his inauguration echoing still, was trying to lift the ban on gays in the military. Senator Sam Nunn of Georgia, a genuine moderate-to-conservative Democrat, was trying to stop him.

* * *

There are two things a politician cannot be and succeed in main-stream national politics: a tax-and-spend liberal and a cultural liberal. (Right-wing extremism might have been a third curse in the early 1990s, though Reagan's presidency seemed too recent to make a definitive case when the Religious Right was establishing itself as a real Republican force.)

Clinton would be cast as a tax-and-spend liberal soon enough, but the extraordinary thing was that he managed to cast himself as a cultural liberal—making gay rights his seeming priority—before he found his way to the White House bathrooms.

There were voters who thought they were getting in Clinton a Nunn-like Democrat, not one who would fight with the Georgian on a basis of social ideology over a volatile issue affecting homosexuals and the armed forces.

Americans are fairly tolerant, by and large. Give them time to think about it and they'll decide it's not really fair to ban gays uniformly from military service. But give them a new president who seems to make that the centerpiece of his early presidency and it makes them uneasy or even frightened. It also makes them angry if they had elected that president for entirely different reasons and on the promise of an entirely different priority, that being laser-beamed attention on the domestic economy.

Americans don't want their presidents to be on or even near the fringes of issues, and, as George Bush learned, they don't want them to tout their presidencies on central points that they then contradict or belie by their actions. They are pro-choice, but anti-abortion, as Clinton smartly understood. The new president enjoyed explaining the difference between tolerance and permissiveness: Americans would tolerate abortion as a legal right of personal choice, but they did not want government encouraging it beyond keeping it legal—i.e., paying for it with tax money, thus being permissive about it. Mainstream voters turned off to Pat Buchanan's declaration of a cultural war or a religion war, but they weren't ready for Barney Frank as president, either.

What had destroyed Michael Dukakis in 1988 was his utter acqui-escence to the Republicans' portrayal of him as a man who wanted to take everyone's guns, let prisoners loose, go soft on criminals even if his wife was raped, and discourage schoolchildren from saying the Pledge of Allegiance to an American flag he didn't mind their burning. Clinton had spent the fall of 1988 decrying Dukakis's bungling of these matters. For weeks he'd walked around with a script for a commercial he'd written that, he asserted, showed how Dukakis should respond to charges of criminal coddling, particularly the Willie Horton matter. (Basically, Clinton wanted Dukakis to turn the issue around and argue that bad guys had been let out on federal furloughs as well. In a dozen years in Arkansas, Clinton had become a good counterpuncher. The nation saw that in the presidential campaign of 1992.)

But now, with one issue, the Democrat who knew much better than Dukakis how to appeal to middle-class voters and win an election was defining himself as Dukakis had been defined by Republicans. He was doing it in the worst way, as a first presidential impression, and thus a lasting one.

That night in San Diego, a man asked, "Is Clinton so naive that he has no understanding of the military culture?" I answered that Clinton was lulled to sleep on the issue in a way that indicated he lacked a full appreciation of the military culture. "Doesn't that scare the hell out of you?" the man asked. "Not at all," I said. But I told the man that he had analyzed the matter perfectly as being naivete and assessed the political problem precisely—as one of Clinton's lack of credibility as commander in chief.

The military culture, which had resisted racial integration more than four decades before, placed great value on unit cohesion based on a surrender of individual rights. The brass saw no prejudice in its position that young men couldn't work together if one might be attracted to another sexually or romantically. Young soldiers sometimes ridiculed each other as "faggots" if they failed to perform their duties with toughness. How could they do that if the unit was infested with actual gays? How in that environment does one insult a gay man? Accuse him of liking girls? These questions, silly though they be, and inherently homophobic, were real.

The draft-dodging, war-protesting career politician named Bill Clinton—the man whom fate would assign to oversee the necessary and sensible downsizing of the military-industrial complex in the post–Cold War—had little to no sensitivity to such questions.

In the new Clinton White House, only three top-level officials demonstrated in those early days a sensitivity to gay rights and an obliviousness to the obvious dangers that were sufficient to keep the issue of gays in the military in the forefront of the presidential debut through a kind of inertia.

Not among them was Mack McLarty, the chief of staff, a moderate-to-conservative businessman and utility executive from a well-to-do Arkansas family who, truth be known, was more in line with his Georgia friend, Sam Nunn, than with Clinton on the issue. Also innocent was Hillary Rodham Clinton, who was otherwise occupied plotting a medical care revolution and who, though more identifiably liberal through some of her associations and causes, often was more calculatingly pragmatic than her husband. She also had a long history of letting her husband make his own mistakes.

One of the guilty was George Stephanopoulos, the whiz kid from the campaign. In his dual role as spokesman and policy adviser, Stephanopoulos kept reminding Clinton that he had made a promise to lift the ban.

On many issues Stephanopoulos demonstrated a pragmatism that made him a valuable presidential adviser. In fact, on most issues he seemed driven by a belief that his best service to his own liberal philosophy was to encourage pragmatic and compromising actions that would help this Democratic president succeed and therefore keep Republicans out of the White House. But his thinking on this issue—that breaking the promise might damage Clinton as much or more than keeping it would damage him, and that there was something to be said for principle and getting the issue out of the way—turned out, by his own eventual admission, to be dead wrong politically. Back in Arkansas I'd once heard a man say, "Sometimes you just have to rise above principle." This, for Bill Clinton, was such a time. At least it was a time to delay principle to a less conspicuous moment of his presidency.

Another with complicity was Anthony Lake, the national security adviser. He argued that if Clinton simply signed the order lifting the ban and then was overriden by Congress, gays would gain nothing. It was better, then, he said, to try to arrive at a compromise. That turned out to be the worst political advice of all. It put the issue at the top of Clinton's agenda as he moved into the White House, and it sent a signal of presidential vacillation.

The third was Bill Clinton himself. As Americans were discovering, he had a heart as big as Alaska and he wore it on his sleeve. He could get teary-eyed over the smallest thing. He'd left puddles of tears beneath his good-bye hugs back in Arkansas.

In his anti-war days, he'd befriended a contemporary young liberal named David Mixner. In time, the bright and articulate Mixner would become a successful businessman in California. In time, he would "out" himself to his friend Bill Clinton, who, through that friendship and others with gays, would come to view homosexuality as an uncontrollable fact of existence for some fine people who, as a result, faced discrimination.

The issue symbolized dramatically the generational change in America that Clinton's election provided. During the 1980s, baby boomers who were well educated, socially conscious, and socially active had become well acquainted with, and in many cases turned out already to be friends with, persons who were gay and had decided to say so.

What happened to this supposedly crafty, overpromising, and overcompromising politician was that he fell asleep at the switch and then got strung out on nothing less than a principle grounded in his generation, philosophy, and compassion. He woke up after he'd broken so many other campaign promises that he decided he had no viable option other than to try to keep this one, or at least appear to try to keep it.

He saw the issue as a simple one of civil rights, one area where his commitment had seldom been questioned. In my many criticisms of Clinton, I'd never even hinted that he lacked compassion or fairmindedness, for he didn't. And he decided that if he was to try to keep the promise, he'd best do it early—as far from reelection time as possible.

He had made the promise to lift the ban in a campaign appearance before a gay group in Boston. He readily makes promises to groups: all too readily when campaigning. It seemed a simple enough issue to him, and there were cost savings. The military was expending millions to defend the policy of gay exclusion in federal court. He didn't stop to think the matter through beyond that. He didn't know enough about the military to think it through. Then—and this is important—he'd heard barely a peep about it, much to his campaign strategists' surprise.

In August 1992, just back from the Democratic National Convention, I'd run into James Carville, Clinton's quirky and celebrated campaign strategist, on a Little Rock sidewalk. What did Carville expect the Republicans to throw at Clinton in the fall? "Liberal, abortion, gays," he said.

It didn't happen that way. The Republicans hit Clinton on taxes, trust, draft evasion, and war protesting. They were snake-bitten on the socioreligious issues. They had sustained severe damage from a back-lash against Pat Buchanan's speech at their national convention in Houston. The socioreligious issues that usually could be exploited to build fear—all falling under the general category of mainstream family values—seemed to be negated in 1992 by the voters' beliefs that they'd been snookered into voting on irrelevancies in 1988 and that the Republicans were being diversionary whenever they raised them.

In 1992, cliché aside, it *really was* the economy. Polls and focus groups repeatedly showed that people simply did not want to hinge their votes on socioreligious issues. It didn't mean they'd all turned into social liberals, abortion advocates, and gay sympathizers; there was something stronger at work in America, a worry about the very future of the American economy, the federal debt, growing global competition, the loss of white-collar jobs, the decline of America's large industries, the dearth of good jobs for college graduates, and whether it might be a good idea for a change to let one party have both the presidency and the Congress so they might get something done instead of stifling each other and, in the process, any hope of progress.

Nothing will put a Democrat to sleep faster than getting elected President of the United States without sustaining Republican exploitation of emotional socioreligious issues. If only George Bush had made an issue of gays in the military during the campaign (which would have made at least as much sense as making an issue of Clinton's student sojourn to Moscow), and if only his attacks had appeared to cut into Clinton's poll numbers, then by election day Clinton would have wiggled his way out of the promise and turned the diversion issue back on Bush, a task for which he had a nice touch. Had that happened, gays in the military would not have been on Clinton's agenda as a seemingly easy vow to keep the minute he took office, requiring only a stroke of the pen.

Gays would have been angry, but they would have voted for him, and he had already benefited from their financial largesse when he needed it most, during the primary. There were countless other issues of concern to gays—AIDS the paramount one, of course—and Clinton was by far the best friend they'd ever had in a presidential candidate.

It was understandable that gays gave little consideration to political pacing. They wanted discrimination to end, and Clinton had promised. But in a way it was horribly unfair for gays to press Clinton on the issue in the beginning: he had at least four years to issue executive orders, but he had no time to waste in trying to establish credibility with, or at least begin to reduce distrust among, the military brass. He had finessed his way out of the draft and organized war protests; he didn't even know how to salute. Tackling gays in the military in his opening fortnight was arguably the single stupidest thing he could ever do.

The political dynamics of the issue bore remarkable resemblance to the reaction early in 1994 to the movie entitled *Philadelphia,* which is about a gay man who is a successful lawyer. He sues his employer after being fired because he has AIDS. Some gays were outraged by the film's sanitized view of a homosexual lifestyle and considered the movie an affront. But in the view of many progressive-thinking people, it was that very sanitized, mainstream appeal that enabled the movie to advance the cause of sensitivity toward gays and AIDS among the movie-going middle class. Clinton needed to appeal to the middle class; it would have been a more mainstream tactic for him to have spent the first two weeks on another issue, any other issue.

Something else had lulled Clinton to sleep. He loved his home state of Arkansas, no doubt. But he'd long looked at Arkansas as a curiously populist place located on the buckle of the Bible Belt where he had to make concessions to keep himself in office and his national hopes alive. Suddenly, as president, he sensed that on some social issues he had greater freedom to be himself. For example, he'd talked around the abortion issue for a dozen years in his home state. Arkansas voters sensed he was pro-choice, but he never came out and said it straight-forwardly until he announced his presidential candidacy and the political advantages were utterly clear.

Likewise, on gays in the military, Clinton sensed that he could stand for something as president that he would have been forced to run from in Arkansas. He was in a broader arena now, with a more widely enlightened constituency; in other words, there would be more cover. As recently as 1991, he'd cowered when a bill was introduced in the Arkansas legislature to repeal the sodomy statute, and was grateful it never got out of a Senate committee where members responded essentially this way: This law is ridiculous, but does anyone in his right mind think I can vote to repeal it and go to church back home on Sunday? Only after he entered the Democratic presidential primary and ACT UP, a gay activist organization determined to make public scenes, sent a couple of agents to Arkansas—threatening kiss-ins and to apply for marriage licenses in the courthouses of rural counties—did Clinton announce that he thought the law should be repealed.

As it turned out, Arkansas wasn't all that curious; it was, in fact, a pretty good training laboratory for the politics of the presidency, except that it contained no urban area and, naturally, offered no exposure to foreign policy. But on social policy, if it wouldn't play there, it probably wouldn't play in Peoria, either.

In Arkansas, Clinton had benefited from challenging, obsessive, protective, and parentlike staffers who used varying, complementary styles to keep him in check and remind him of what might not play. He wasn't getting that kind of staff counsel in the first days of his presidency.

His longtime friend and fiercely devoted Arkansas aide, Betsey Wright, had not joined the White House but had gone to work for the Wexler Group, a liberal Democratic lobbying concern, instead, because key campaign aides such as Carville and Stephanopoulos had seen her, probably rightly, as overemotional, counterproductive, and high-maintenance. "The last thing we need around here is more stress," a White House aide said.

But the frequently emotional, often tearful Wright, a longtime advocate of women in politics, had been effective in Arkansas disciplining Clinton, keeping him from making too many commitments or errors of judgment, even if it required a screaming match. A heated challenge was the kind of thing that got through to the emotion-driven and temperamental Clinton. He would respond first in kind, then often with an apology and a tacit acceptance that probably she was right. Another gubernatorial aide once told about being screamed at by Hillary over the telephone while Clinton and Wright stood on each side of her and screamed at each other.

Say what you will, it worked. Seldom were there hard feelings. As I knew from experience, the new president had great capacity for spontaneous anger, but little capacity for sustaining it beyond twelve hours. He loudly cursed me over the telephone late one night—because I hadn't written that his Democratic run-off opponent in 1982 was being backed by Republicans—then apologized the next morning.

But as he became president, his inner circle contained no overwrought screamers willing to get in his face or treat him as someone needing handling—as someone who, left to his own devices, would make too many commitments, trust too many people, display a lack of personal discipline, and barrel into trouble armed with nothing but supreme confidence and optimism. Instead, the inner circle contained personal friends who treated him with the deference they believed that not only the office deserved, but that the well-meaning and accomplished young occupant, a meritocrat who had risen by his own abilities from consummately modest beginnings, deserved. It was reminiscent of Clinton's ill-fated first gubernatorial term in Arkansas—of a wrong-headed inertia that Clinton wouldn't stop and that none of the young, well-educated, self-congratulating, left-leaning activists around him could influence.

Stephanopoulos (excepting his damaging advice on gays in the military) and Bruce Lindsey, Clinton's dear friend from Little Rock and their youthful days on Senator Fulbright's staff, were in the beginning the nearest thing to the kind of valuable adviser on the intersection of policy and politics that Clinton needed. They were familiar with his weaknesses and possessed campaign experience, practicality, unswerving loyalty, enough nerve to challenge him, and enough self-assuredness to stand in and take the kind of profane abuse he could sometimes dish out. But Stephanopoulos wasn't settled into such a role in the early days of the presidency; he was preoccupied and miscast dealing with the media. Lindsey was given the massive task of coordinating the appointment of subcabinet officials throughout the government; it was a nine-month job, at a minimum, that would wear him down and temporarily take him out of Clinton's inner circle of advisers.

Mack McLarty, the courtly chief of staff who saw his job as more a low-profile facilitator than high-profile dictator, could be firm, but in a subtle way. His style was corporate and proper, not political and gritty. He was well suited to deflect the president's temper, but not to match it or to draw positive energy from it.

He and the president had been friends since kindergarten in Hope, and Clinton respected McLarty because his chief of staff represented many of the things that the president was not: a product of a prominent, well-to-do family, schooled in the corporate world, a decent high school athlete, meticulous, ever proper, and organized to the point that he put time with his sons on his written schedule.

Back in Arkansas, McLarty had been more conventionally popular than Clinton. In 1963, Clinton was elected at the American Legion's Arkansas Boys State Convention as a delegate to Boys Nation, where he shook the hand of John F. Kennedy in the Rose Garden. But Boys Nation was a consolation prize; McLarty had been elected governor of Boys State. Clinton was a political prodigy when at age twenty-seven he nearly unseated a veteran Republican congressman; McLarty had been elected to the Arkansas legislature at the age of twenty-three, two years after he'd been elected president of the student body at the University of Arkansas at Fayetteville and his father, who owned and operated Ford dealerships that Mack later inherited, delivered the vans to keep his son's campaign promise to implement a shuttle system on the campus.

But there's a big gap between kindergarten and the age of forty-six, which is when these boyhood friends reunited in the White House to work side by side for the first time.

McLarty liked to say that the president had never raised his voice to him—a concession to their friendship and to McLarty's unending personal courtesy. But it also provided a clear indication that as they reunited in the White House, there was too much cordiality and too little energy and free expression in their relationship.

Clinton directed temper tantrums at a half dozen other White House aides—Stephanopoulos, Lindsey, doorkeeper Nancy Hernreich, deputy chief of staff Mark Gearan, national security adviser Anthony Lake, and especially his young personal assistant Andrew Friendly. None could see his or her way clear to shout back at the President of the United States. They compared notes on how they deflected these tantrums, and everyone agreed that Hernreich, who was from Fort Smith, Arkansas, and had known Clinton for two decades, was the most adept. She'd sigh, maybe smirk a bit, shake her head, deliver a firm reply, and go on about her business.

McLarty told everyone not to worry about it. The president yelled at them when he should have been yelling at his chief of staff.

The fact was that in the latter years of his governorship of Arkansas, Clinton had grown bored in the job and weary of Wright's obsessive, hovering style. The fact was that he didn't want a strong chief of staff. He didn't like being controlled; he didn't like surrendering freedom; he didn't know anyone he considered significantly smarter than himself on a general basis.

McLarty only later came to realize that Clinton had needed, and would accept, a kind of parenting from him. The president had wanted his friend and chief of staff to apply his self-discipline and organizational skills to Clinton—to keep him closer to schedule and in focus. But McLarty was new to Washington, filled with a bit of wonder in the beginning, and initially uncomfortable breaking up a national security briefing or a cabinet meeting by scolding the President of the United

States or the Secretary of Defense for unproductive, intellectual verbosity. (Les Aspin, the Defense Secretary, was even more professorial—more inclined to analyze options than choose one—than Clinton.)

By late in the year, McLarty had begun to pass Clinton notes saying such things as, "Get to the point, Haiti, and wrap this up." Once McLarty literally took the president by the arm to free him from a self-indulgent discussion with aides so that they could discuss scheduling. Clinton, when confronted in that almost parental way, would follow instructions. McLarty also worked up the nerve to tell Clinton late in the year that he thought his temper tantrums were unbecoming, and the president agreed. But they merely subsided for a while. When things go wrong, Clinton lashes out at those around him.

McLarty told me late in the year that working with Clinton had been revealing. "I told the President the other day, only half-jokingly: 'I'm convinced more than ever of your greatness, and I'm convinced more than ever of your goodness. But what I'll never understand is how a man with such genius for organizing his thoughts and articulating them could be so disorganized in managing himself.' "

McLarty was not a policy man in the beginning, and only occasionally did he seek as the year progressed to influence the president with his centrist views, which were pretty much in line with those senators such as Nunn and John Breaux of Louisiana, both high officials in the "new Democrat" Democratic Leadership Council to which McLarty, as a corporate president, had contributed thousands of dollars through the late 1980s. Instead, McLarty functioned as the White House staff's chairman, a presidential facilitator and aspiring "honest broker," a liaison to businesspeople, and the White House's best connection to moderate-to-conservative Democrats in Congress.

In White House structural parlance, an "honest broker" is a chief of staff who uses his access to the president to lay out options and reasonings provided by the staff and cabinet, but not to editorialize or lobby. "I really took the 'honest broker' thing too seriously in the beginning, I think," McLarty said late in the year. Eventually he realized that since the chief of staff got a lot of blame when things went wrong, it might behoove him to offer his own two cents' worth on policy, which he did by pressing Clinton to accept more spending cuts in his budget and then go to the mat for NAFTA.

Clinton had also benefited in Arkansas from the sage if unsophisticated counsel of what we called good ol' boys who were father figures, undoubtedly filling the great vacuum in Clinton's life. Maurice Smith, for a time Clinton's gubernatorial executive secretary, was the proto-type: an old guard pol from a tiny place called Birdeye, a country banker and farmer whose political operations dated to the Orval Faubus days in the 1950s, he had an ever present cigarette, a graveled voice, and a subtly firm hand that Clinton respected. Another fellow not much older than Clinton wore cowboy boots with his business suits and hailed from a slow little place called Yell County between Little Rock and Fort Smith. His name was Jim Pledger, and Clinton made him the state director of the Finance and Administration Department and, for a time, when Clinton and Betsey Wright were on the outs, his chief of staff. Countless times Pledger had said over the years, "Gov'ner, we'll do that if you want to, but I don't think they're gonna go for it up in Yell County." Usually, his quiet admonitions prevailed.

Just as there were no screamers in the presidential inner circle, there were no cowboy-booted good ol' boys, either. Maurice Smith was ailing physically and in a job he liked as director of the Arkansas Highway and Transportation Department. Clinton talked to Pledger about a Washington job, some kind of job, but the discussions were aborted early: moving from Yell County to Little Rock had been adventure enough for the country boy.

McLarty, Bruce Lindsey, and Senator David Pryor of Arkansas thought of themselves as Clinton's common-sense advisers from back home, but while McLarty was more surefooted on management than policy, Lindsey was buried in résumés as head of personnel, and Pryor wasn't with the president all the time. Dale Bumpers of Arkansas was reasonably close to the president, but he was more independent-minded than Pryor. Whereas Pryor could be counted on to devote himself to the president, Bumpers, who once had been touted for president him-self, was more inclined to leave the balance of presidential bidding to Pryor.

Bumpers's best service to Clinton was his wit, irreverence, and level-headedness. For example, he told Clinton that the White House is "the crown jewel of the federal penal system."

All of that is to explain that in the beginning Clinton essentially was on his own in the big city, surrounded by Arkansas friends who were Washington virgins, a circle of Rhodes Scholars, a circle of Californians, and otherwise by names from his networking Rolodex—friends from academia, think tanks, the business world, and the national Democratic apparatus who had no experience working with him day to day. They knew him from an earlier phase of his life, or through notes and telephone calls, or through occasional get-togethers. They knew he was a spectacular political candidate and as smart as anyone they had encountered. But they didn't know anything about the naivete and recklessness with which he could sometimes govern if not confronted either with a scolding or a homey piece of common-sense advice.

Young aides in the White House called Clinton "the icon of hope." Back in Arkansas, aides had called him a project to be watched lest he hang out with the wrong person—a utility executive whose company was trying to raise rates or an investment banker under investigation by a federal grand jury or a wheeler-dealer who destroyed a savings and loan—or do something foolish such as announcing an Arkansas legislative session from Boston or getting a haircut on an airport runway from a Hollywood stylist who regularly charged $200. He was amid higher IQs now, with greater intellectual stimulation, but less common sense.

It went without saying that Clinton's White House staff lacked on-the-job experience. It had to be so. Democrats hadn't been near the White House for a dozen years. There was no on-the-job experience to be had among them except with refugees of the failed Carter administration. Clinton couldn't load up with Carter retreads lest he appear another Carter.

As it was, he decided that the need for experience necessitated that he turn to Carter retreads in the area where he needed the greatest compensation for his own inexperience and inattention: foreign policy. But instead of compensation, these appointees turned out to be Clinton clones: cautious, agonizing, indecisive, overly pragmatic centrists. They were Secretary of State Warren Christopher, a corporate lawyer and second-ranking State Department official under Carter, whose conciliatory, careful style conveyed blandness; and national security adviser Anthony Lake, who had a reputation as an academically oriented composer of position papers but not as a forceful decision maker. Lake was known as a "first second," meaning he would speak up for a policy only after someone else had recommended it. It had been Stephanopoulos who chanced a recommendation on gays in the military: keep the promise. It had been Lake who said that was a worthy idea, but mayber the president should compromise.

Clinton had wanted Christopher, a veteran of the State Department and of the delicate negotiations of corporate law, to manage the world for him—keep it on hold if he could—while he pursued a dizzying domestic agenda. It's doubtful whether anyone could have managed the world in 1993. But Warren Christopher certainly could not.

The gap between Clinton the campaigner and Clinton the governor was evident in the absence of campaign officials in the high echelon of the West Wing. James Carville, who didn't want a government job and certainly wasn't suited for one, was a bit taken aback after his first trip to the White House in late January. He didn't see many people he knew well from the inner sanctum of the gritty, tough, and widely acclaimed campaign. Other than Stephanopoulos and Lindsey, whom Carville labeled "solid," he saw strangers.

McLarty had been running the Arkansas Louisiana Gas Company, trying to steer the troubled *Fortune* 500 company through natural gas deregulation, plummeting stock prices, and steep debt, during the campaign. Carol Rasco, the surprise choice as domestic policy adviser, beating out the centrist products of the Democratic Leadership Council and Progressive Policy Institute, had been toiling on Clinton's gubernatorial staff back in Little Rock, but on policy, not politics, handling his health care and welfare reform initiatives before the National Governors Association. Bernie Nussbaum, the White House chief counsel and an old friend of Hillary, had been practicing law with a prestigious New York firm. Vince Foster, Jr., the deputy counsel, had been doing the same at Hillary's Rose Law Firm in Little Rock.

These were the best and most trusted mutual friends of Bill and Hillary. The point of their selections was that they would devote their talents to the president's agenda, not their own. It was not unheard of to rely on different kinds of aides for campaigning and governing. Bradley Patterson, a fourteen-year veteran of Republican White Houses, was quoted in *The Strategic Presidency* (1988), by James Pfiffner, as saying: "The virtues needed in the crucible of the campaign are almost to the opposite of the preparation needed for life in the White House."

But the problem on Inauguration Day was that the Clinton White House wasn't politically trained or Washington-seasoned or ready for prime time. The chasm between Clinton the campaigner and Clinton the president was demonstrated by more than grand promises and retreat; it was demonstrated by the replacement of the campaign's cynical, gutty political manipulators with businesspeople, corporate lawyers, issues specialists, and the Clintons' best pals. Clinton had consistently defended himself back in Arkansas against charges that he didn't know how to run government like a business. Now he appeared ready to run the White House with business executives and corporate lawyers, not politicians. He would be politician enough for the White House.

Beyond that, so much effort had been put into synthesizing a cabinet that looked like America and provided a nice balance of traditional Democrats and new Democrats, and in getting it in place by Clinton's needlessly imposed Christmas deadline, that the White House staff had been thrown together almost as an afterthought. On the day the staff had been announced in Little Rock, several transition employees hadn't known if they were on or off.

Carol Willis, a black preacher's son from McGehee, Arkansas, and a twelve-year Clinton aide who was as responsible as anyone for Clinton's intimacy with black constituencies, wanted to go, as he put it, to "the big house." On the day Clinton's staff was announced, Willis still hadn't been told anything. He boycotted the announcement, then turned his back on Clinton afterward. "What's wrong with Willis?" Clinton asked McLarty, who explained Willis's displeasure. "Well, make it right. Make it right," Clinton said. Willis was named a vice chairman of the Democratic National Committee, heading voter participation. The West Wing of the White House would be almost exclusively white.

Months later, key White House officials would reflect that it had been a mistake to base Clinton's transition operation back in Little Rock, introducing the new team to Washington barely in time to take over the most powerful office in the world. A couple of months of learning the way around D.C. could not have hurt.

"You can put in your book that I said there are some people working for Bill Clinton who don't work for Bill Clinton, if you know what I mean," Carville said after his early visit to the White House. Stephanopoulos, a Carville ally, said later, "I think James must have been referring to the people in the White House who didn't work in the campaign." Most likely Carville was referring instead to people in the new administration who, unlike campaign staffers who had devoted themselves to the tunnel-visioned goal of Clinton's well-being and thus his election, were determined now that the election was over to push their own policy proposals or personnel considerations with a primary regard for their own interests and a secondary regard for the president himself.

Carville did manage to invoke a comparison. "I was proud of the fact that in the campaign we never had to retract anything or correct a bad leak." That, notably, was the day after Clinton had abandoned his second prospect for Attorney General, Kimba Wood. Her impending nomination had been widely leaked the day before. Presumably it was leaked by someone advocating her selection and not yet sensitized to the Clinton style: no decision is final until it's irretrievable. Until then, like a late-night veto, it can be snatched from beneath the door.

Bruce Lindsey later reflected that the administration might have been assembled backward. Rather than assembling the cabinet and then the White House staff, it might have been wiser to have reversed the process.

What of Vice President Al Gore, who was emerging as the most connected and integral vice president of the modern era? He and Clinton had become good friends during the campaign bus tours, but they had been only casually acquainted generational rivals before that.

One of the great ironies of the campaign was that Clinton's choice of Gore as running mate solidified the nominee's moderate reputation and appeal. The fact was that Gore was perceived as a moderate because he said so, because he exhibited knowledge on arms issues, and because his wife had led a campaign to label rock music. But Gore's voting record in the Senate was solidly liberal by modern definition, and his best-selling book on the environment was hardly a centrist manifesto. Clinton's credentials as a centrist governing Arkansas—support for the death penalty, pro-business tax policies, neglect of the environment in the interest of development—were far better than Gore's as a senator, although, to be fair, a governor could choose his issues and escape the occasionally defining votes that were required in the Congress.

Gore's early influence was to push for expeditious lifting of the ban on gays in the military, which would have been promptly overridden in the Senate (to the president's utter humiliation), and to persuade Clinton to propose a complex tax on the energy content of fuels that struck many others in the Clinton administration as ill-conceived and that died an ugly death at the hands of Southern moderates in the United States Senate.

What of Hillary Rodham Clinton, widely accused of being the real president, or at least widely believed to be the new president's strongest influence and enforcer?

The fact was that in Arkansas she had been busy with a law career and had exerted her considerable influence not generally, but mostly on matters of her choosing and of special interest to her, such as education and children's services. Now, as the president's wife, it would be much the same: She busied herself with health care. She had never been, and would not now be, her husband's shadow or baby-sitter. Clinton's aides and associates in Arkansas told this story from August 1986: He was on Hilton Head Island in South Carolina to assume the chairmanship of the National Governors Association. When supporters arrived there a day after Clinton had arrived, and a day before the acceptance speech that would provide his biggest step to date into the national arena, they found him very ill with a stomach virus. Had Hillary, who was with him, called a doctor? Given him a pill? No, she told them. He could handle himself. She was no nurse.

Actually, Hillary often behaved in the White House in 1993 as a special-interest advocate for health care reform without regard for the broader presidential strategies. She pushed her own agenda while others were left to try to blend it into the whole. That caused resentment among some of the practical-minded presidential advisers. Bruce Lindsey, for one, found himself at odds with the resolute First Lady over appointments and strategic planning. She pressured him both on personnel choices and the pace of appointments; he, in turn, thought that someone close to the president needed to concern himself with overall strategies because his wife was obsessed with health care and his vice president was obsessed with his assignment: "reinventing government."

Hillary's influence over appointments and the health care issue contributed toward Clinton's finding himself portrayed slightly and precariously to the left of his Southern moderate heritage, and thus losing his connection to middle-class white voters. It is true that Hillary can be more calculating and pragmatic than her husband, but in image and personal alliances, she is to his left. The real difference is that although they think much alike and compose a brainy team of symmetrical strengths (she, more focused and analytical in the lawyerly sense; he, infinitely warmer and more talented intellectually and politically), he has broader interests and will retreat, while she might not.

When Hillary intervened in policy or strategy, sensing a need, one of two things happened: Her husband would take her advice or they would argue, Clinton explaining to her that he, not she, was the president. Her influence was overstated. For years she was a children's advocate in Arkansas, but not until the Center for Youth Law in San Francisco sued him while he was a presidential candidate did her husband acquiesce to spending more money and reforming the state's abysmally failing system of children's services.

In early 1993, Washington was rife with rumors of loud fights between the president and First Lady. In fact, they were known to disagree vigorously in private at times, which is not believed to be uncommon in modern American marriage. It was their style, not unlike Clinton's relationship with Betsey Wright. When they had conflicts, they aired them without reservation in private; but in public, solidarity was always the rule. Perhaps it was understandable that the raw-edged volatility of this private relationship—one in which two bright, independent, strong-willed people were mutually respectful but sometimes rivals for intellectual and tactical superiority—might have unnerved the hovering Secret Service or the White House permanent staff, leading to gossip.

Hillary was forever challenging her husband's judgment about people, telling him that many of those he deemed his friends weren't his friends at all. Often she was right; her husband was entirely too trusting. Sometimes he'd listen; sometimes not. Sometimes he'd agree with her, then prove unable to overcome his soft touch and basic instinct for warmth and gregariousness.

(I should note that while the president and leading White House officials generally cooperated with me in gathering information for this book, a lawyer representing Hillary sent a letter saying she was too busy and would not. The point is that Clinton could not say no but Hillary certainly could.)

Hillary is better than her husband at focusing on a specific issue or assignment, mastering the complexities, and remaining resolute. But she doesn't have her husband's natural political instincts and talents for relating to people and winning affection, a shortcoming she bared through harsh and ill-advised comments during the presidential campaign that led to a self-imposed low profile.

Nor is she as smart as he. The most common refrain among those who know the Clintons well is that although Hillary is smart, the brilliant original thinker in the family is Bill.

I recall the fall of 1980, riding on a plane with Arkansas's First Couple to a campaign stop in Fort Smith, after which we were to take a brief flight to Fayetteville. My assignment was to stay with them all day, but the Clintons were excited that the county sheriff and prosecuting attorney in Fort Smith would hold a news conference later in the day to defend Clinton's handling of the crisis of rioting Cuban refugees at nearby Fort Chaffee. His Republican opponent was using the riot against him rather shamelessly and demagogically, saying Clinton should have "stood up" to his friends in the Carter administration and told them to take the Cubans elsewhere. When I mentioned that I would be with them in Fayetteville, and therefore unable to cover the news conference, Hillary began barking orders: I would stay in Fort Smith for the news conference, then a state police trooper would drive me up the road to Fayetteville. That, of course, would have been an improper use of a state trooper, as Clinton and I knew. He later thanked me for making other arrangements. Hillary was a take-charge person, but she wasn't always attuned to political sensitivities. The sound judgment of a lawyer is not the same as the sound judgment of a politician.

Then, in 1987, the Arkansas legislature was preparing to end its regular session and stayed late one April night to tend to last-minue conference reports and amendment concurrences. It had been a generally unsuccessful session for Clinton: He had proposed expanding the sales tax base to apply a 2 percent gross receipts tax to many business services that were exempt, and had been dealt a decisive defeat by the state's powerful business lobbyists.

These last-night sessions were historically colorful in Arkansas: legislators were tired and playful (one fellow always dressed the last day to look like Colonel Harlan Sanders of Kentucky Fried Chicken fame), and there were reports and circumstantial evidence of alcohol consumption. All the big-time lobbyists had left the Capitol to gather for fellowship at the nearby headquarters of the Arkansas Poultry Federation, a.k.a. the "Chicken House." Suddenly, about 8:00 P.M., Clinton's floor people in the House of Representatives began making motions to suspend the rules and pull out of committee those failed bills extending the sales tax to certain services. The lobbyists down at the "Chicken House" had to rush back in horror and anger, and there were a couple of near fistfights. It turned out Hillary had finished her lawyer's work for the day and joined her husband downstairs in the governor's office, where she had taken charge of strategy and introduced a stranger—combativeness—to it.

Then, in 1990, Clinton's renomination for governor in the Democratic primary was challenged by a lawyer and foundation director named Tom McRae, who ran from the left and began making modest gains in polls about three weeks out. Limited in money, he relied greatly on news conferences, and one day he conducted one in the rotunda of the state Capitol to blast Clinton for being out of state too often and accumulating too much power through a decade in the Governor's Mansion. "Oh, Tom, give me a break," came a familiar female voice. It was Hillary, who ambushed him and engaged him right then and there in a debate that she won handily because, as many members of Congress were to find in 1993, it's difficult to figure out how to deal with the First Lady. But at best her stunt, which the Clintons insisted was spontaneous, was a washout, admired by some and considered untoward by others. Later that year, a group of advisers and contributors met with Clinton to plot his general election strategy. One of them, lawyer Ark Monroe of Little Rock, a second cousin of Gore, worked up the nerve to say he hoped Hillary would not perform any more ambushes. After a pregnant silence, Clinton stonily replied that he thought Hillary's attack on McRae was the highlight of the primary campaign.

Regardless of the president's occasional arguments with his wife, no one could feel comfortable criticizing her to him. One day in 1982, Clinton said to me that campaign aides had told him I didn't like Hillary. It was true. I had told them that. But I resisted being drawn into the conversation; I did not wish to discuss the merits of the governor's wife with the governor. But he badgered. Finally, I said, "Well, yes, I said I find her a little cold and rigid." At that point Clinton proceeded to lecture me about overcoming cultural disconnections—male-female, Chicago-Arkansas—and explain to me that what I didn't understand was that his wife was the single most brilliant and compassionate person he knew.

He might not have been wrong about those disconnects. Consider another campaign plane incident in 1982: Hillary, with two-year-old Chelsea in tow, accompanied her husband on an uncommonly exhausting one-day fly-around to the Arkansas media markets from Little Rock to Texarkana to Fort Smith to Fayetteville to Jonesboro. At the end of the day, flying back to Little Rock, the seemingly tireless and boyishly exuberant Clinton got the idea for a card game of hearts in which he and I would be participants along with his press secretary and campaign travel aide. As we set up a makeshift table, and as Clinton prepared to deal the cards with his left hand, a stern voice came from a seat in the back of the plane where Hillary was holding Chelsea, "Bill—no." As Clinton looked to Hillary sheepishly and explained that a hand or two would relax him, she admonished that he could best use the time to relax, sleep, or work on the script for a radio spot he would tape that evening. After a few seconds of uncertainty, Clinton said he'd play just one hand because it would relax him, and we played, not altogether comfortably. For the longest time I recalled that incident as one in which Hillary displayed a most unattractive iciness. But later I began to mitigate the view; she had spent the day attending to her husband's political needs, piling in and out of a small airplane with her toddler in her arms, presenting the picture of an attractive family to the television cameras that waited at the end of every runway. She was tired; she was cranky; and in those conditions, the fact that Bill wanted to play cards simply irked her. None of us is at his or her best after a day such as she'd had.

Hillary clearly was more combative, unforgiving, and disciplined than her husband. She therefore was occasionally valuable as an enforcer. But her raw political skills weren't anything to brag about. All things considered, she was best suited to applying her skills of organizing and maintaining resolve to work on the second floor of the West Wing, overseeing a massive task force delving into the most complex problem facing the federal government, occasionally finding time to influence her husband and exhort him to straighten up. The only problem was that the nation's most complex issue now had an added complication in the White House: Anyone wanting to challenge the approach to it had to challenge the most brilliant and compassionate person the president knew.

In the touted "collegial" White House atmosphere, all of these personalities and styles—McLarty's, Stephanopoulos's, Lindsey's, Hillary's, and Gore's—pulled at a synthesizing president who lacked a gravitational force toward a solid center.

Some of Clinton's old friends at the "new Democrat" organizations, the Democratic Leadership Council and the Progressive Policy Institute, grumbled that the president was leaving them behind and behaving as an old-style liberal Democrat. They didn't blame Clinton, but the people around him. They weren't merely extending politeness toward the president; they genuinely believed that he was not the master of his own domain, but a prisoner of his advisers.

Mainly, their complaints at that point had to be with the influence of First Lady Hillary over appointments and health care, Vice President Gore over the energy tax, Labor Secretary Robert Reich for pushing an economic stimulus bill, and George Stephanopoulos and Tony Lake over the big one: gays in the military. But if the charge was lurching to the left, Clinton had personal complicity.

Within a week of his election, a reporter asked Clinton in Little Rock if he intended to keep his promise for an expeditious early order lifting the ban on gays in the military. Yes, Clinton said. But the issue, he explained, was how to address gay behavior, not gay orientation, in the code of military conduct. That was a complication, he said. He was beginning to wake up; he was telegraphing the familiar retreat. But when the reporter asked Clinton if he was backing down on the specific promise to lift the ban, Clinton said absolutely not.

Senator Bumpers saw Clinton the next day when they met at a Little Rock hospital to visit Senator Pryor, who had undergone bypass surgery. Bumpers told the president-elect that he was handling himself well. But he advised that the gays-in-the-military issue would be nothing but trouble. It was odd. Bumpers's record was more uniformly liberal than Clinton's, but here was the more liberal mentor advising the would-be synthesizer and supposed new Democrat that he was wading into shark-infested waters. Clinton replied that he had no choice. He had promised.

The Republicans in Congress, with the tricky electoral equation now moot, swung into action. Maybe George Bush couldn't use the issue in the campaign, but now they certainly could wrap it around the new president's neck. They could rough him up and paint him as a liberal. They would try to override the order with legislation, they said. Sam Nunn, who chaired the Armed Services Committee and was the Democrats' most credible militarist, would help them, although Clinton had the too-trusting idea that eventually Nunn would do the partisan thing and help him smooth over the issue.

Sandy Berger, a foreign policy specialist on the transition staff who would become assistant national security adviser in the White House, asked for the help of one of Clinton's best and most able friends, John Holum, a lawyer in Washington and a former Air Force officer who wanted to be Secretary of the Navy. Holum was assigned to examine the military policy banning gays and determine what it would mean to lift it, and how it could best be done.

When Clinton had abruptly bowed out of running for president in 1987, Holum had flown down to Little Rock to help him write the speech he would deliver the next day at the event that had been planned originally as a formal announcement of his candidacy. In September 1991, when Clinton met with friends to decide whether to seek the presidency, Holum was there. When it came time to write the platform at the Democratic National Convention in 1992, Holum protected the nominee's interests.

During this time, Clinton had briefings from military leaders and a session with General Colin Powell, the chairman of the Joint Chiefs of Staff, with whom he would eventually become fairly friendly. The resistance to gays in the military was strong and ominous.

In fact, two days before Clinton's first meeting with Powell, a couple of curious phone calls came to Arkansas State Senator Vic Snyder of Little Rock, who had sponsored the bill seeking repeal of the state's sodomy statute. The first one was from Don Judges, a member of the faculty at the University of Arkansas Law School at Fayetteville. He said he had been called by Air Force Major Carol Brennecke, an attorney and aide to Powell on the staff of the Joint Chiefs. Judges asked about that sodomy bill and Clinton's reaction to it, and Snyder reacted angrily that the Joint Chiefs seemed to be going behind the back of their commander-in-chief-to-be. Later Major Brennecke called Snyder to say she was merely doing research. Snyder told her that if Powell wanted to know Clinton's thoughts on the sodomy bill in Arkansas, he ought to ask his new boss.

Snyder also accused Major Brennecke of trying to dredge up information that Clinton had embraced an anti-gay position back in Arkansas so that Powell could confront the new president. The truth, which he declined to tell her, was that Clinton had told Snyder privately that he would sign the bill if it was passed in the legislature. That, of course, was a hollow promise to make privately, passage being an absolute impossibility. Brennecke, by the way, was a graduate of the University of Arkansas Law School.

Clinton also spoke occasionally by phone with Nunn, who had endorsed Clinton early in the presidential race as a moderate brother of the Democratic Leadership Council. But their relationship was not quite as warm as they had hoped.

Both the Clintons were still a bit resentful of Nunn for not having shown up to campaign with Hillary in Georgia, as had been planned, on that winter day in early 1992 after Gennifer Flowers made her public accusations against Clinton. Hillary can hold a grudge. Her husband can't unless Hillary feels strongly enough about it to influence him. (In the early 1980s, the Clintons had stayed mad for a couple of years at Bumpers for having said at a roast in Little Rock that Clinton couldn't finish his income-tax return because he couldn't find Hillary to sign as head of household.)

Since being the Democrats' leading militarist was Nunn's claim to fame, and since the defense establishment was his powermaking constituency, and since his home state was pro-military and conservative, he would protect the military's interests and his own home state political interests over those of his party's new president, who seemed to be not quite the moderate brother that Nunn had hoped. Nunn believed Clinton needed him more than the other way around, and Clinton was not sufficiently combative to tell him or show him differently.

By mid-December 1992, John Holum had filed a report. It was balanced and objective. It contained a draft of an executive order to lift the ban. But its most notable suggestion was that the best way to proceed on lifting the ban on gays in the military might be slowly, with a six-month period of study. The military brass's resistance was strong. So was Nunn's. The issue might not be so simple. Six months of study might be worthwhile substantively as well as politically. There were tricky questions about how to accept open gays for induction, but then regulate their conduct once gays were in service.

About that time, in late December, *The New York Times* published a front-page article reporting inside information, based on a leak of Holum's report, presumably by a Clinton insider worried about the president-elect's vacillation, that the president-elect might take six months to ease in the removal of the ban, during which the issue would be studied by the military and the Congress.

Gay groups, who had emerged as a strong Democratic constituency in 1992, and major contributors, felt betrayed and were outraged. They said so in the article. Clinton hadn't promised a study; he had promised an order.

It so happened that Clinton was in the process of breaking, bending, or at least deferring several campaign promises, and getting a lot of unfavorable publicity in the process. The press, mostly friendly to him in the campaign, was gunning for him now. The pattern was unfolding: Cut the Democratic challenger slack as a candidate; deny him any as president.

There would be no middle-class tax cut. There would be no accepting of Haitian boat people. There would be no health care reform without significant added costs. There would be no cutting the deficit in half in four years through economic growth. Clinton talked now in a conciliatory way about China; days before, as a candidate, he'd talked in a combative way about demanding human rights and holding China's "most-favored-nation" status in abeyance.

It's a fact of life in politics: the bravado of campaigning versus the reality of governing. But with Clinton, the gulf was wider than normal.

So the new president, unusually sensitive to press criticism in general and hypersensitive to the charge that he was retreating on everything, since he knew it to be true, decided to try to keep the promise about gays in the military—or, more precisely, to *appear* to try to keep it.

"We knew by December that the Republicans in Congress would act to override us, and succeed—absolutely," Stephanopoulos said months later. In other words, an executive order as promised would have prompted legislation in Congress to slap the new president and codify the ban on homosexuals.

For a short while, but only a short while, Clinton and key advisers considered issuing the executive order in the first weeks of his presidency and letting Congress do whatever it wished. The promise would be kept. The president would have stood for principle.

But soon everyone seemed to agree with the argument that this new president, the first of his generation to lead the country, a man without foreign policy or military credential, would appear dangerously anemic, maybe devoid of presidential stature, if he were overridden on an emotional sociomilitary issue at the very onset of his presidency.

Clinton and some of his people continued to think, wholly erroneously and naively, that Nunn might help facilitate a reasonably smooth and effortless compromise that would let the president cling to his position while getting the issue off his front burner. Months later a leading White House official would explain that the pace of the transition and inauguration planning was so frenetic that it didn't occur to anyone until the week of the inauguration that Nunn hadn't ever indicated any inclination to do anything other than oppose the lifting of the ban.

Then in that first week, a memorandum written by new Defense Secretary Les Aspin to the Joint Chiefs of Staff was leaked to the press. It ordered the Joint Chiefs to come to a meeting not to provide input, but to be told of the president's commitment to lifting the ban so they could begin plans to implement it.

The memo was composed on a computer system at the Defense Department that was on line with the system at the Senate Armed Services Committee. Whoever leaked the memorandum did the president no favor; logically, it could have been done by someone opposed to the ban or by someone favoring it. Those opposed to the ban wanted Clinton to stay firm, and public pressure might help. Those favoring the ban wanted to engender negative reaction to Clinton's intention to lift it.

One effect of the memo was to infuriate Nunn, who didn't like the tone, the stated intent, or the fact that he was being ignored or taken for granted. Even if he had been inclined to facilitate a smooth compromise, he lost the inclination the day that memo showed up on his staff's computer screen.

What an irony, then: The clever pragmatist who tried to balance conviction with mainstream electability found himself a cultural leftist within hours of his joyous Inaugural Parade. It drove him crazy. He wanted to shed the issue. He snapped at Andrea Mitchell of NBC News, who prefaced a question by saying he seemed preoccupied with gays in the military. "No, *you're* preoccupied," he said.

In the second week of his presidency, in the middle of the raging debate, he went over to the Marriott Hotel in Washington and delivered a speech to his old friends at the National Governors Association about the standby issue of would-be new Democrats: welfare reform. It was a non sequitur. Welfare reform wouldn't be undertaken until much later in the year, at the earliest. Clinton was trying to steal a page from the master of changing the subject, Ronald Reagan. It didn't work.

A Clinton friend and frequent campaign volunteer from Arkansas wrote the president a three-page letter to chastise him over his seeming obsession with the issue and lament what he was letting it do to his presidency—i.e., define it unattractively and contradict his campaign image. Clinton wrote back to say he'd bet he hadn't spent three hours on the subject. (Clinton would repeat the line so many times in coming months—including an Oval Office interview with me on June 18— that surely he spent more than three hours claiming to have spent only three hours on the subject.)

Then in his first televised news conference he indicated he might go along with a supposed compromise that would segregate gays within the military, a total betrayal of the principle he'd espoused. He'd lost his celebrated political equilibrium. David Mixner, the old and dear gay friend, attacked the president for betrayal on ABC's "Nightline."

In strict political terms, Clinton made serious miscalculations. He overestimated the goodwill toward a new president, especially one who got only 43 percent of the vote. He underestimated the intensity of the press coverage. He misjudged Sam Nunn. He failed to grasp the extent of the signal he would send by dealing with the issue at the very outset of his presidency. He was not yet sensitized to the modern media's fixation on the presidency: the Cable News Network's on-the-hour news reports, repeating the issue incessantly, and the growing popularity of one Rush Limbaugh, a highly entertaining right-wing talk-show artisan, not to mention the television and radio programming of the Religious Right. If nothing else, they generated telephone calls and mail.

This is what America thought it saw: A young president who had passed himself off as a new kind of Democrat with a "new way," who would "focus like a laser beam on the economy," instead couldn't wait to move into the White House and revert to his days as a long-haired operative for George McGovern's presidential campaign by trying to force a military he loathed to accept open homosexuals. But it wasn't that at all. Clinton wanted the brass's respect and approval. He was merely in a fix of his own making, torn between the massive gulf he tends to create between too much promise and pragmatic retreat. The American people who had elected him and reserved judgment were now getting an eyeful, and, like the people of Arkansas in 1979, they didn't like what they were seeing.

Clinton also failed to sense that once he was into the issue, not even he was clever enough to find a safe harbor or safe exit. He'd either betray gays, alienate a distrustful military, or look like a weakling if he straddled the fence. He couldn't even mention the issue without sustaining a blow in the polls. He had great confidence in his ability to synthesize, but this was an issue that defied his best efforts.

There was one other political miscalculation, fairly basic. The gay rights movement was a social movement, not a tight political organization. A friendly but wise president would have advocated gay rights in a general and educational way. But a savvy president would never have made a specific promise of a specific policy, one so easily enacted that it required only his signature, to a social movement. This was not like promising a policy to the AFL-CIO, then sitting down to horse-trade with Lane Kirkland and other labor pols. A social movement is driven by emotion and a basic principle of rightness that a politician trying to finesse his way through the system is bound to betray.

Amid such rampant miscalculation, the first couple of weeks of Clinton's presidency were truly miserable. The White House switchboards were overloaded; people were calling by the thousands. Half the White House staff was sick. McLarty became chief of staff with a case of strep throat and an important assignment: As a moderate who had contributed to the Democratic Leadership Council and who shared close mutual friends from Georgia with Nunn, he was to help Defense Secretary Aspin and Howard Paster, the chief congressional liaison, work out a time-buying compromise with the senator.

Nunn himself had a cold. He declined to sign off on a compromise one night because, he said, he was under so much medication that he didn't trust his judgment.

During this time, White House aides, especially Paster, were becoming growingly impatient with Nunn. The aloof Georgian was speaking against the president on the Senate floor, granting interviews in which he said he was at a loss to explain Clinton's thinking, and ceding very little in private negotiations.

"We wouldn't have been strung out for as long as we were if Nunn hadn't kept fucking with us," a young White House aide said months later.

Eventually, Nunn would agree to the six months that John Holum had recommended in the first place and that Clinton had already resigned himself to accepting. For a half year, the military would not ask about sexual orientation. Gays could still be discharged for making their preference known. Nunn would conduct Senate Armed Services Committee hearings that would firmly establish himself as the national point man on the issue. Clinton didn't get much. He'd been kicked in the teeth, actually.

Holum never had a meeting with Clinton on his sane and sage report on the issue. His recommendation for a six-month phase-in was forgotten quickly, even as it became reality. "The Holum Report? Gosh, no one's asked about that in a long time," Dee Dee Myers, the press secretary, would say months later.

Nor did Holum win the appointment he sought as Secretary of the Navy. He couldn't get a military appointment, some Clinton aides insisted, because he was associated with the issue of gays in the military. "Just another example of a friend of Bill getting screwed," said another friend of Bill, who also thought she'd been insufficiently appreciated. Eventually Holum got the top job in the disarmament office, and by all accounts enjoys it.

"In retrospect, yeah, we should have settled this issue in December before we got to town," Stephanopoulos said months later. "The President should have put Colin Powell, Les Aspin [Clinton's Defense Secretary], and Sam Nunn in a private room and said, 'I'm committed to changing the policy. Now you guys work it out and tell me in six months how you're going to do it.' "

Holum's report would have offered a perfect excuse: Deferring six months in December would have taken the issue off the new president's plate as he arrived on the job. He would have averted the strong first impression of cultural liberalism. He would have been accused of betrayal by gays, but so what? He was accused of that in July, anyway. Nunn, Powell, and Aspin would have arrived at the same eventual muddled compromise—the military wouldn't ask, gays wouldn't reveal their orientation, and the military wouldn't investigate mere rumors of gay activity.

It would have been judged a retreat from a campaign promise, but one of Clinton's own volition, not as a whipping inflicted on the new kid in town by the brass and Sam Nunn. As a result, some might have been more inclined to see the compromise as a minor advance rather than a total capitulation. Clinton had somehow managed what seemed to be both, and had arrived at that point without the least aplomb.

In the strangest twist of all, the Clinton administration would find itself in late October 1993 appealing a federal court ruling that any discrimination by the military on the basis of sexual orientation was unconstitutional, effectively fighting legally the very point the president had once made on principle.

But four months later Clinton's White House would issue a general statement opposing any state laws restricting the rights of gays. *That* is precisely the kind of position Clinton could and should take regarding a social movement: a general statement about principles.

The real story of this horrible beginning was that Clinton wasn't quite the governing genius as had been portrayed, a shortcoming complicated by a staff of political novices who hadn't ever worked with him at governing and were divided between the left and the center. But the perception that resonated was that Clinton himself was of the cultural left, and a slick, dishonest character who passed himself off in the campaign as something he couldn't wait to betray as president.

The credibility problem would plague the first year of the presidency that Clinton had long dreamed of, maybe since he was nine years old and sat in front of the black-and-white television set back in Hot Springs, mesmerized by the adulation given Adlai Stevenson as he was nominated by the Democratic National Convention.

Clinton's love of cheers and the stage was palpable; staff aides in Arkansas had long half-joked that his instincts for playing to crowds would have made him a good rock and roll performer or televangelist. But from the new presidential stage, before standing-room-only on Pennsylvania Avenue, the new performer was reading no rave reviews after opening night.

His only hope was that he had made one accurate calculation: By

confronting gays in the military in the beginning and getting a resolution, such as it was, in six months, the issue might recede in the
notoriously short span of public attention and become less defining by
the time everyone voted again.

White House aides hoped that would be the case, but the fact was
that Clinton had sustained residual damage among some voters in the
one group he most needed if he was to develop a governing constituency
and get reelected: middle-class whites.

Hopes of his ever again carrying a Southern state besides Arkansas
may have been dashed. And the folks weren't too pleased back in
Arkansas, where, by the way, another attempt to repeal the sodomy
statute had failed.

Things would get worse before they would get better. The man whose
political career had been an action-adventure story would turn the
opening act of his presidency of the United States into a thrilling
highwire act.

CHAPTER 3

The Great Synthesizer,
or the Synthetic Man?

"**A**re you surprised?" Mack McLarty asked with a chuckle.
It was early February 1993, and the issue of gays in the military had been deferred, mercifully.

I had remarked that Bill Clinton seemed determined to address assertively and immediately the real problems of the country—the budget deficit, health care, campaign financing, and a pattern of governmental neglect of urban, social, educational, and job-training needs—and that he also appeared willing to do the politically risky and ask for a bit of sacrifice from the middle class to which he had pandered in his campaign.

Yes, I was surprised.

With all due respect, the Bill Clinton I had known in recent years had been more pragmatic than that. Certainly it surprised me that the man who, after winning back the governorship of a needy state such as Arkansas, had managed in a decade to emphasize only two matters—schools and economic development—to the exclusion of industrial and agricultural pollution, regressive taxation, an outdated constitution, and a bureaucratic quagmire in children's welfare services, would set out to address every serious problem in America in his very first month as president.

By his timetable, he'd reverse Reaganomics by June and revolutionize one seventh of the gross domestic product, the medical industry, by August. After the New Deal and the Fair Deal, this would be Clinton's Hell of a Deal.

"You shouldn't be [surprised]," McLarty explained: Clinton was a bright and voracious student of history, especially the history of his favorite subject, the American presidency. He knew that many presidents' defining successes came early in their first terms when they benefited from congressional reaction to a national spirit of goodwill and high hope. (In *The Strategic Presidency,* H. R. Haldeman, top presidential aide to Richard Nixon, had been quoted as saying, "Your power is going to start eroding from January 20 on.") Clinton knew, too, that the toughest battles should be fought as far from elections as possible, for everyone's sake, as a matter of pure practicality. He also knew that as president he would be judged ultimately and most importantly by history. And Clinton had the idea that nearly two in three Americans had sent one message loud and clear in November: Shake things up.

Others made similar points. "This isn't the Bill Clinton you and I knew in Arkansas," Dale Bumpers said. "He'll be judged by history now." David Pryor, the other Arkansas senator, told me, "Bill Clinton doesn't think he was elected for national tranquility. He thinks he was elected to have a national—oh, what's the word?—catharsis."

I suspected a related factor, one already observed in the debacle on gays in the military. Clinton thought he was largely liberated as president; that he was free of some of the constraints and necessary political pacing of a state that had been settled largely by independent, unsophisticated people fleeing government intrusion. His good friend Diane Blair, a University of Arkansas political science professor whom he would name to the board of the Public Broadcasting Corporation, had in the mid-1980s written a history of Arkansas politics that analyzed the anti-government heritage of the state. Early in Clinton's presidential campaign, she had been quoted in *The New York Times* as saying that there was only so much anyone could accomplish in Arkansas, considering local attitudes and the Arkansas legislature's reflection of them.

Some of Clinton's friends from Arkansas would accuse me in 1993 of that which I had frequently alleged of Clinton: of trying to have things both ways. I accused him of not doing enough as governor of Arkansas, then of disregarding the lessons of Arkansas to try to do too much as president. The criticism certainly deserved an explanation. The record in Arkansas encompassed a dozen years; the overly ambitious agenda in Washington encompassed a few months. Mainly, I believed Clinton could have addressed more issues than schools and job development in a dozen years in Arkansas had he not been primarily concerned with staying snugly perched in the governor's office until the right opportunity came along to seek the presidency. At times I thought Arkansas needed a governor more than it needed the national Democratic Party's great white hope.

"He wants me to do things that'll get me beat," Governor Clinton once said of me to a competing newspaper columnist in Arkansas. Now, as president, he seemed inclined to take those kinds of risks by his own choice, reminiscent though they were of his youthful and ill-fated first term as governor.

Sheer energy surely was a factor. In Arkansas, Clinton had run the state part time and moonlighted as a national political networker gearing up for a run for the presidency. Now he had only one job and there was nothing on his agenda but to do it. His office was at his house.

James Carville walked in to see the new president in early February. A few days later, waiting to deliver a speech in Phoenix, he recalled having had this thought: "We've got to get this guy something to sell. This ain't him, sittin' there waitin' for somebody to drop something in his 'in' basket."

Still, I hardly was alone in my surprise at the substance, ambition, length, breadth, and pure audacity of Clinton's initial presidential agenda.

Up in Lowell, Massachusetts, failed Democratic presidential candidate Paul Tsongas had been quoted as saying he was both surprised and pleased. It was understandable. He and Clinton had argued in their primary about the issues of sacrifice and the deficit. Tsongas ridiculed Clinton's pandering to the middle class, and Clinton, sliding deftly to flank Tsongas on the left, ridiculed him as a moralizer who in fact espoused a kind of Republican premise with trickle-down underpinnings. Now as president, Clinton would abandon the middle-class tax cut and espouse sacrifice for deficit reduction and generational responsibility. In other words, Clinton would attempt to govern as Tsongas had campaigned. This was vintage Clinton: Do what it takes to win, then try to soar unnoticed over the mighty gulf between reckless promise and responsible governing.

In an early February meeting in the Oval Office with the Democratic congressional leadership, House Speaker Tom Foley of Washington said he couldn't hold Democratic votes on the deficit and campaign reform. Democrats might risk their political careers by voting for higher taxes, but it would be too much to ask them to then turn around immediately and repeal some of the incumbents' advantages by limiting political action committee contributions and providing incentives for campaign-spending limits. The president suggested that they move on. Then he turned the discussion to health care reform. Foley asked, "Mr. President, you're not really planning to do health care this year, are you?" Clinton responded that he'd hate to think that with health care the greatest barrier to a balanced federal budget and of grave concern to millions of Americans, the Congress couldn't do something about it in the space of twelve months.

Clinton was wedded to attacking health care, so to speak. His wife had enhanced the centerpiece of his governorship of Arkansas—education reform—by chairing with tenacity and deftness the commission charged with writing new minimum school standards. Now with no law career to continue, she needed, and in fact required, a role. Her husband wanted and trusted her help on substantive matters.

The Clintons thought it ill-advised that Hillary exert influence generally by virtue of being the wife of the president. That would lend itself to criticism and do little for the cause of a woman's independent accomplishment. Hillary wanted a project where she could make her independent mark, and she told her husband she would take the biggest and toughest of them all, health care. He agreed without compunction.

Clinton also had the idea—based on polling data and the advice of strategists such as Carville, who had risen to fame by helping elect Harris Wofford to the U.S. Senate from Pennsylvania on the promise of health security—that health care might be an even better connection to the white working middle class than welfare reform. The 37 million uninsured Americans weren't disproportionately minorities or welfare recipients; they included people who had jobs without full benefits, or who had medical conditions that caused insurers to avoid them, or who changed jobs, or chose self-employment and couldn't afford the non-group insurance rates.

He thought at the time that he could sell health reform as a means of saving money and reducing the long-term deficit and debt, appealing to Perot voters while winning goodwill from working-class people frightened about the continued availability of insurance and affordable health care. In time, research would show that a better sales pitch than deficit reduction was the promise of security—of a middle-class entitlement that couldn't be taken away. American people, it seemed from research, didn't mind a social program if everyone got something from it. What they didn't like was a Great Society program that took from the working class to sustain the cycle of poverty for the deprived and disenfranchised.

Clinton wanted health reform by the mid-term elections so that Democratic incumbents could say they had solved the nation's greatest problem and helped the middle class. Considering the complexities and minefields of such a battle, he thought it wise to start as early as possible. In the back of his mind he thought it might be a second-year issue, but he held to its possibility as a first-year one. And the issue was so complex that even a second-year end game required a first-year timetable.

Foley, who knew Congress if nothing else, was a bit overwhelmed. He saw a long-term agenda requiring the kind of political pacing Clinton had learned in Arkansas. But in the euphoria of the moment, in deference to the historical context of his new station, and with what would turn out to be an exaggerated and overly optimistic reading of his mandate and possibilities, Clinton himself seemed to have disregarded the lessons he had learned the hard way in Arkansas.

In his first gubernatorial term back home, when he was but thirty-two, Clinton had declared war on timber clear cutting, raised automobile licensing fees for a road program, created an Energy Department to fight utilities on their building plans and to push for alternative investment in conservation and renewable resources, set up a rural health program designed to allow nurses to provide some services historically reserved for doctors, and changed the name of the Industrial Development Commission to the Economic Development Department. He changed its focus as well, from chasing smokestacks to pursuing a broader, cleaner strategy to develop the state's economy at least in part from within its boundaries through education and job training. His Republican conqueror attacked it all, benefited from the powerful special interests' fear of Clinton's activism, then repealed the whole agenda. When Clinton came back two years later, he lifted not a finger to try to put any of it back. He'd said to me during his two-year hiatus, "If I ever get the chance again, I'm not going to try to force people to do what's good for them."

Now, as on the issue of gays in the military, Clinton seemed to think his new job transcended those Arkansas experiences.

The new president was confident in his skills as a synthesizer; he was an incurable optimist and a fervent analyst of election returns and the trends they represented. He was as well a firm believer in the virtue of an activist government with a program, if only a pilot one, for whatever ailed you.

It was true that Clinton had learned to focus in Arkansas, but that never seemed to limit the number of items proposed in his areas of focus—education and jobs—or the length of his extemporaneous State of the State speeches. He'd drone for more than an hour with main points, secondary points, and brain-numbing detail. (He always wants to tell you everything he knows, and he knows plenty.)

If you applied those qualities to the presidential election in 1992 and the inauguration in 1993, you got a new president with an optimistic analysis of the election's mandate, making him overconfident about what could be accomplished in reviving government activism through his clever synthesis of the various elements of a pervasive national mood for change.

David Broder, the political writer for *The Washington Post* who had been so impressed with Clinton, wrote that the new president was limited by the fact that he'd won only 43 percent of the popular vote. But Clinton was buoyed by the possibility that he actually might have won 62 percent. That was the combined support for Clinton and Ross Perot, both of whom had preached change. Typically, Clinton saw the glass as more than half-full, even if, technically, it was more than half-empty.

Clinton thought he was clever enough to embroider his support with much of Perot's. He would seek first to recruit Perot. Failing that, he would seek to use him. Failing that, he would seek to neutralize him by emphasizing the issues of interest to his followers: deficit reduction, political reform, and ending what was called "gridlock."

Failing that? He had no plan. Clinton is an optimist.

For the better part of a decade, Broder had watched Clinton at annual meetings of the National Governors Association and been mightily impressed. Clinton was smart as a whip, articulate, congenial, moderate, and level-headed. He seemed to be a thinker, a mediator, and a leader. He seemed to have a predisposition for bipartisan solutions, and a certain charm and knack for them.

That was pretty much the take of David Osborne, a writer from Boston whose first book, published in 1987, was called *Laboratories of Democracy*. Clinton liked the book so much he gave Osborne a job working with Vice President Al Gore on "reinventing government," which happened to be the subject and title of Osborne's second and better-selling book.

Laboratories of Democracy studied a few stellar governors who were confronting problems and, in Osborne's view, reinventing government on their own. His point was that while Reagan practiced a kind of detached federalism, the states were left to confront the real problems of schools, infrastructure, welfare administration, and competition for economic growth. He profiled several governors whose performances, he believed, were effective, and demonstrated what would come to be known as a "new paradigm," or new model—not strictly liberal or conservative, but progressive, creative, competent, consensus-building, and based more in the brain than the heart.

Of the mid-eighties governors he chose to highlight—Clinton, Michael Dukakis, Lamar Alexander of Tennessee, Bruce Babbitt of Arizona, and a few others—Osborne clearly deemed Clinton the cream of the crop. He wrote of his amazement that Clinton could stand in a fairgrounds arena in rural Arkansas and work a crowd to frenzy by preaching for better schools. Osborne lacked cultural perspective: in Arkansas, entertainment offerings are limited. The best forms can be found in the blues-based music of honky-tonks on Saturday night and the dramatic theatrics of preachers in Southern Baptist pulpits on Sunday morning. There was one other venue: the political stump, where the best performers rolled up their sleeves and worked crowds like entertainers or fire-and-brimstone preachers.

This—not Georgetown, Yale, or Oxford—was Clinton's strongest cultural influence, at least in terms of political style. On policy, he was a prisoner of academia and conciliation who could provide a professorial analysis of an issue more easily than he could take a stand on one side or the other. It made him a marvelous moderator of discussions. Combined with his personal charm and desire to be liked, it also made everyone think he agreed with them. The Arkansas landscape was strewn with people who believed Clinton had lied to them, double-crossed them, or left them out to dry.

At Governors Association meetings, which required four or five days of public political performance, and thus were tailormade for Clinton's strengths, the Arkansas governor had taken the lead on writing a set of education goals for the year 2000 that George Bush's administration embraced. In fact, Bush invited Clinton to attend his State of the Union speech in 1990 and mentioned him favorably in the speech, to the considerable chagrin of the long-suffering Republicans back in Arkansas.

Clinton had also taken the lead on writing an NGA position paper on welfare reform. He literally took charge of the process, pen in hand, to choose the words to fashion the right bipartisan compromise.

If the governors had ever elected a Mr. Congeniality or a Most Valuable Player, Clinton would have been it. But David Broder and these other governors did not come back to Arkansas to live with Clinton and get the full story, one based not on four or five days of writing reports, but on 360 days a year offering the good—admirable goals and strong salesmanship—and the bad—poor administrative skills, hedging, retreat, and legislative sessions for which he was seldom well prepared.

Broder thought this new president might use the skills so evident at governors' conferences to expand his political base and build a moderate, pragmatic, mainstream national government, perhaps with one or two Republicans in key positions in the cabinet.

It wasn't an altogether unreasonable expectation. I always joked that Clinton's goal in life was someday to get 100 percent of the vote. And Clinton seemed curiously able to abide Republicans.

At the governors' conference in 1985 in Boise, Democratic governors were livid upon learning that President Reagan had signed a fund-solicitation letter for Republican opponents of so-called liberal Democratic governors. It turned out that the governors had pledged bipartisan cooperation on issues such as education and welfare reform. Now the Democrats felt double-crossed by Reagan's partisanly offensive rhetoric.

All except Clinton, that is. He said he understood that politics was a contact sport. He suggested that maybe the national Republican Committee sent out the letter without any real input from Republican governors. He said the last thing the governors needed to do was to behave like Congress. When a select group of governors met in a summit to address the controversy, reporters could watch through a glass door. At one point it appeared that Michael Dukakis, the Democratic governor of Massachusetts, and John Sununu, the Republican governor of New Hampshire, whose paths would collide in the 1988 presidential campaign, were about to come out of their chairs at each other. There between them, his hands extended palms-forward as if to make peace, was Bill Clinton.

But Clinton's attempted synthesis as president would not be bipartisan, at least not in the beginning. First it would be within the Democratic Party, which was badly split. Yes, he could get things passed with the exclusive support of his own party, but he had to bridge Sam Nunn and Ted Kennedy to do it.

He needed to straddle the gap between traditional liberals who had elected him and DLC-type moderates and "new Democrats" who had essentially nominated him by jump-starting him to major primary victories across the South. Both factions in the Democratic Party could claim credit for Clinton's election, and thus ownership of him. His best votes in November had come in typical liberal congressional districts. But he couldn't have appealed to working-class white voters without advancing such DLC concepts as welfare reform and distancing himself from the Reverend Jesse Jackson. Just as he was adept at relating to diverse groups, so was he beset by those competing groups claiming proprietary interests in him.

This typifies Clinton's predicament and challenge: his wife was a former board chairman of the Children's Defense Fund, which reacted coolly to the welfare reform idea of cutting off aid to welfare recipients after two or three years. Clinton, however, had been affiliated with centrist Democratic groups who believed such a proposal was at the very heart of redefining the party's message as one of responsibility instead of entitlement. Typically, Bill Clinton was firmly on both sides. Confidently and optimistically, he thought he could synthesize these competing philosophies with an all-encompassing third way that would require welfare recipients to seek and take work, but with some kind of safety net for blameless children. Most likely that safety net would be a costly system of public jobs and subsidies for private employers hiring welfare recipients. It usually turned out that Clinton's synthesized solutions required money.

Actually, there were three kinds of Democrats in Washington in 1993: old-style liberal ones; "new" ones, who tended to be moderates and conservatives; and Clinton, trying to be the bridge between them by splitting their differences.

After trying to bridge the gap in his own party, Clinton would confront the great complication of American attitudes: he would seek to develop a governing majority by extending his synthesizing instincts to Ross Perot voters, soon to be labeled "the radical middle," people who seemed to want one thing, which was action.

Clinton assembled a cabinet of a few traditional liberals, a few moderates, a few deficit hawks, and a few advocates of greater federal spending, but no Republicans. These diverse, even contradictory Democrats would provide the components for Clinton's synthesizer, with which he alone would make the music of his presidency.

For example, Leon Panetta, who was made director of the Office of Management and Budget, was an acclaimed deficit hawk who advocated deep spending cuts. Robert Reich, a Harvard instructor and old Clinton friend from Rhodes Scholar days, was an articulate advocate of new kinds of investments—i.e., spending—to rehabilitate and stimulate the economy, largely through public works spending and lifelong job-retraining programs. Clinton agreed with both, and differed with both; each man had a good idea, but maybe each carried his noble view to the point of political impracticality without sufficient regard for the opposing view. Clinton was by nature a versatile, see-all-sides thinker.

But it remained to be seen whether smart, congenial, conciliatory, conflict-averting leadership among governors at their brief annual conferences was relevant to the presidency. It remained to be seen whether phrasing a plank in a report to appease Democrats and Republicans had anything to do with leading the Congress and the people as president. It remained to be seen whether professorial analyses of issues would serve a president well. It remained to be seen whether Clinton, desiring to bridge so many gaps, would try to do so many things partially that he would do nothing profoundly. And it remained to be seen whether Americans would trust music blended in a synthesizer. Might they find it phony? Would the Great Synthesizer be seen instead as the Synthetic Man?

Clinton had tuned his synthesizer over a dozen years in Arkansas, a place of anti-intellectual populism. It forces its politicians to be clever, even veiled, and to rely on personal political skills, since it is relatively small in area and sparse in population. What they always said in Arkansas was that Bill Clinton, Dale Bumpers, and David Pryor never forgot a name. I'd ridden down many an Arkansas country road with Clinton, my eyes glazed over as he told me who lived where and explained why he had lost or won this precinct or that in a previous election.

Whenever he campaigned in the Arkansas hinterlands, Clinton would drop the g to say he was "workin' " real hard on "helpin' " people. He'd say things like, "You don't have to be all broke out with brilliance to know . . . ," which, actually, he'd picked up from Bumpers.

Once on the reelection campaign trail in a small town in Southeast

Arkansas, Clinton suddenly vanished from Main Street. Some elderly fellow had wanted to show him something at his house, and Clinton jumped in the man's car and took off with him as a campaign aide exclaimed, "What the hell?" and set out in hot pursuit. Already Clinton was about a half-day behind schedule, typically. Another time, on a downtown street in the town of Morrilton, a fellow drove up to a stoplight in a pickup with two dogs in the open bed. "Hey, man," Clinton yelled, and started trotting toward the idling driver while whispering to a campaign aide, "what kind of dogs are those? How old are they?" When he reached the driver, Clinton said, "Hey, buddy, those sure are good-looking birddogs. What are they, about three?" They were four years old, the delighted driver replied.

Those are the skills and tricks that a left-leaning politician must learn and apply in a rural, populist state that is small enough to place a continuing premium on personal, or retail, politics. They'd served Clinton well in his presidential campaign, especially on the bus tours. He could relate in a way that his predecessors as Democratic presidential nominees could not.

More substantively, consider how Clinton used clever political and policy synthesis in Arkansas to build a national reputation as an education reformer.

Confronted in 1983 with an Arkansas Supreme Court ruling that school funding had to be equalized, Clinton knew he had to raise taxes to redistribute state school money upward, not downward. That was the underlying reason he proposed a sales tax increase. But he knew he needed greater accountability for raising taxes. He also knew that Arkansas needed desperately to improve its public schools.

So he assigned Hillary to write and sell tough new school standards—smaller class sizes, elementary school counselors, and new requirements for courses in foreign languages and advanced mathematics and science. Still, it wasn't enough. He decided to alienate a typical Democratic constituency, the National Education Association (NEA), and force all the state's schoolteachers to take a basic skills test, designed on about an eighth-grade level in reading, writing, and arithmetic. He declared he would veto his own sales tax bill if he didn't get teacher testing.

He was using teachers as whipping boys. Politically, he achieved a popular machismo: Let's identify the dimwits in the teaching profession and get them out. As policy, he had accomplished precisely nothing except to disparage the teaching profession: About 10 percent of the teachers failed the test the first time, but they could take it again. In the end, only 3 percent failed. Many states embarked on education reforms in the early 1980s, but Bill Clinton's centerpiece—teacher testing—was repeated nowhere else.

This is what he'd succeeded in doing: He'd finessed a court-ordered tax increase to redefine it as a matter of educational advancement, with the considerable help of his wife; he'd proposed a typical tax-and-spend solution but alienated a typical liberal constituency, the NEA, to do it; he'd made a bold advancement in Arkansas, but done it with a bit of trickery and a dose of demagoguery.

This was our nation's new president, and Americans got their first glimpse of him at his best—as an effortless moderator of a policy discussion and an uncanny synthesizer of information taken from experts with diverse points of view, as a kind of Phil Donahue of politics and policy—in December between his election and inauguration.

Elite businesspeople, top-level bureaucrats, and think-tank experts assembled around Clinton at a large table in Little Rock as C-SPAN and CNN beamed the president-elect's "economic summit" on live television. Clinton called on those who were to speak and responded to each of them. He accepted viewer call-ins, handling them with the aplomb of Larry King or even Regis and Kathy Lee. He saw merit in everything everyone had to say. Nearly everyone agreed that the budget deficit had to be trimmed. Most everyone agreed that the costs of health care had to be controlled. A majority believed there was a need to invest to rebuild America's infrastructure, assist the inner cities, and develop new high-technology information networks. A couple of people stressed that the new president had to move quickly to strike while the iron was hot.

Clinton gleaned it all, regurgitated it, spun it, and made it all seem part of a master plan. He was the nation's "Great Moderator." Longtime political observers were in awe: he had assembled a diverse group and essentially co-opted everyone into backing whatever economic program he would outline after he became president. Or so they thought.

Pundits could be forgiven if they put too much stock in, and drew too many optimistic conclusions from, Clinton's ability to speak extemporaneously in complete, coherent, well-organized sentences. After Clinton's first news conference as president-elect, R. W. "Johnny" Apple wrote a front-page analysis in *The New York Times* applauding the president-elect's ability to do just that. For a dozen years, Americans had listened first to a president who read a TelePrompTer beautifully but sometimes needed a whisper from his wife to answer a question, and then to a pleasant president whose syntax was forever mangled.

Basically, Clinton had merely demonstrated the skills that had been so impressive at five-day governors' conferences: command of policy detail, synthesis, cleverness, articulation, and charming persuasion. He seemed to make the presidency look easy. But he wasn't president yet. All he had done was perform admirably as a discussion leader, not a nation leader.

He had a plan.

Clinton knew that he benefited from a Democratic majority in Congress that needed him to succeed, which gave him a leg up.

He would centralize power in the White House, much as Nixon and Reagan had done. Cabinet members would not so much govern as they would make arguments for the president's synthesizer. Within the White House, Clinton would centralize power in the Oval Office, much as John F. Kennedy and Jimmy Carter had, the latter to the point that he was accused of micromanagement.

Clinton selected his boyhood friend McLarty, a courtly and meticulous businessman, as a chief of staff who would not be in the style of the prototypically powerful chief of staff—not the lone gatekeeper or co-president or White House tyrant. McLarty would function somewhat like a chief executive officer in a firm that had a fully engaged president, an active and influential wife of the president, an active and influential vice president, and a collegial atmosphere in which more than a dozen people would be granted free access to a president who loved to talk, brainstorm, energize, and theorize. To that extent the White House would function somewhat like, though not exactly like, the old "spokes-of-the-wheel" model in which the president was the hub of numerous co-equal aides and advisers, a system that, by the way, had been widely discredited by White House veterans who had tried and failed to make it work in past administrations. As with everything else about this new president, the Clinton White House would be a hybrid of other models—a learned and applied synthesis. But Bill Clinton would be at the center.

The new president also believed—and his pollster, Stan Greenberg, advised him—that he might be clever enough to augment his support with about half of the vote that Ross Perot had received in the previous November, thus providing a governing majority and a reelection base.

Clinton intended to use Perot's popularity as leverage over Democrats who clung to politics-as-usual: Reduce the deficit or watch Perot's

United We Stand movement wreak havoc for your reelection campaigns; adopt campaign finance reform or see the same. Those were his admonitions.

Meanwhile, he would preach the Perot sermon of personal sacrifice to reduce the deficit to make a case for, and engender support for, higher taxes. But for Clinton, higher taxes actually served two broader purposes beyond merely reducing the deficit and reversing the trend toward generational irresponsibility, if not eventual national bankruptcy.

First, they would provide him an excuse to redistribute the tax burden, assigning more of it to the well-to-do, who had benefited far more than any other group from the tax policies of the Reagan-Bush era, while increasing the income-tax credits for people who worked but couldn't pull out of poverty. That was a fairly typical Democratic concept, transferring from the rich to the poor, but at least to the working poor, not the welfare poor. Second, raising taxes and cutting programs would provide or free up money not only to reduce the deficit, but to spend on reversing Reaganomics further by paying for new or expanded programs like Head Start, national service, job training, innovative education projects, and aid to urban areas. That strikingly resembled the old Democratic traditions of an activist government practicing social engineering. And the new president hoped to divert some money into roads, bridges, high-speed rail, and information networks—public works, the virtues of which were established with the New Deal.

Altogether, Bill Clinton was trying a hat trick of more mammoth proportions than the one he had pulled back in Arkansas in 1983 when he put a court-ordered tax increase under a hat and pulled out bold education reform. Now he would put Paul Tsongas and Ross Perot under the hat and come out with some modernized FDR and LBJ.

He would have something for everyone, which is his customary goal. There would be deficit reduction. There would be cuts in government programs and an overall reduction in the rate of growth of federal spending. There would be new programs for activist causes. There would be a short-term spending plan for economic stimulation, mostly in the neglected urban centers. These would be a more progressive tax structure.

But there's a fine line between smart politics and sleight-of-hand, and Clinton teetered on it. In Washington, unlike Little Rock, there were hundreds of Republicans whose job and genius were to dog him, challenge him on his trickery, and brand him with unpopular labels. Those Republicans with whom Clinton had cooperated at governors' conferences would become the scourge of his early presidential existence.

It was not in Clinton's nature to fight a strictly partisan battle or to exclude anyone from friendly and cooperative overture. But it *was* in his nature to examine the political facts, figures, and dynamics, and react according to what appeared to be the path of least resistance. Those facts were the following, and they led him headlong into a partisan quagmire:

- The Democrats outnumbered Republicans by a wide margin in the House and by a reasonably comfortable margin in the Senate.

- The Democrats were inclined to support their new president because the onus was on them to break gridlock and deliver action.

- Clinton had walked into a partisan hornet's nest in Washington. Democrats were resentful of what they saw as the fiscal irresponsibility and rhetorical deception of the Reagan-Bush era, and of Republican appeals to patriotism that suggested the Democrats were somehow unpatriotic. Republicans were resentful of what they saw as the Democratic congressional majority's rude and unfair treatment of Republican presidential nominees such as John Tower, Robert Bork, and Clarence Thomas. They weren't prepared to lie down. They were prepared, whenever the right opportunities arose, to give the Democrats a bit of their own medicine. Republicans thought the press had handled Clinton with kid gloves in the campaign. They would treat him approximately as respectfully as the Democrats in Congress had treated Bush. It's doubtful Clinton could have bridged this gap even if he'd felt it politically necessary and applied all his talents for charming and cajoling.

- Polls and focus groups showed that Clinton's most effective bits of rhetoric were those about "failed Reaganomics" and "reversing trickle-down economics." Focus groups were especially revealing: middle-class voters didn't demonstrate warm feelings toward Reagan anymore; they thought they'd been sold a bill of goods. It is difficult to reach out on a bipartisan basis when your own partisans resent the opposing partisans and when your best selling point is to ridicule the legacy of your opponents.

Synthesizing the liberal and moderate Democrats and then reaching out to Perot voters would be a sufficiently tough assignment for the beginning. The conciliatory consensus builder would open his presidency by trying to solidify and bank on Democrats, split the difference between the old and new versions, reach out to Perot supporters, and overpower the outnumbered Republicans.

Later, if needed, he'd refine his skills of bipartisanship. He suspected it would be necessary on health care reform, especially if he could manage to frame the issue as one of economic stability and deficit reduction rather than as a social or tax issue. It might not be necessary to attack Reagan's legacy and all that Republicans espouse to push health care reform.

But in the beginning Clinton and his inner circle were determined to borrow only from Reagan's magic for communications and message control. McLarty and Stephanopoulos carried on a continuing conversation about how to control the president's message. McLarty talked with Hamilton Jordan, the chief of staff for Jimmy Carter, and found him to have "several very good ideas." He talked with other former chiefs of staff, including Sununu, who seemed eager to advise on the strategic nuances of serving as a presidential chief of staff. Stephanopoulos visited with former communication directors and press secretaries—among them David Gergen, the moderate, thoughtful spin doctor for three Republican presidents, who was high in the Washington punditocracy.

One idea, pressed by Stephanopoulos from his campaign experience, and by his deputy, Jeff Eller, was to exploit Clinton's audience skills by having him conduct town meetings with regular citizens from regional television studios around the country. New satellite equipment was set up at the White House so that Clinton could speak to local television news anchors. It was important, they believed—as communications specialists for every president in recent memory had believed—to maneuver around or over the White House press corps, which, for the first time ever, would be excluded from the second-floor press offices in the West Wing.

That exclusion was fully practical because Stephanopoulos, the main press spokesman, was a policy insider as much as a spokesman.

Furthermore, everything a reporter might reasonably need in the way of press services was available through staff members on the lower press level, which was accessible. Anyway, reporters who had to rely on access to official spokespeople were in trouble for real news. But as a symbol, especially when combined with other communications strategies, one of which was to conduct briefings devoid even of the tiniest news morsel, even an occasional bone for the dogs, it was a mistake for which the White House would pay. Hillary Clinton, not surprisingly, had encouraged it.

As Marlin Fitzwater, the longtime spokesman for Reagan and Bush, had known, a spokesperson ought to enter every briefing armed with at least one actual answer to an eminently predictable question. It was known as "playing the game." Stephanopoulos instead engendered this kind of reporter-grumbling: "No one is as good as George at not answering a question."

When I conveyed that comment to Stephanopoulos, he said, "Some days that's my job—go out there and don't make news." He was contemptuous of some of the reporters. He told me that major newspapers, trying to compete with television and 24-hour news organizations, had stooped to printing editorial analysis as front-page news and engaged in "mock investigative reporting." He said, "They call us spin doctors. But they're spinning, too." When he was taken off the press beat, promoted—really—to being the president's shadow and key adviser on political and policy strategy, journalists chortled. More than one said that George got his deserved comeuppance because "he wouldn't play the game."

Stephanopoulos's failing as chief spokesman was a deadly and youthful combination of naivete and hubris, but it facilitated his promotion to senior adviser on politics and policy, which was where he belonged and where he was eminently more comfortable and valuable.

Clinton wanted to open his presidency by talking about five issues and keeping attention focused on them. Gays in the military was not one of them, and now the White House had finally managed to get it off the front page for six months.

Those subjects, in order as listed by McLarty, were: 1. The economy and deficit. 2. Health care. 3. Campaign finance reform. 4. Welfare reform. 5. National service (which was Clinton's plan to pay for college education for youths who would agree to two years of public service).

All of that in one year?

"Well, they're building blocks," McLarty said. "You don't necessarily pass them all at once, but they all go together, and one lays the foundation for the other."

The economy and health care were the central themes of Clinton's candidacy, and now Clinton hoped to blend them into a broad philosophy that would appeal to liberals, moderates, Perot voters, and the vast middle class. Reaganism would be reversed, the deficit would be reduced, some spending would be cut, cities would get more money, taxes would rise on the rich, and universal health care would be a goal that liberals would embrace as a social reform and middle-class moderates might embrace because of the financial security it offered them.

Campaign finance reform would appeal to Perot voters who despised the influence of money and the self-perpetuation of incumbency. Welfare reform would introduce a new kind of Democrat and appeal to blue-collar voters who resented the welfare state. National service would excite the youth, who had voted in record large numbers for Clinton and, naturally, represented the future of the electorate.

That was the clever, ever-calculating, ever optimistic plan of America's would-be Great Synthesizer. At that point, reinventing government and the North American Free Trade Agreement didn't even show up on the radar.

Clinton believed his era would be dominated by two dynamics: a spirit for change, and a set of new problems in the post–Cold War global economy that defied traditional ideologies and could best be addressed by a leader who was in effect a savvy follower—taking the views of others, whether they be strident, polarized, or simply principled, and concocting a magically blended solution.

At the very least, Clinton would be the antithesis of the most successful of his immediate predecessors: Ronald Reagan. The only thing he had in common with Reagan was that he hoped to coast through foreign policy in his first year.

He was young where Reagan was old. He was vigorous where Reagan was detached. He was a one-man presidential band where Reagan was a delegator. He was a finesser and synthesizer of ideology while Reagan was an ideologue. He believed in government above all else; Reagan didn't believe that government could do anything helpful other than get out of the free market's way.

And, much unlike Reagan, Clinton wasn't very good at reading a TelePrompTer, as the nation would soon find out.

CHAPTER 4

A Tale of Two Speeches

Most politicians demonstrate consistency if nothing else in their public speaking. Either they are embarrassingly bad (Bill Bradley comes to mind), numbingly mediocre (nearly everyone else), or so good and compelling that partisans become titillated at the prospect of their command performances and are almost never disappointed (Mario Cuomo, a bit of a poet, and Ronald Reagan, an actor).

Bill Clinton is an exception, typically. He can be all of the above: both very good and really bad, which defines his political existence.

For years I'd heard him inspire rural audiences on the Arkansas campaign trail. But I'd also heard him send civic clubs into after-buffet siestas. I'd heard all his opening jokes ("The difference between Baptists and Methodists is that Methodists will call each other by name when they meet in the liquor store"). I'd heard him wend his way from opening anecdotes to arduous, fatigue-inducing, point-by-point analyses of how his policies and programs for schools and job development were designed to educate, train, and otherwise prepare Arkansas youth for competition in the new global economy. That was a stretch through the 1980s for a state still fighting to become a full partner in the *national* economy.

These were the only consistent strains:

- He almost always was good when in trouble and in need of a frantic rally of salesmanship and sermonizing, blending the used-car dealer and the Baptist preacher, and making up the speech as he went along. In New Hampshire in the winter of 1992, for example, he abruptly lost 15 points in the polls. In rally after rally in the closing days of the primary, he sent chills down the spines of veteran political watchers like Curtis Wilkie of the *Boston Globe,* who declared he'd never heard anything so good, and James Carville, who had just signed on to advise the Clinton campaign and thought that although his product was damaged goods, he'd found something special. "I'll be with you until the last dog dies," Clinton bellowed in the New Hampshire cold. People wondered what it meant. Was it some kind of Southern-fried Checkers speech? But they cheered like crazy.

- He was almost always bad when reading a text from a Tele-PrompTer; it robbed him of his soulfulness and the audience with which he needed to relate. A machine has no expressive eyes to signal feedback to a speaker who is essentially insecure. It is my long-held belief that Clinton connects well with audiences because he desperately needs to connect. "How did I do?" Clinton would ask after a speech when a more self-assured politician would have assumed he had done quite well. Clinton plays well off audience reactions because he is hypersensitive to them.

He could adapt to his audience, a talent refined through the variety of his associations, from rural Arkansas to Washington to Oxford to Yale. "Are you staying with me for the NAACP event tonight?" he asked me once on the campaign trail. When I said yes, he said, "Well, I'll have to change my speech." With a white reporter in tow, he would tone down the imitation of Dr. Martin Luther King, Jr. But he was far from being the Great Communicator, Ronald Reagan, the professionally trained romancer of the camera. Who can forget perhaps the most notoriously monotonous speech ever delivered at a national political convention? Surely it was Clinton's in 1988 in nomination of Michael Dukakis. On the flight from Atlanta back to Little Rock two days after that speech, Clinton sat across from me in coach class and explained the dynamics of the disaster. He knew immediately he was in trouble. He knew his audience, and that it was restless. But he had before him a TelePrompTer rolling a lengthy prepared text—and a bad one that had been approved by Dukakis's people after hours of tinkering and overediting that turned it into a tome. He thought that perhaps the party's nominee expected him to deliver it in full for the television audience. His instinct was to blow off the machine and give the audience about 15 minutes of extemporaneous hell-raising. But instead, thinking the speech might play better at home than in the arena, he plodded on, and on, and on, falling on his sword and endangering his own political future.

But not to worry. Within a week, thanks to an appearance brokered by his Hollywood friends, Harry and Linda Bloodworth-Thomason of growing sit-com fame ("Evening Shade," "Designing Women"), he'd gone on "The Tonight Show" to make fun of himself and play "Summertime" on the saxophone. For her part, Hillary dismissed the convention debacle in a typically direct, unapologetic way. "If the charge is that Bill made a long, boring speech," she said, "then that is a charge that could be made in spades against Mike Dukakis or Bill Bradley." It always seemed to her that people asked more of her husband than they asked of politicians normally.

One aspect of the presidency that doesn't always serve Clinton is that he has a staff of speechwriters, and, considering the time constraints of the job, he often simply reads their texts. What he needs for most occasions is a staff of speech outliners who will present him with a framework of talking points, leaving plenty of white space between them. He's best as a freelance orator. Once Clinton handed me a note he had written on the back of an envelope. On the front of the envelope, it turned out, was a minimalist outline for the smooth 15-minute speech he'd just delivered.

Clinton hadn't been president a month before he showed the nation his full range as an orator. He delivered a horrible speech and a great speech on the same subject in the space of 48 hours.

What he said both times was that he would stand up to the tough and responsible assignment that the voters had given him—leading the country through a perilous time caused by the fiscal mess left by Republican administrations and an economy that was spotty and no longer the envy of the world.

He vowed to get the federal budget deficit down through the only credible means possible: real, verifiable spending cuts and fair, progressive tax increases. He vowed at the same time to reinvest in the matters most important to global competitiveness and the quality of life: America's schools, cities, infrastructure, and people. He apologized for the necessity of having to raise taxes minimally on the middle class, to whom he'd promised in the campaign an income-tax cut or a new child care credit.

In seeking to explain his about-face on middle-class taxes, Clinton explained that the deficit was worse than he had thought. That was, at least, misleading. He'd had ample opportunity to review the fact that new estimates of the deficit for the ongoing fiscal year were in the $300 billion range—this after George Bush had imperiled his presidency by acquiescing to a Democratic plan to get the deficit down by an estimated $490 billion over five years, a plan gone awry in a recession. But perhaps Clinton had not known fully—because he hadn't stopped campaigning long enough to think about it—just how ominous the trend appeared for coming years, with the deficit rising dramatically and the national debt compounding.

That fact hadn't been explained to him fully until the transition period, when his key economic advisers gathered around him at Blair House, across the street from the White House, and laid out the harsh realities. They told him he couldn't afford the middle-class tax cut. They told him his campaign pledge to raise $40 billion by collecting outstanding taxes owed by foreign corporations doing business in America might be overstated by, oh, 1,000 percent. Clinton's reaction was to argue mildly about the tax on foreign corporations and declare, ever optimistically, that the figures on the deficit and debt presented him with a great challenge and a great opportunity.

The horrible speech was from the Oval Office in prime time on Monday, February 15, 1993, and, naturally, read to a live television audience from a TelePrompTer in an otherwise empty room.

The new president's Arkansas buddies—Senators Bumpers and Pryor—were with him at the White House as he delivered this first address to the nation. They were invited to go with him into the Oval Office for the speech itself, but declined, not wanting to be a distraction. Their presence might have helped. As it was, Clinton was awash in his own heroes, sitting behind John F. Kennedy's desk with a bust of Abraham Lincoln to his left.

The brief address was infamously memorable for four reasons. One was the way Clinton looked—small, boyish, and uncomfortable, with his suit coat appearing oversized and bunched up in the back, leading Tom Shales, the television critic for *The Washington Post,* to write the next morning that the address should have been titled "Home Alone 3." The second was that people seemed to hear only one word: "taxes." The third was the intimation of class-warfare rhetoric: Let's punish the rich with higher taxes because they made out like bandits during the Reagan-Bush years. (To be fair, that was more of an inference by listeners than a direct statement by Clinton.) The fourth was the way he chose to close it: He was sorry he couldn't keep the promise about a middle-class tax, and instead would propose a tax to be paid by the middle class on the energy content of heating oil and motor fuels (British Thermal Units); when he was a boy, making a sacrifice for your country was called "patriotism."

The invoking of partisan patriotism was the brainchild of Paul Begala, James Carville's younger partner from Texas and Clinton's favorite phrasemaker. He'd written the well-received speech that Georgia Governor Zell Miller had delivered at the Democratic National Convention. Carville and Begala—and Clinton—felt it fair for the Democrats to "play the patriotism card" because Reagan, Bush, and the Republicans had played it against Democrats for a dozen years.

Months later Begala told me: "It might not be ethical for me to say I wrote that line, but I'll say this: Whoever wrote it, Vice President Gore [an uncommonly active vice president already] improved it. When he saw that closing line about people calling sacrifice patriotism when he was a boy, he added, 'And we still do.' I don't agree it was a bad line, but I will say that the vice president's editing made it seem less like a lecture."

The line was based in part on research by Stan Greenberg, the pollster who, like Begala and Carville, was working for Clinton through a contract with the Democratic National Committee. Greenberg's surveys showed people willing, maybe anxious, to rally to a cause of self-sacrifice. But "patriotism" fell a little flat as a synonym for "sacrifice." Patriotism could be invoked effectively by Republicans in regard to foreign policy to suggest that Democrats were soft militarily. Patriotism could be invoked effectively by Republicans as symbolism—at a flag factory, for example, when the Democratic presidential nominee had once vetoed a bill to require the recitation of the Pledge of Allegiance, as Michael Dukakis had done (quite appropriately, since a mandated recitation was unconstitutional in Massachusetts). But waving the old red-white-and-blue to rally support for paying higher taxes? It wasn't one of the talented Begala's better ideas.

Clinton walked out of the Oval Office and told his Senate friends from Arkansas that he didn't think the speech had gone all that well. They knew as much and changed the subject to the substance of what he had said, which they admired, instead of the style with which he had said it.

The next morning, chief of staff Mack McLarty assembled the White House speechwriters and tried to break through his own courtliness and chew them out. He'd been reading countless profiles of himself in newspapers emphasizing his politeness and collegiality. He needed to show someone he could be a real boss. He'd thought about hiring Hillary's tough friend from New York, Susan Thomases, as his chief deputy and bad cop. Then he'd decided on the politically savvy Harold Ickes, also of New York City; but Ickes couldn't join the administration until he was cleared of allegations that he had ties to organized crime through his representation of labor unions. As it was, McLarty's chief deputy was the only man in the White House who might have been as cordial and courteous as he is—Mark Gearen.

Whoever had anything to do with that speech seemed a good choice for McLarty's first shot at tough criticism. Apparently he performed well enough. "Oh, yeah, he was a little hot," Begalá said. "At the time, I didn't know Mack very well. I love him now, of course, like everybody does, but the problem at the time was that we hadn't worked together and we weren't connected yet."

McLarty thought one of his best services to the president would be to tug him gently rightward on occasion and remind him of that "new Democrat" rhetoric that had elected him. He hadn't liked the Monday-night speech at all because Clinton talked about tax increases more than he talked about spending cuts, and because it seemed to declare or invoke class warfare.

It probably wasn't coincidental that McLarty was joined in that view by the other multi-millionaire in the White House, economic czar Robert Rubin, a Wall Street mogul.

"This class-warfare stuff [hit the greedy rich with higher taxes] is not what the president got elected on," McLarty told the speechwriters. Then he went in and told the president the same thing. Clinton said he hadn't meant that at all, and, in fact, the text didn't say what so many seemed to have heard.

"I've got a bet with Robert Rubin," Begala said months later. "If he can find one reference in that speech that is perjorative against the rich, I'll give him $100 or donate it to his favorite charity. He can't find one, and you can't either."

No, not specifically.

Clinton got elected after a campaign in which he consistently promised to extract taxes from the wealthiest who made out best during the
1980s. But McLarty was onto something, and time would show him
to be a pretty good barometer: With a two-pronged attack to deficit
reduction, the prong that needed to resound was the one about cutting
spending. The call to arms had to be "shared sacrifice," which should
not be interchanged with "patriotism." We are patriotic on the Fourth
of July; we sacrifice on April 15.

On February 16, the stock market fell 83 points, the biggest one-
day slide since November 1991. They had heard "class warfare" on
Wall Street. They weren't feeling too patriotic.

The triumphant speech was February 17, an address to a joint session
of Congress, with a boisterous, partisanly divided Congress as the
president's audience—live and in-person people who were interested,
alert, and responsive. Clinton had a text that had been finished only
moments before, but he took off on extemporaneous jaunts whenever
the audience reaction compelled him. About a fifth of the speech was
ad-libbed, and that was the best part.

When he declared that he would make his budget based on the
estimates and projections of the Congressional Budget Office, since it
was independent and bipartisan, Republicans hooted at the very idea
that anything affiliated with the Democratic-controlled Congress could
be bipartisan. Clinton played off that. "Now, you laugh, my fellow
Republicans," he began, and then he embarked on an extemporaneous
lecture about the phoniness of Republican administrations in the past
as they relied on false and overly optimistic assumptions and tricks
played by the Office of Management and Budget to make their budgets
appear better than they turned out to be.

Later, he said, "To those who call for more spending cuts, I say fine,
but *be as specific as I have been*." Democrats roared approval. "That's
wonderful," Bumpers said to a colleague next to him, Senator Jim Sasser
of Tennessee, a Democrat and the chairman of the Budget Committee.
Democrats resented that Republicans loved to talk about balancing the
budget through a constitutional amendment or general spending caps
without seriously addressing where and what to cut, getting general
approval while avoiding responsibility for any specific ramifications.

To temper the partisanship, or to try to transcend it, Clinton declared
that it mattered not to the people nor to him who took the blame for
the problems the country faced, or the credit if the deficit was lowered,
the economy jump-started, and campaign financing reformed.

Clinton went back to the White House that night to stay up late with his Hollywood friend, Harry Thomason, a likable soulmate who, like Clinton, had risen from small-town Arkansas beginnings to great national success.

Clinton knew he had triumphed. His objective had been three-fold, and it might have seemed inherently contradictory to one who didn't have supreme confidence in his internal synthesizer. Clinton had needed to emphasize the virtue of shared sacrifice and spending cuts while deemphasizing those tax increases as much as possible. He had needed to demonstrate to the American people—particularly Perot voters—that he was a man of action committed to budget reform, political reform, and economic focusing, and that he would not behave as a Democrat-as-usual, playing partisan games of credit and blame. He needed to demonstrate to the Democrats in Congress, who could pass his budget by themselves, that he shared their contempt for the Republican budget games of the past and would provide them cover for support of his package.

For one night, at least, he'd done all that, triumphing inside the Beltway and outside. As of February 17, this new president, by nature overly optimistic and overly confident, had empirical evidence that he might be every bit as clever and capable as he thought. An overnight poll conducted for CNN and *Time* magazine showed that 79 percent of the respondents liked the speech and supported what the president had to say.

He'd accomplished even more. Alan Greenspan, the chairman of the Federal Reserve, had sat beside Hillary Rodham Clinton during the speech. Some people thought he had been co-opted. Greenspan had been persuaded that a presidential speech promising leadership for honest deficit reduction, which he'd long advocated, was something he could at least show up for. At the very least, Greenspan's presence signaled credibility to the financial markets.

For his part, Clinton knew that he was proposing a long-term economic strategy and that his best hope for short-term good news was keeping alive a trend toward subterranean interest rates, which had set off a spate of mortgage refinancings begun in the last year of the Bush administration, and which might spur general economic expansion to mitigate the downsizing of the defense industry. Low interest rates were helpful to Clinton's desired political constituency, members of the middle class: they could refinance their homes.

How could two speeches of such substantive similarity outlining the same objectives be received with such marked difference in the space of 48 hours?

It wasn't quite enough to explain that it was Bill Clinton, the prince of volatility, making the speeches. Nor was it quite enough to cite that the American society had been conditioned to react to the influences of style over the intricacies of substance. It was a combination of those factors: a volatile political figure as the leader of a superficial people, a prescription for a wild ride. And it was as simple as this: The American people wanted spending cuts more than they wanted their taxes raised, and they reacted favorably to the former and haltingly to the latter.

If public attitudes, political fortunes, and policy courses were to be driven by style over substance, by which component of his program the president emphasized and which he cleverly skirted, then it was pretty clear that this battle over the budget and the economy would be decided more by rhetoric than by truth.

That is precisely what would happen. The Republicans would rise from the near dead to unleash a rhetorical Blitzkrieg. And Clinton, in the fine tradition of his Arkansas history, would not provide quality service after the sale. Back in Arkansas, he'd given compelling (though long) speeches to kick off legislative sessions; then the bills wouldn't be introduced for weeks even though he had two years to prepare between regular sixty-day legislative sessions.

Paul Begala explained months later that he and Carville had insisted that the truth about taxes had to be confronted in that first Oval Office address. They were frightened by the lessons they had learned consulting New Jersey Governor James Florio. Facing a budget crisis, Florio had made deep cuts in state spending. Then he proposed a tax increase. In other words, he had followed a supposedly smart formula: Demonstrate governmental accountability and belt-tightening first, then ask for taxes. But what happened was that people remembered only the taxes, and resented them.

But maybe the simple lesson, the unavoidable truth, was that any Democrat raising taxes will be clobbered rhetorically by Republicans— period. "Yeah," Begala chucked. "It might be that simple."

Substantively, America needed in 1993 either a great moral leader or a clever policy synthesizer. Since so-called gridlock was the main concern, the country may at that moment have needed the latter more than the former. In other words, Americans might have been in a mood to get something, *anything,* accomplished and to save the preaching for later. Clinton thus was the right man for the moment, if, that is, he could be tough enough, gather up some credibility, and perform as cleverly as he believed himself capable of doing.

With an annual budget deficit of maybe $300 billion, and a debt of $4 trillion, and with Americans growing fretful about the strength of the economy, the quality of education, and the frightening increase in violent crime, pure and unyielding ideology by the nation's leader might have been polarizing and stifling. It would have been precisely that unless the leader had the inclination and credibility to be a great moral persuader for middle-class sacrifice and new ideas to restore personal responsibility and a sense of community among those who were angry, violent, and lost, mostly in the cities.

Clinton was more at ease seeking political and policy solutions and accepting compromise than embracing and proclaiming a strong moral vision from which one could not easily retreat. It's easier to bend on a policy than a sermon.

More than that, what America had was a 43 percent president who got fewer votes in each congressional district than the congressman or woman elected from each of those districts. For that reason, Clinton was more equipped to synthesize than preach.

In terms of politics and policy, Clinton knew that Americans had lost faith, becoming cynical and pessimistic. He knew that they couldn't decide whether to blame Democratic tax-and-spend liberalism or borrow-and-spend Reaganomics, so they blamed both and wanted no more of either. (That would be borne out months later when New Jersey voters elected a governor. Exit polls showed that a majority disapproved of Governor Jim Florio's tax increase, but that a majority also rejected the supply-side throwback idea of the challenger, Christine Todd Whitman, to phase in a 30 percent tax reduction.)

Clinton was onto something in his belief that the American people wanted a "third way." But the question was whether he could actually fashion a new way and convince the American people that it wasn't more of the same with different packaging.

Nuances notwithstanding, there were in Congress in 1993 two basic and stubborn establishment philosophies on the budget and general economics. One, fiscally conservative, encompassing Republicans and moderate-to-conservative Democrats, was to cut spending deeply to get the deficit down. The other, socially liberal, was to undo the Reagan Revolution and restore the Democratic Party's modern heritage with greater spending on neglected cities, schools, jobs programs, and public works.

Neither was a responsible position by itself, economically or politically.

Tunnel-visioned deficit hawks, driven either by a sense of generational responsibility or an erroneously simplistic belief that high deficits caused poor economic performance, tended not to take into full account the fact that government had become so large and integrated into the full fabric of the American economy that deep, severe, immediate cuts in programs designed to bring the budget into quick balance would have shrunk the economy by harmful proportions. Military installations meant jobs. So did hospitals getting reimbursements on entitlement programs. So did the Rural Electrification Association with its interest-rate subsidies, and so on down the line.

Most spending cuts would extract a price somewhere else for consumers. Hell-bent deficit reduction would have been a kind of unnecessary shock therapy for those employed by the government, providing services to it, receiving subsidies from it, and reaping direct and indirect benefits from it.

The nation was not close to bankruptcy. It could pay its bills. It could find the money for emergency disaster relief. The problem was the trend, not the existing state of affairs. The crying need was not to get rid of the deficit; it was to embark on a credibly downward trend.

Actually, the problem was more acutely political than economic. People didn't trust a government that spent more than it collected as a matter of worsening habit. They didn't trust politicians who seemed impotent to stop it. Clinton knew that he couldn't make his beloved government a viable force again unless he first restored its credibility to spend money on new-idea programs. He was motivated less by the dollar signs of a budget battle than by the poll figures showing that Americans hated politics. He was a politician, not an economist. He wanted political repair, which meant he had to concern himself with economic repair.

On the other hand, old-time liberals who wanted to spend more for social engineering probably would have led the Democratic Party to political suicide, since a majority of the people clearly wanted leaner, not bigger, government. Barring an economic upturn of proportions not predicted by anyone, the old-line Democratic liberals would have run up the deficit and angered the electorate on the mere hope—a suspect theory that was widely discredited in the minds of pivotal suburban voters—that all the social spending would reap long-term dividends in a healthier, better-educated population.

It was Clinton's job, not to mention his natural inclination and talent, to weave these opposing forces into a plan that was passable and workable. "Passable" was as key as "workable," since "gridlock" was the enemy. The plan would need to get the deficit down, but not too fast, and it would need to rearrange federal spending to get more money, but not too much, into cities, schools, and jobs programs. Clinton needed to keep the liberal Democrats in the House on board as well as the conservative Democrats in the Senate. He needed a little of this and a little of that, politically and economically.

Clinton declared in his State of the Union speech that there was nothing intrinsically good about deficit reduction alone. It was a rare moment of commendable candor in which he tried to put aside rhetoric and explain the truth of the matter. The worth of deficit reduction, he believed, was in reversing a trend toward a government that couldn't be active, meaning it couldn't afford to develop programs to help people, because it would eventually be forced to devote too much of its money, and too much of its gross domestic product, to debt servicing.

Months later, in his second temporarily triumphant address to Congress, on health care, Clinton would warn of a government that, unless set right, would eventually be able to do only three things: maintain a national defense, pay for entitlement programs, and pay interest.

He wanted to do more than merely bring government's accounting ledgers closer to symmetry. He needed to pump the economy. A Democratic president needed to produce economic results. James Carville kept reminding Clinton not to go overboard pandering to the Perot-driven deficit mania. Every poll showed the American people more worried about their jobs than the deficit. It had not been "the deficit, stupid," that had been posted on the wall in Clinton's campaign headquarters back in Little Rock.

Therefore, Clinton's budget itself was hardly bold, but a synthesized middle ground. It came to be known as bold only because he had the courage to propose higher taxes. It was the legacy of Ronald Reagan and the rhetoric of Republicans that made a very simple and time-honored concept—progressive tax rates in which the wealthiest with the greatest ability to pay more would be required to do so—seem dangerous.

Americans hated taxes by nature, but Reagan had soured them further. His rhetoric at the national level had made lower taxation a seeming virtue, while his policies forced state and local governments to raise taxes to meet needs neglected by the national administration. So the American people were spoiled by a president telling them taxes were bad while they had governors, mayors, state legislators, and city council members who raised them out of necessity because the federal government was doing less.

I recall Clinton's speaking early in 1983 to a group of businesspeople in Little Rock shortly after he regained the governor's office. He knew what lay ahead: He'd have to raise taxes while Reaganism became the national vogue. "Would you rather be the president who cut taxes or the governor who had to raise them?" he asked rhetorically and with frustration. In the rest of the decade, he would raise the sales tax twice, the corporate tax rate once, the corporate franchise tax once, not to mention so-called sin taxes and myriad user fees. He tried and failed to broaden the sales tax by applying it to certain professional services.

Now he would be the president who raised taxes after Reagan. Clinton's fate, it seemed, was to be the anti-Reagan.

"Bold" proposals from a great moral leader would have been a 50-cent-a-gallon increase in the gasoline tax, which is what Paul Tsongas and Ross Perot had recommended as campaigners, though Perot seemed to have forgotten about it in his growing criticisms of the new administration. "Bold" would have been means testing on Social Security and Medicare, meaning a proportionate reduction in, or elimination of, benefits for persons whose retirement incomes were higher than average. "Bold" might have been asking real sacrifice of a middle class that was pampered more than it knew or would admit through the full deductibility of mortgage interest and the full deductibility of health insurance costs for employers. It might have been a broadside attack on the vast bureaucracy and subsidy programs of the federal Agriculture Department, an agency that had grown in inverse proportion to the decline in the number of people engaged in agriculture. "Bold" would have been making actual reductions in discretionary spending, not "caps" or reductions over a period of five years in the rate of expected spending increases.

On the other side of the equation, the liberal one, "bold" would have been pumping anywhere from $30 billion to $100 billion, or more, into an economic stimulus program emphasizing public sector jobs, job training, community programs, and public works in the inner cities where the social crisis was worsening each year with more violence, more ethnic and racial divisiveness, and greater despair and disorder.

Clinton believed that either side of the equation would carry a political price too high, an economic risk too great, and a general threat to the ability of government to provide needed services for the moment and build viability for the future. He believed the economic and political considerations were essentially the same, requiring careful and incremental tinkering.

As he pored over the budget in early February 1993, he kept asking advisers one question, and it was the question of a politician and synthesizer trying to finesse his way out of gridlock, not of a moral leader seeking to blast his way through it: "What can we pass?"

This was the essence of his program, most of it having been promised in the campaign: Persons with high incomes, defined as couples with adjusted gross incomes exceeding $140,000 and individuals with adjusted gross incomes exceeding $115,000, would have their income-tax rates raised from 31 percent to 36 percent; those with incomes exceeding $250,000 a year would pay a 10 percent surtax; corporate income taxes would be raised to 36 percent; Social Security recipients with incomes exceeding $30,000 or so, depending on whether they were single or married, would pay income taxes on 85 percent of their incomes rather than 50 percent; defense spending would be cut by $88 billion over five years; spending on Medicare and Medicaid would be cut by $62.6 billion over five years; another $100 billion or so would be cut from the rate of spending increases in about a hundred categories; a few federal subsidies would be eliminated or reduced; the earned-income-tax credit for persons who worked but didn't rise above the poverty level would be expanded (a classic liberal-minded transfer of money from the rich to the poor); and, finally, the bugaboo, since it asked something of the vast middle class—everyone would pay a tax on the BTU content of fuels, which would be reflected in home utility bills and gasoline purchases, costing an average of $40 to $50 a year. Gasoline prices would go up about 7 cents a gallon. An ancillary benefit of the BTU tax was that it might stir a bit of conservation.

The BTU tax, which would eventually be scaled back to a simple and small gasoline tax increase, was the favored initiative of Vice President Gore, who prevailed over more fiscally conservative economic advisers because of his concerns about conservation benefits and his credibility on environmental matters.

Meanwhile, a short-term economic stimulus program would contain a modest $16 billion to be pumped that very summer into parks, swimming pools, youth centers, and jobs programs that were on a list of ready-to-go projects at the Housing and Urban Development Department.

Finally, Clinton reserved the right to start at least a few programs of his own, all scaled back dramatically from his campaign bravado. Key among them were a national service plan for youth to pay for college educations for those who would perform two years of public service work, school-to-job programs designed to merge advanced classroom instruction with real-life job training in high-tech fields, and government-run childhood immunizations. These were what he called "investments" rather than "spending," trying to give them a glossier veneer and make the point that the government, like the American people, needed to invest more and consume less.

If the assumptions of the Congressional Budget Office were correct, the plan would reduce the deficit by $500 billion over five years from what it would have been otherwise. The deficit would go from nearly $300 billion a year to about $200 billion. The debt would rise by about $1 trillion over the five years.

What the president had pieced together through hours of late-night meetings with economic advisers in the Roosevelt Room of the White House was an amalgam of competing ideas that, on balance, represented a step in the right direction.

David Broder wrote that Clinton suffered his own "trust deficit" because he was preaching deficit reduction while piling a trillion dollars on the debt. It was true that Clinton had continued his campaign mode of over-promise and sleight-of-hand. Outside of defense, he wasn't cutting spending; he was reducing the projected rate of spending growth. He wasn't raising taxes merely to reduce the deficit; he was raising taxes partly to reduce the deficit and partly to pay for new programs. As usual, confident in his cleverness, he followed an instinct to be disingenuous: rather than explaining to the American people what has just been explained here, and the reason and virtue of it, he leaned on the political selling points, which were sacrifice and deficit reduction, and tried to veil the full meaning of his amalgam of pro-posals. That's the very reason I'd sometimes availed myself of the moniker given Clinton back in Arkansas: "Slick Willie."

Even so, Clinton's plan, if the assumptions proved correct, would substantially reduce the deficit as a percentage of gross domestic prod-uct (GDP), which his economic advisers assured him was the most important calculation. Interest rates would stay low, inflation would remain in check, and the economy would recover choppily, according to a study by the Congressional Budget Office. Any hope of wiping out the deficit altogether depended on economic growth and health care reform, the latter to reduce the ever-growing drain on the government and the private sector of medical treatment and health insurance costs.

Clinton promised that his wife's task force would unveil its health reform package May 1. He talked about weaving some elements of health care reform, which would be the biggest social program ever undertaken, into the budget reconciliation bill by July. The blind optimism of that, or the sheer audacity of it, or the utter naivete of it, left congressional leaders shaking their heads. Naturally, it would not happen.

In early March, as the congressional clamor began for deeper spending cuts—mostly among Democrats nervous about tax increases as the legacy of Reagan, the specter of Perot, and the growing ratings of the blustery right-wing radio talker Rush Limbaugh frightened them— Clinton met at the White House with Prime Minister John Major of Great Britain. The visiting Tory, a man of credible conservative credentials, remarked that he thought Clinton had proposed just about enough spending cuts. This leading ally didn't want the United States to do anything precipitous or reckless; to an extent, he was endorsing as wise a key part of the economic plan that American Republicans and conservatives were calling bogus and wildly liberal.

The bloom of the State of the Union triumph lasted about a month, give or take. Clinton's pattern in Arkansas—noble speeches, great initial salesmanship, then a lull while his staff tried to actually write bills reflecting his speeches—repeated itself in Washington. The difference was that a lull or void could go unfilled in laid-back Arkansas, but not in the nation's capital.

Effective initial rhetoric by Clinton gave way to more effective follow-up rhetoric by detractors. The Republicans redefined the plan not as one of sacrifice and deficit reduction, but as one of the same old tax-and-spend liberalism. Now Clinton was seen as both a cultural liberal and a tax-and-spend liberal, the two things he couldn't be and succeed as president or win reelection.

The kind of synthesizing practiced by Clinton, so effective at a national governors' meeting and surely useful in a corporate boardroom, was fraught with danger in Washington and big-time partisan politics. Politics is easier to play from one side of the field or the other, and it's much easier to play without the responsibilities of the chief executive.

In the middle, one can be seen as standing for nothing, or one can be seen by opposing sides as standing more for the other side than for theirs. An amalgam of competing ideas runs the risk of containing too little of one and too much of another, leaving no one happy. Polishing an intricately responsible plan with superficial and deceptive rhetoric can backfire in a job that gets more scrutiny than any in the world.

All of that happened to Bill Clinton in the few weeks after his address to Congress.

His problems were exacerbated by pragmatic retreats for which he was becoming famous, and the tactical blunders to which his inexperienced and unsavvy White House was prone.

Liberal Democrats representing districts that Clinton carried handsomely grumbled less than anyone else, since Clinton had in fact begun governing from the left with the issue of gays in the military and by proposing higher taxes on the rich with new tax breaks for the poor. Eventually, though, they began to complain that soulless budget cutting was overpowering any kind of social conscience or urban policy, long neglected under Reagan and Bush.

Moderate-to-conservative Democrats, most from Clinton's South, grumbled much more loudly about Clinton trying to raise taxes and cut spending at the same time, when he should be cutting spending first, and more, while taxing second, and less. Their argument resonated in the White House because moderate-to-conservative Democrats sounded eerily like those pivotal and slippery Perot voters who preached this sermon: Cut spending; reduce the deficit, a virtue in itself. To do less would be to break faith and practice politics-as-usual. These moderate-to-conservative Democrats in Congress had friends and soulmates in Mack McLarty, Leon Panetta, economic security adviser Robert Rubin, and Treasury Secretary Lloyd Bentsen, all of whom wanted more spending cuts, and none of whom was enamored of a complicated tax on British Thermal Units.

Again, Clinton was a bit to the left of his heritage—the Democratic Leadership Council. Republicans who had feared a mainstream Democratic president with middle-class appeal saw Clinton play into their hands. Sam Nunn walked around complaining that he could not fathom why Clinton wouldn't govern "from the center." Even David Pryor, the president's popular Senate friend from Arkansas, was privately wondering if there was any way Clinton could moderate a bit. He eventually suggested doing away with any middle-class tax altogether, even a little gasoline tax increase.

Republicans weren't in the game until Clinton's $16 billion economic stimulus bill, having passed the House easily, came to the Senate in March, handing them rhetorical firepower. Here, they charged, was a bill laden with pork barrel for big-city Democratic mayors—i.e., old-style Democratic politics-as-usual. Here, they charged, was *prima facie* evidence that the new president's talk of cutting government spending to reduce the deficit was hollow. These were *new* expenditures. Here, they charged, was the the handiwork of a tax-and-spend liberal.

Until then, people in Washington had remarked that the Republicans were fighting in this new environment to remain a relevant political force. The Republicans had been arguing among themselves about whether they needed to offer an alternative to Clinton's budget or merely vote against his.

It was Clinton himself who summed up best what began happening to him about mid-March. "We're losing the rhetorical war," he said.

Then there was the matter of the tactical war, which he was losing as well.

The argument would rage for months in Washington over whether Senate Republicans intended all along, without regard for the parliamentary heavy-handedness of Senator Robert Byrd of Virginia, to filibuster against the president's $16 billion economic stimulus bill to buy time for the rhetorical war and show themselves to be alive and kicking in time for the GOP's spring President's Dinner, a fund-raising festival that had raised record amounts when Reagan and Bush were in the White House and offered access for cash. But this much was certain: The White House played squarely into the GOP's hands.

The stimulus bill sailed out of the House on a purely partisan vote where liberals dominate the Democratic Party. It came to the tougher Senate, where Southern Democrats were more apt to vote like Republicans. The White House's chief congressional liaison, Howard Paster, a veteran Capitol Hill operative on the House side but without as much experience in the Senate, brought in Senator Byrd, chairman of the Senate Appropriations Committee, to meet privately with the president to plot strategy. Remarkably, Senate Majority Leader George Mitchell was not present, an inconceivable error for which the president would soon apologize.

Byrd, who would handle the bill since it was an emergency spending measure, was a crusty, old-style senator who had been the Democratic leader of the Senate for a few of the Reagan years, but was at heart, according to a friendly Senate colleague, "a president's man." What he had desired for years was a Democrat in the White House for whom he could use his influence in the Senate.

Byrd asked Clinton, "Do you want this bill without amendments?"

"Yes," the president said.

That answer in the affirmative reflected only a general desire by Clinton, who not too long afterward would acknowledge to Senate Minority Leader Bob Dole that the stimulus bill hadn't been something he had campaigned on. But it was taken as an LBJ-style marching order by the veteran senator from West Virginia, who knew every rule in the book about limiting debate and denying even the consideration of amendments.

(It reminded me of a day back in Arkansas in 1983, when Winthrop Paul Rockefeller, son of the late Governor Winthrop Rockefeller, who was a reform Republican governor of Arkansas from 1966 to 1970, showed up at the Arkansas Highway Department to meet with the director about the volatile issue of truck-weight limits. He said Governor Clinton had asked him to try to settle the issue. The highway director called Clinton, who for the longest time couldn't imagine what Win Paul was talking about. Finally, he remembered. Win Paul had come to see him and offered to do anything he could to help him. Clinton had responded, not seriously, "You could settle this truck-weight thing for me.")

The heavy-handed Byrd-Paster strategy in the Senate offended Republicans, galvanizing them and giving them an excuse for acting for purely partisan reasons. All forty-three of them stayed together on a filibuster to deny the 60 votes needed to end it, killing the stimulus bill and giving the new president his second rude introduction to the big time, gays in the military having provided the first.

But before galvanizing the Republicans, the Byrd-Paster strategy had managed to stifle two Southern Democrats who seemed to be ahead of the curve. Senators John Breaux of Louisiana and David Boren of Oklahoma wanted to delay spending the money in the stimulus bill until budget cuts of an equal sum could be made. That proposal by conservative and moderate Democrats—cut spending first, tax second—would come to the fore in a few months. But for now the White House denied them. It was an ominous mistake.

The unwillingness to oblige the Breaux-Boren proposal advanced the image of a president veering to the left and betraying the Southern moderate influences of the Democratic Leadership Council that arguably had propelled him to his party's presidential nomination.

If Clinton had obliged Breaux and Boren, he might have delivered a preemptive strike against Republican rhetoric. He would have sent a signal to the American people that while he believed in new spending in some areas, he was too fiscally responsible to spend recklessly.

The failure of the stimulus bill set off the second round of backbiting and finger-pointing in the White House—the first having been directed toward Bernie Nussbaum, the New York City lawyer and friend of Hillary who was chief White House counsel, over his mishandling of the nomination of Zoe Baird for Attorney General and the near nomination of Kimba Wood for the same. (Nussbaum had recommended that Clinton stand behind Baird even as her nomination crumbled because she had hired illegal aliens for domestic help and not paid Social Security taxes on them; then he neglected to get to the bottom of Wood's arrangements with domestic help, which were far less egregious—no illegal aliens were involved—but troublesome, nonetheless.) Now, in view of the stimulus defeat, several of the younger White House aides went sour on Howard Paster, who had ill-advisedly pursued a high-handed policy more suited to the House of Representatives, where the Democrats' majority is greater and a minority filibuster is not allowed, than to the Senate.

The ineptness of the new administration was evident in the fact that its chief congressional liaison had proposed a 51-vote strategy in the Senate, not realizing until too late that with a filibuster allowed on an emergency spending measure, he would need a 60-vote strategy to break a standoff.

There was, in fact, a generation gap developing in the White House. Young aides, many Stephanopoulos's disciples, were irked by press criticism of a fuzzy-cheeked White House when, in fact, the big blunders had been made by the older guys. McLarty was a much bigger fan of the young but uncommonly bright Stephanopoulos, who knew both politics and policy, than of Nussbaum or Paster, who seemed to have lead feet politically. But the president? He was a friend of all. No one could imagine him firing anyone, especially Nussbaum, who had been Hillary's boss when she worked on the counsel's staff for the House Judiciary Committee considering impeachment of Richard Nixon. Nussbaum had been one of the first people she had told about her plans to marry a young man from Arkansas who would be president someday. The Clintons had turned to Nussbaum for advice back in the winter of 1992 during the Gennifer Flowers near debacle.

In time Howard Paster would improve as congressional director, then resign in the fall in a blaze of glory. Nussbaum would not appear to improve.

At their core, the tactical errors of the stimulus bill stemmed from Clinton's early preoccupation with doing nothing the way that Jimmy Carter had done it. The comparisons were too easy between these Southern governors without reinforcing them. One of Carter's failings was that he persisted in maintaining the role of outsider in his dealings with Congress, and therefore had limited effectiveness. Clinton decided to play the Washington game and hired a confirmed Democratic insider like Paster to direct his congressional operation.

During the 1980s, Democratic insiders had won their favors by using the powerful Democratic committee chairmen. By deploying Byrd, Paster merely followed that dozen-year tradition. The problem was that Ronald Reagan had redefined the presidency as an outsider game, appealing to voters outside the Beltway to indirectly effect action by the Congress. So while Clinton, Paster, and Byrd played an inside game based on inapplicable Democratic strategies from the Reagan years, the Republicans won the outside games of rhetoric and public opinion.

It is said of Clinton that he is incapable of sustained error. By the fall, on another major issue, he would cleverly effect a desired congressional result by playing the outside game and sending his vice president to the Larry King Live show to debate Ross Perot.

It was hard to imagine later that in the early stages of the Senate fight over the stimulus bill, the rap on Clinton was that he wouldn't compromise. Conventional wisdom can change on a dime in Washington, especially with a president who, when burned, can change with equal abruptness. In Washington in 1993, the combination of a fickle punditocracy and a groundless presidency made the conventional wisdom as wildly changing as the weather back in Arkansas.

In mid-March, Clinton went from a tactical blunderer who wouldn't compromise to a tactical blunderer who was a mushy over-compromiser. The only constant was that he was certainly a blunderer.

With the stimulus bill in trouble in the Senate, and as Clinton began to see potential problems for his make-or-break budget in a Senate of solidly opposed Republicans and wavering conservative Democrats from the South and West, the president agreed to meet with a dozen or so Democratic senators from Western states.

The meeting, like most of Clinton's, was cordial. It began with the Western senators thanking the president for even seeing them. Several recalled never getting to meet as a group with Jimmy Carter. They said they found out in the newspaper early in that Democratic presidency that Carter intended to kill water projects in their states. But already Clinton had shown himself different from Carter: he had carried a few of their states, the first Democratic presidential candidate to do so since Johnson in 1964, and now he was actually sitting down with them.

Their concern was the provision in Clinton's budget for increases in grazing fees and mining royalties on public lands, which dominated their Big Sky country. They wondered if maybe the administration wasn't behaving a bit precipitously in trying to get a little extra money while sending a pleasing signal to environmentalists. Their staffs hadn't been consulted, but each of them had aides who were quite knowledgeable on the subject. The issue was complex, they said. Higher grazing fees didn't necessarily mean better land management, and there were hundreds of small-ranch operators who might be imperiled as a result of the fee increases. What they wanted from the president, they said, was only one thing: Would he assign someone in the White House to work with their aides who had become expert on the subject? At least the White House ought to have the benefit of the expertise and thinking of party allies who had long studied the matter. Some of the senators, especially Max Baucus of Montana, talked tougher outside the Oval Office. But in the meeting, that was all they asked.

Why, certainly, he would assign a staff person, said the conciliatory president, and he turned to McLarty and asked him to appoint such a liaison.

McLarty gave the assignment to Greg Simon, who worked on Vice President Gore's staff. He chose Simon because of Gore's own expertise and credibility in environmental matters as well as Simon's reputation for thoroughness.

Over the next couple of weeks, Simon studied the matters and came to several perfectly reasonable conclusions. The proposed rates of the fees and royalties seemed to be pulled from thin air. No one could offer him any sound reasoning for the estimates of what they would raise. He found the estimates of the Congressional Budget Office and the Office of Management and Budget on the amount of money to be raised to be unacceptably disparate, based on admitted guesswork by both, indicating there was a dearth of empirical information. Meanwhile, Interior Secretary Bruce Babbitt—popular with Democrats in the West, and a Clinton-style synthesizer who had credibility with environmentalists and business interests—was in the midst of a study of public land management and could, as part of that, raise grazing fees later by administrative action, subject, of course, to congressional override. Finally, the Senate's leading advocate of increased mining royalties—who happened to be Dale Bumpers of Arkansas, who had long argued that the government was squandering millions in mining rights—had said publicly days before that he expected a full airing in the fall on a comprehensive mining reform law that could cover the issue of royalties.

Simon recommended to Gore and McLarty that there was no need, and in fact no logical reason to fight the issue of grazing fees and mining royalties as part of the budget battle. It could be handled otherwise with more thoroughness and efficiency, and perhaps less political complication. McLarty and Gore talked it over, and they made the decision to delete the fees and royalties. The president passively agreed, trusting that Gore knew the Senate since he had served there, and that McLarty was nothing if not positively pragmatic.

(Gore, it turned out, hadn't been extolled in the Senate as a clever legislative strategist. And McLarty, like Clinton, had a history of choosing conciliation over fighting. As chairman of the Arkansas Louisiana Gas Company, McLarty had inherited several so-called take-or-pay contracts with exploration and production companies, entered into before he took the corporate helm and during a time—around 1980— of widespread industry fear of gas shortages and the competitive pressures of deregulation. If paid in full, the contracts would have bankrupted the company. McLarty had two choices: negotiate for settlements or fight the contracts in court. He chose to negotiate for settlements, fearing the risks of protracted litigation. Settling the contracts saddled McLarty's company with such steep debt that the stock price, once well over $20, had dropped to about $7 in December of 1992 when he resigned to become chief of staff to the president-elect. Some utility experts said he should have gone to court and taken a chance. Mack McLarty did not take chances, except for the big one: coming to Washington as chief of staff to his friend.)

Actually, House-Senate conferees meeting on the budget resolution had decided on their own to remove the grazing fees from the measure moments before a White House official sent word that the administration wanted them taken out.

Senator Baucus of ranch-rich Montana, anxious to show his constituents that he could deliver, promptly put out a news release suggesting that he and his Western Democratic colleagues had won this major concession by getting tough with the president.

Senator Bumpers, having heard reports of White House wavering, had tried for a day and a half to get in touch with McLarty to recommend that he not cave in quickly. By the time McLarty called him back, the deed had been done. Baucus has already blanketed Montana with news releases, McLarty told Bumpers.

The action set off a firestorm of pundit and environmentalist criticism.

The pundits said the president had revealed that he was a hasty retreater who, in the Washington vernacular, could be "rolled." Clinton had emphasized from the moment the fees and royalties were removed from the bill that he intended to address them separately later and that, contrary to popular opinion, he had made no substantive concession at all, which was true. But he'd appeared to retreat before the opponent fired anything other than a warning shot.

Environmental groups interested in stricter regulation of public land use said the president had betrayed them, giving in to powerful business interests. Several of them met with McLarty, who promised that the Clinton administration would follow through on grazing-fee reform. Most weren't satisfied.

The promise to revisit the fees eventually was kept, in August, a week after the budget was passed by the margin of Gore's tie-breaking vote, when Interior Secretary Babbitt announced grazing-fee increases that the Western Democratic senators said they could accept and that environmental groups praised uniformly. They subsequently were reduced in a conference report, and filibustered by a Senate minority; but essentially, Clinton had arranged both to win his budget and to keep viable the prospect of higher grazing fees.

What the president had endured was a classic Clinton case of ugly "process" versus worthy "product."

The inside word that stunned Washington, quite properly, was that the Western Democrats were surprised that the White House acquiesced so quickly: A group of senators had asked only for a dialogue; a few days later they were handed a convincing victory that cost them nothing.

Bumpers summed up the issue this way: "First of all, the White House was right. They couldn't have passed that budget with those provisions in there. But my point in trying to reach Mack was that by keeping those fees in the budget bill a little longer, they could have won some other concessions. I've been a trial lawyer. Even if you know you're going to have to concede a point, you don't want to signal it until it's absolutely necessary. The White House did the smart thing, but they may not have done it at the smartest time."

Months later, McLarty said, "I agree with that. I'll take the blame."

If not for the kind of leverage Bumpers was suggesting, why did the White House decide in the first place to lump grazing fees and mining royalties into the budget bill? Actually, it had been done for mathematical and cosmetic reasons: Clinton wanted to propose deficit reduction that exceeded the amount Bush had agreed to in the budget reconciliation package in 1990. He was seeking to blend so many facets, a little of this and that, that he needed every few million dollars he could lay his hands on.

"Sometimes our biggest problem around here is that we publicly declare our own goal," Bruce Lindsey said one day. "Then the Republicans and our critics can blast us with our own definition of success when we fall a little short of it. We need more long-term strategic planning."

What we had by the end of March was a weak president who at first hadn't compromised when he should have, over the stimulus bill, and then compromised too readily when he shouldn't have, over the grazing fees and mining royalties.

The Congress was seeing the Bill Clinton I had seen in Arkansas: an over-compensator and a strategic blunderer who spent half of his time during state legislative sessions walking a tightrope, wheeling and dealing wildly at the end to pass something reasonably bold and meaningful. In Arkansas, Clinton had ended one legislative session by literally running from one end of the third floor of the state Capitol to the other to get the chambers to agree to his clever last-minute wording of amendments.

Meanwhile, the Bob Dole–led Republicans were suddenly back from the dead. They gleefully pushed the perception of a weak dissembler who not only broke a promise to the middle class, but was a president who ran from a fight and, deep down, was just another nasty tax-and-spend liberal. As a result of the Republican murder of the stimulus bill, conservative groups began raising funds at rates reminiscent of the glorious Reagan years.

Hayley Barbour, the Mississippian and Republican national chairman, went around the country delivering the same line over and over: "Bill Clinton has done more to unite the Republican Party than I ever could."

The Clinton administration did itself no good—in fact it played into the Republicans' hands again—by proceeding headfirst on health care reform as the budget battles were unfolding. One revolution at a time was plenty. Health care reform would cost big money. And then Health and Human Services Secretary Donna Shalala said publicly that a European-style value-added tax was an option.

It unnerved the American people, this idea of another massive tax on the heels of all these proposed already. Just what kind of tax-crazed liberal was this new president?

Actually, most of the economic thinkers in the Clinton administration believed the country would be better off if it replaced the personal income tax, which draws from personal success, with a value-added tax or luxury-oriented national sales tax, which takes its bite out of personal consumption. But that was a second-term issue, not a second-month issue, and Shalala was quickly showing herself to be one of the weakest and most politically inept members of the president's cabinet.

Meanwhile, Clinton was learning that being a "new Democrat" would be trickier in the White House than the Governor's Mansion. One of his claims to fame in Arkansas had been a generous investment tax credit for firms that expanded to employ more people. He had designed it to keep the International Paper Company from leaving Pine Bluff, Arkansas, for another state. The credit, widely criticized by liberals in Arkansas, was in fact a useful tool in the state-to-state competition for jobs that was so prevalent in the 1980s. But when Clinton proposed a similar investment tax credit on the federal level, two key Democrats—Senator Daniel Patrick Moynihan of New York, chairman of the Senate Finance Committee, and Representative Dan Rostenkowski of Illinois, chairman of the House Ways and Means Committee—explained to him that it was pure folly. Companies that planned expansions anyway would merely expedite them to get a tax break, and, once again, tinkering with the tax code for policy purposes would backfire. Clinton's investment tax credit—his calling card as a business-friendly new Democrat—was dead on arrival.

He couldn't always perform the presidency as a kind of governor in chief. The dynamics were quite different when you were responsible for all fifty states.

In less than one hundred days on the job of his dreams, the synthesizing baby-boom Democrat in the White House had been branded naive, a cultural liberal, a tax-and-spend liberal, a dissembler, a tactical blunderer, and a weakling—and, actually, had behaved a bit like all of them. The would-be Great Synthesizer had become a synthesis of negatives.

What happened to all that goodwill for a new president? It was short-lived; in fact, it may never have existed for a minority president with credibility problems. David Broder had been right about that 43 percent; Clinton had been wrong about 62 percent.

In a short time, Bill Clinton would set modern-day records for early presidential unpopularity.

People who'd known him in Arkansas were accustomed to the pattern: Start out poorly, walk the highwire, rally frantically. Remember the words of Betsey Wright: "He'll figure it out."

White House officials took solace in an old admonition of Senator Sam Ervin: In politics you'll never be satisfied at the end of the day; only at some point in the future, looking back on the body of work, examining the baby without living the labor pains, can one hope to feel good about what he has done.

But Clinton had never failed at this level, and things weren't yet as bad as they soon would get.

CHAPTER 5

April Fool

At a staff meeting one April morning, as Clinton's approval rating plummeted, Mack McLarty tried to lift spirits with the kind of pep talk to which he was inevitably and sometimes irritatingly prone.

He related that Ronald Reagan's poll numbers had dropped early in his presidency, and, actually, didn't begin to shoot up until he was shot outside the Washington Hilton Hotel.

"Oh, Mack, it's not that bad, is it? What are you suggesting?" cracked Rahm Emmanuel, a young Chicago ballet dancer educated at Sarah Lawrence whose fund-raising exploits in the campaign had landed him the choice job as White House political director.

Emmanuel would lose the job several weeks later in a White House personnel shake-up, reassigned as deputy director of communications. His arrogance and abrasiveness made him a widely unpopular young man inside the White House. Black humor, it seemed, did not become a White House political director.

Actually, it was telling that Emmanuel was reassigned to another high-ranking White House job rather than axed or sent to an agency. Though he was widely disliked in the White House, he happened to be liked by the chief of staff, who had befriended him during the fund-raising days of the campaign back in Little Rock.

Here was one of those odd friendships: A chief of staff criticized for being too soft and a young political operative criticized for being too brash. But on the day of Emmanuel's wisecrack, McLarty took him aside and politely suggested that one-upping the chief of staff with a one-liner was not appreciated by the chief of staff.

Emmanuel's ups and downs seemed to parallel the president's. Both hit lows in April and May. Both would be greatly rehabilitated by November.

Black humor was the only intentional comedy emanating from the White House in the late spring and early summer. But unintended comedy was rampant.

The new president's problems were compounding rapidly and most of his wounds were self-inflicted. But there was one powerful external problem that gained strength in inverse proportion to Clinton's polling decline. His name was Ross Perot, the anti-politician in an age of anti-politics. Perot was the scourge of a young president, a consummate politician who had never worked at anything else save brief stints as a law professor and practicing attorney, both of which he performed with one eye on the job and the other on the imminent race for public office.

In one April poll, the ubiquitous Perot was in a tie with Clinton in a head-to-head race, a rather noteworthy development considering that five months earlier, Clinton had won the votes of 24 million more Americans than Perot.

The mercurial Texan was hard to figure, and not only for the White House. Veteran members of Congress of both parties told stories about getting seemingly altruistic telephone calls over the years from Perot in which he advanced ideas for reducing the federal deficit or making government responsible or, in the case of his special interest, getting to the bottom of the matter of Americans still unaccounted for in Vietnam. Members of Congress had long considered Perot sincere and worthy of respect and admiration, though uncompromising, dictatorial, possibly paranoid, and therefore unsuited for the travails of elective politics. But now he behaved as a cynical political candidate, expediently disregarding his own budget-reduction plan of the campaign with its 50-cent-a-gallon tax increase to lambast Clinton's, a proposal that was 43 cents a gallon cheaper. He sounded like a Republican for the moment; but Republicans knew he was entirely too unpredictable for cozy bedfellowing.

The White House—youthful, expressive, self-absorbed, contemptuous of critics, and megalomaniacal in places—offered widely divergent theories on what it all meant. Some dismissed Perot's relevance to Clinton on the argument that Perot voters were essentially conservative white people, thus more likely to be Republican voters anyway. That theory meant that Clinton needed only to protect the classic Democratic constituencies to win another three-way race. Others asserted that Perot's negatives made him unelectable, never able to get 50 percent of the vote plus one, and that he shouldn't be a source of great worry even as the Republican presidential nominee, a possibility suddenly discussed. Others again viewed Perot's outsider popularity as leverage to keep nervous Democratic members in Congress in line to enact Clinton's deficit-reduction and campaign finance reform measures. Yet others saw Perot gaining strength only from Clinton's weakness, and could find nothing but bad news in that.

Each assertion had arguable merit, but it was the last one that began about this time to preoccupy a president who treasured popularity and lacked the self-assurance to dismiss with stoicism the growing popularity of a harsh critic.

Clinton analyzes election returns with great insight into trends and meanings, and Perot's 19 percent had sent him a clear, unnerving message about the depth of Americans' exasperation with government. His pollsters and strategists had explained to him that what Perot voters wanted more than anything else was action—any action. Nothing brought a Perot crowd to its feet faster than the Texan's line that it was time to take a shovel and clean out the barn.

The danger, then, was that setbacks such as Clinton's on the economic stimulus bill would trap him in a deathly cycle: Perot would grow stronger with each failing, therefore lessening Clinton's stature and his ability to persuade Congress next time.

Clinton also knew that if Perot hadn't behaved so curiously in 1992—getting out of the race, then back in, and accusing Republicans of plotting to sabotage his daughter's wedding—he would have landed an even greater share of the vote. Now Perot's frequent missiles imperiled Clinton's ability to govern, defying the president's best efforts to recruit, use, neutralize, or otherwise handle his celebrity critic.

On the afternoon before he delivered his State of the Union speech on February 17, Clinton had telephoned Perot to extend a courtesy and seek support for a program that was designed in great part to appeal to the Perot mania for deficit reduction. Perot was respectfully complimentary in general terms, but did not commit himself. When Perot appeared that evening on ABC's "Nightline," saying Clinton's plan sounded pleasant but that the devil would be in the details, White

House aides called during the show to correct or clarify, again respectfully, a couple of Perot's assertions. The parties were sparring with kid gloves.

From the White House, McLarty—the president's chief liaison to businessmen—talked with Perot by telephone several times in the early months, always finding him reasonable in his advocacy and advice. McLarty described one conversation as "very constructive; it couldn't have been more appropriate." He said he'd encountered Perot's pique only once. Clinton told a dinner audience that Perot had telephoned McLarty to apologize to him for having said at a congressional hearing that the White House was devoid of anyone with business experience. Perot, after reading that Clinton had made that public comment, called McLarty to say he thought they had been speaking privately. McLarty said he'd only told Clinton—since, after all, his job was to serve the president—and hadn't expected the president to blab publicly.

Perot had made the comment about the absence of White House business experience during testimony to the Joint Committee on Congressional Reform, where he ran into two of McLarty's staunchest defenders—David Pryor of Arkansas and David Boren of Oklahoma, where McLarty's gas company had done business. Perot had backed down when he appeared on the very verge of escalating his crtiticism. He said the Arkansas Louisiana Gas Company had endured "problems" under McLarty, but he chose not to exploit the company's burdensome debt and declining stock price.

Perot soon began to blab aplenty in public, sniping at Clinton incessantly: not enough spending cuts, too many taxes, too much compromise, too many broken promises, not enough credibility, more politics-as-usual. He treated Clinton approximately as disrespectfully as he had treated George Bush, and he did so offering no specifics, bearing no personal responsibility, and escaping the need to reconcile what he was saying now with what he had proposed as a candidate, as well as the need to explain how he could work with Congress when he'd displayed difficulty getting along with associates for years.

Inevitably, the temperamental Clinton snapped. It happened on April Fool's Day.

Clinton went to Annapolis to speak to the American Society of Newspaper Editors. During a question-and-answer session, an editor asked about something Perot had mentioned to the group the day before: The rumor that a woman in the White House had insulted a military officer working at the White House for the Joint Chiefs of

Staff. According to the rumor, she had declined to return the simple greeting of a lieutenant general, telling him she didn't speak to men in military uniforms.

Clinton was reeling from reports that he loathed the military, which he didn't, and lacked credibility as commander in chief, which he did. He was reeling from rumors in general. One was that he and Hillary fought like alley cats, exchanging loud profanities, and that Hillary had thrown an ashtray at him. These bits of gossip emanated from the Secret Service and the White House permanent staff, and they had made their way into *Newsweek* magazine.

Angry that Perot talked nicely in private but repeated an unsubstantiated report in public, Clinton declared Perot a rumormonger. He portrayed the story about a woman's rude treatment of the military officer as "made of whole cloth."

He got into his limousine after the appearance and said to an aide, "I stepped on my story, didn't I?"

Stepping on a story means making unintended news—relegating the intended message to secondary status through an extemporaneous declaration that bears greater interest for reporters. Ronald Reagan never had a problem stepping on a story since he knew how to stick to a script; but the accessible, energetic, extemporaneous Clinton sometimes appeared to be stomping grapes. More than once it had to do with Perot. (One day in the fall he would step on his intended story by declaring a day ahead of schedule that Al Gore would challenge Perot to a debate.)

Clinton's testiness at Annapolis netted him a front-page story that next morning in *The New York Times* in which Perot, given the opportunity to respond to the president's attack, stepped up his charge that Clinton lacked credibility not only as commander in chief but in general. Being called a liar by Bill Clinton was "a truly unique experience," Perot said to Gwen Ifill of the *Times*.

Clinton read the *Times* article on his way to Portland, Oregon, to conduct a promised summit on the dispute between environmentalists and the timber industry in the Pacific Northwest. From there he would go to Vancouver for a summit with Boris Yeltsin.

"The president knows that," McLarty said, when I suggested that Clinton had played into Perot's hands and committed a tactical error by taking the bait of a man whose support he needed to tap and exploit, not galvanize. "He was tired, mentally and physically, and a bit frustrated. These rumors. . . ."

Yes, what of those rumors?

The one about a woman's insulting a military officer at the White House was not "made of whole cloth," as Clinton had said. "Something happened, and we regret it. The President was very unhappy about it," McLarty said. "But it didn't happen quite the way it's been described."

As for his supposed loathing of the military, few things could have been further from the truth. "It's just not Bill Clinton," McLarty said. It could not possibly be true that Clinton was obsessed with trying to please everyone and simultaneously contemptuous of the military. Actually, he most desires approval from those who don't readily extend it. In Arkansas, our joke was that the quickest way to Clinton's ear was to criticize him publicly. Even the now-famous letter he wrote as a twenty-three-year-old draft evader to an ROTC colonel to whom he'd lied about his intentions seemed in part an effort to win the colonel's understanding, if not acceptance.

In Vancouver, Clinton jogged with the lieutenant general who had sustained the impoliteness, whatever its form. Pool photographers, usually seen as intrusive by the Clintons, were encouraged to observe and shoot pictures.

The rumors about Hillary were at least overblown, and mostly false and malicious. They were based on a cultural inability to cope with her powerful role. She can hurt more with a brisk comment or a glare than an ashtray. A governor's staffer in Arkansas told of the time he was at the Governor's Mansion on business and spotted Hillary's father, the late Hugh Rodham, in the kitchen. He'd always enjoyed Rodham's company, so he stepped into the kitchen to say hello. It turned out that Hillary's mother and brothers were there, too. The staffer said that Hillary gave him a look he'd never forget, one that sent an unmistakable message: How dare you infiltrate my private family time? Get the hell out of here.

The rumors sprang from embellishments of her palpable displeasure about the hovering, controlling nature of the Secret Service, which invaded what she called her "zone of privacy" and conflicted with her own controlling nature. And, yes, she, like her husband, has a temper.

Here is a good, albeit mild, example: On the week of Clinton's inauguration, the Southwestern Bell Telephone Company, which serves Arkansas, sponsored a tribute to Hillary for her championing of children and education. The event at the Kennedy Center included a satellite hookup with First Daughter Chelsea's classroom back at Horace Mann

School on the eastern, mostly black side of Little Rock. George "Skip" Holland, lobbyist for Southwestern Bell in Arkansas, was on stage awaiting Hillary's arrival. With him was the company president, Mike Flynn, and two technicians whose job was to make sure the satellite hookup came off without a hitch. A Secret Service agent walked up to Holland and told him the company could have only two representatives on stage when Mrs. Clinton arrived. After a bit of contention, during which the Secret Service man asked insistently that Holland please let him do his job, Holland decided that if only two company employees could be on stage, they would be the vital technicians. When Hillary arrived, she greeted Holland and Flynn warmly. As she prepared to walk to the stage, she asked, "Aren't you coming?" Holland told her of the orders of the Secret Service, and Hillary blew a fuse. "Damnit, this is my event, not the Secret Service's event," she said. "I'll decide who gets on the stage."

Told of that story and asked if it represented the First Lady's widely rumored colorful language, a White House official said, "No. I'm talking about something a bit more colorful."

Matters would get worse.

Clinton accepted that Reagan had made the president's job seem manageable enough through the magic of simplicity, superficiality, firm ideology, delegation, detachment, message control, foreign policy coasting, and communications mastery. But Clinton's message wasn't simple or superficial; it was nuanced and diversified. And he had been anything but detached except in one fateful matter.

One of the exclamation points on Clinton's April from Hell was the FBI's offensive on cult leader David Koresh's Ranch Apocalypse outside Waco, Texas, after weeks of standoff resulting from a bungled raid on the compound by agents of the Bureau of Alcohol, Tobacco, and Firearms (ATF). The ATF agents had acted on charges that Koresh oversaw an arsenal of illegal weapons.

In one of Washington's cruel twists, Clinton paid a bitter price of seeming cowardice for the one situation he'd kept away from at a time when he was widely panned for trying to do too much.

The White House seemed rather cavalier about the events that Monday morning, April 19, when the FBI moved on the Waco compound with tanks knocking holes in the walls and releasing tear gas inside. Asked about the offensive by a reporter early in the day, Clinton responded that Attorney General Janet Reno had told him a little about it the day before. During the noon hour, as CNN broadcast the offensive live, Clinton went about business as usual. He addressed a labor convention at the Washington Hilton, delivering an uninspired appeal for his stimulus program. He knew it was doomed.

About 1:00 P.M., George Stephanopoulos came out for his daily news briefing determined, as always, to avoid definitive action verbs. He joked about the loudness of the necktie worn by Bill Plante of CBS, and this exchange, typical of Stephanopoulos's answer avoidance, ensued:

Q: Does the President or anybody in the White House have any input into the operation in Waco?

Stephanopoulos: The Attorney General informed the President yesterday that they were planning on going ahead with this operation. But it's a decision by the Attorney General and the FBI.

Q: George, since the Attorney General works for the President, isn't it fair to say that it's a presidential decision not to stop it?

Stephanopoulos: The President was clearly informed of . . .

Q: He apparently gave approval to it. Or he could have stopped it.

Stephanopoulos: Well, he didn't stop it. No, he didn't stop it. The Attorney General informed . . .

Q: So in not stopping it, he approved it?

Stephanopoulos: We can get into a philosophical or semantic discussion, but . . .

Q: Well, he assumes responsibility?

Stephanopoulos: Certainly he is responsible, but it's the Attorney General and the FBI that have operational control over this. But clearly he was informed.

Q: Did she ask him for authorization?

Stephanopoulos: No, she informed him. She said this is what the
FBI would like to do.

After a few more minutes of this byplay, with reporters trying vainly
to get Stephanopoulos to say the word "authorize," Wolf Blitzer of CNN
asked Stephanopoulos if he was aware that the compound was at that
moment on fire.

There was a bit of inappropriate laughter in the press briefing room,
a dungeon that shuts out the real world and warps its inhabitants into
caring more about political implications than burning children. Stephanopoulos looked around and an aide handed him a note. "This just
in," Stephanopoulos said, adding to the jocularity.

Stephanopoulos said he could confirm what CNN was showing the
world. The compound was ablaze. He had no other information.

Afterward, as Stephanopoulos walked back to his cordoned office,
young aides gathered around him to say the cultists had started the
fire. "This is not good," he said. They said they'd debated whether to
give him that information. "You probably should have," he said.

Stephanopoulos went back to his office to turn up the volume on
CNN's telecast. "Not good," he said again. And then again. He went
to his desk and placed a call to the Justice Department, asking for
Webb Hubbell, the nominee for associate attorney general who was
one of the best friends of the Clintons from Little Rock. Hubbell wasn't
immediately available. He was in the situation room monitoring the
horror.

Then Stephanopoulos scurried to the president's office. Dee Dee
Myers, the press secretary, said to a deputy, "You know what they'll
say. They'll say we should have waited them out; that they would have
run out of food."

Down the hall, Clinton had seen aides gathered around a television
set and asked almost idly, "What's going on?" Clearly, Waco had not
been on his mind. As the horror sank in, he remarked that surely the
children had been placed in the underground bus on the compound,
where they'd be safe. But that was not the case.

What followed was a 24-hour period of public silence by the President of the United States and the emergence of his third choice for
Attorney General, Reno, as a national heroine. She'd approved an operation that proved ill-conceived and tragically bungled, but she

promptly held a news conference to accept blame, said that the buck stopped with her, offered to resign, and, by midnight, had made four live appearances on national television news programs to repeat her explanation that the buck stopped somewhere shy of the place it stopped in Harry Truman's day. Seldom, if ever, had a *mea culpa* resounded with such instant strength and impressiveness.

On NBC with Tom Brokaw, Reno acknowledged that she hadn't spoken with the president. That struck Brokaw, and others, as odd. It heightened the appearance of a cowering president, leaving the lonely dirty work to his Attorney General. Actually, Clinton had been in touch with Hubbell, Reno explained, but that merely added to the curiosity about Hubbell, the president's golfing partner and Hillary's law partner from Little Rock—and the man they had dispatched to the Justice Department as their eyes and ears while struggling with the selection of the actual Attorney General.

In truth, Reno had been driving back from a luncheon speech in Baltimore when the fire started. Hubbell was monitoring from the situation room. Hubbell had several conversations that afternoon with Stephanopoulos, Bruce Lindsey, and Vince Foster at the White House, but none with Clinton. Reno had been busy assessing the situation and making public appearances, and assumed incorrectly that at least one of Hubbell's White House telephone conversations was with the president himself.

Clinton suggested that afternoon that he needed to say something publicly, but Stephanopoulos advised him not to do it. George advised sitting tight until more was known. This would turn out to be Stephanopoulos's second major political mistake—the first having been his pushing Clinton to try to keep his promise about lifting the ban on gays in the military.

The appearance of a cowering president stung Clinton, and was not altogether deceptive. A politician first and always, he didn't know how to react initially and he put Stephanopoulos's advice ahead of personal instinct. A stronger man might have disregarded an aide's advice because of a sense of personal responsibility.

The president went public the next day, praising Reno, but correcting her: The buck stopped with him, he said. By this time he had decided that even he could win a popularity contest with David Koresh. Don't forget, he said, that it was Koresh who was chiefly responsible for eighty-seven deaths; that it was Koresh who'd commanded a cult that practiced child abuse.

I couldn't help recalling my first conversation with James Carville. It had taken place in March 1992 in the coffeeshop of the Palmer House Hilton Hotel in Chicago, where Clinton was winning the Democratic primary. Aware of my criticisms of Clinton, Carville endeavored to explain to me that while some of what I said might be on target, Clinton was an extraordinary political figure. He said he'd finally found an electable Democrat "who has the ability to go on television and inspire the country the way Reagan did after the Challenger disaster."

Now we'd seen the first televised blaze of the Clinton era, and Janet Reno had played Reagan's role. Clinton's first-day response was limited to telephoning Reno about midnight, after her "Nightline" appearance, to say, "That a girl."

In time an investigation would show that Reno had no real evidence of ongoing child abuse. Justice Department sources would leak information that she had been indecisive about approving the raid, finally capitulating to the urgings of the FBI. Her star would fade a bit, which was of no concern at all to White House aides who were tiring of this mythology of a wondrous Attorney General who made the president look weak by comparison and insisted on independent reactions to presidential proposals.

In time Reno would oppose the merger of the FBI with the Bureau of Alcohol, Tobacco and Firearms, proposed by Vice President Al Gore's report for the so-called reinvention of government. She would react less than enthusiastically to the president's crime-fighting calling card of 50,000 to 100,000 additional policemen. She would advocate censoring television violence without telling the White House she intended to do it. She would make what appeared to be an inappropriate campaign appearance for New Jersey Governor Jim Florio.

Altogether, the matter of Waco was as thorough a disaster as could be imagined: The initial ATF raid was ill-advised and then lied about; the Reno-approved FBI offensive was ill-advised and rationalized by unsubstantiated reports of child abuse. Clinton looked nothing if not weak, and Stephanopoulos could only kick himself over his error.

Meanwhile, the media's fascination with hundred-day reviews, prompted partly by Clinton's typical over-exuberant promise of a first hundred days of unprecedented activity and accomplishment, led to a spate of mostly bad notices the last week of April. The prevailing judgment was that Clinton was in trouble, a bit Carterish, overextended and unfocused, and that he had naively tried to do too many things at once—the budget and health care and campaign finance reform and national service with an occasional reference to coming welfare reform—while depending on a White House staff that appeared to have fallen off a turnip truck from Arkansas.

This was not the best time for the president to be stabbed in the back by his affable director of the Office of Management and Budget—Leon Panetta, a.k.a. "Neon Leon," or "Doctor Spin," as he was dubbed by his friends in the White House after he became the lead story in *The Washington Post* on Clinton's ninety-eighth day in office with comments that were remarkable for their horrible timing and brutal candor.

Panetta pronounced the Clinton presidency sick, very sick, and this was only eighty-seven days after a cabinet retreat to Camp David where Clinton, at the behest of Vice President Gore, brought in a "facilitator" after dinner to lead the cabinet members in bonding exercises designed to enhance trust and the spirit of teamwork. (Within a week, *The Washington Post* had reported on specific personal revelations made by leading administration officials during the bonding session; so much for trust and teamwork. "That was the one that stunned me. I knew after that there was no such thing as a secret in this job," Stephanopoulos said.)

Panetta was a product of the Capitol Hill culture, where members of Congress and reporters bump into each other in the halls of the Capitol and the congressional office buildings, talking freely about the ins and outs, and where legislators frequently behave as lone rangers, able to advocate their points of view freely. The White House and cabinet cultures were quite the opposite; leading officials were sequestered and insulated, speaking through press aides, answerable to the president, and advocates of his synthesized message, not theirs.

But Panetta was respected and nearly beloved in the Clinton administration for his jolly, hearty demeanor, his ferocious work habits, and his credibility among his longtime former colleagues on Capitol Hill. That was a good thing. Otherwise Clinton might have tried to capture the front page on his hundredth day by firing him. Oh, probably not. That was not Clinton's instinct. Firing his key budget man on his hundredth day would have made the first hundred days seem even worse. And the fact of the matter was that next to Reno and Interior Secretary Bruce Babbitt, Panetta was at that moment the best thing about the Clinton administration.

Panetta had begun his Washington career as a Republican appointee from California, converting to the Democratic Party in the Nixon era, largely over the issue of civil rights. Already he'd established himself as independent-minded; no one owned him. In time he ascended to the chairmanship of the House Budget Committee, where he distinguished himself as chief among the "deficit hawks," generally progressive Democrats who resisted Reagan's scheme of lower taxes and increased military spending, and preached that only tough choices for real and substantial deficit reduction would save the country's future.

During the presidential primary of 1992, Panetta made the obvious observation that Clinton's budget pronouncements—middle-class tax cuts, cutting the deficit in half in four years, reforming health care without a tax increase—simply didn't add up. That provided more evidence that Panetta thought and spoke for himself.

Then Clinton became president-elect and began his usual retreat from say-anything-to-win campaign bravado to the pragmatism of reality. He acknowledged the harsh facts that he had put out of his mind for months: It was true that his numbers didn't add up, and that the deficit would grow much higher than his campaign blueprints indicated.

So as he assembled a cabinet where a little old Democrat would blend with a little new Democrat, he sent for Panetta, reputed to be right on the social issues and obsessed with fiscal conservatism. The congressman flew to Little Rock and had a warm private conversation with Clinton, an equally outgoing and likable man, which convinced the president-elect that Panetta was the person he wanted in charge of the Office of Management and Budget, maybe the toughest job in Washington, especially with all that Clinton had in mind.

On the early December day at the Old State House in Little Rock when Clinton announced the appointment of Panetta along with that of Treasury Secretary Lloyd Bentsen and chief economic adviser Robert Rubin, a reporter reminded Clinton of Panetta's assessment months before that the president-elect's numbers didn't add up.

"Well, I'm going to give him a chance to teach me some math," Clinton said. Panetta, as always, laughed heartily in the background.

In office, Clinton set out to draft a budget plan in consultation with about a dozen aides and advisers who worked long hours in the Roosevelt Room in the West Wing. Panetta lost several battles there; he wanted deeper spending cuts than Clinton agreed on. But Panetta was reasonably satisfied that his new boss was making the first honest and earnest presidential attempt toward deficit reduction. He went up to

Capitol Hill to do his duty, testifying for long hours before congressional committees, sometimes combatively when Republicans implied they could make deeper budget cuts. "Let's see 'em," he asked at one point, and Republicans backed down.

Panetta's role as point man made all the more significant his session in late April with journalists at a regular breakfast with newsmakers sponsored by Al Hunt, at the time the Washington bureau chief of *The Wall Street Journal*.

This is what he said:

- Clinton had lost focus and needed to delay release of his wife's health care plan at least until June so he could focus on his budget plan.

- That budget plan was imperiled because Clinton had lost momentum and Panetta was beginning to hear "the same things I heard around here in the eighties," meaning expressed aversions to tax increases and cuts in spending and subsidy programs.

- Clinton's much-needed aid plan for Russia probably couldn't pass at the moment.

- The North American Free Trade Agreement with Mexico and Canada was "dead."

- A false sense of security that the economy was performing acceptably was dangerous, especially with the coming ripple effects of military base closings.

- Clinton's defeat on the stimulus package had emboldened opponents. The challenges of keeping House liberals and Senate conservatives happy were enormous.

- Others in the Clinton administration seemed to feast on the frenetic pace, "but I'm not having any fun yet."

It was all true. Every word. But that wasn't the point. Clinton was reeling from bad notices; the last thing he needed was one atop the front page of *The Washington Post* from his main budget man.

The White House hadn't been altogether blindsided. Word had gotten around later Monday about Panetta's blunt pessimism.

About 9:00 P.M., Stephanopoulos called McLarty to say he thought they might have a "problem with Leon." McLarty said he'd already heard.

But they didn't expect the front page of the next morning's *Post*. Newsmakers seldom are shocked by the content of articles; the headlines and prominent display provide the surprise. There, in the top right corner of the front page, over David Broder's byline, was the full story of Panetta's pessimism, its placement and tone indicating that the sky was falling.

Stephanopoulos got up around 5:00 A.M., having decided to go to the gym for a session on the StairMaster before work, rather than afterward, around midnight, as was his custom. He picked up his *Post* on the way. "I thought to myself, 'God, this is just what we need,'" Stephanopoulos said. "But then I worked out and thought about it, and I calmed down a little. I understood how it could have happened. It was a good thing that I worked out early. If I'd had to go straight to work, my mood would have been much worse."

During Clinton's early-morning jog, a reporter shouted to the president, "Are you mad at Panetta?" Clinton said, "About what?" and ran on as the shrill and distinctive voice of Helen Thomas of UPI rang in his ear: "He says everything is going down the drain."

Panetta walked into McLarty's office about five minutes late for the eight o'clock meeting of key staff members. His colleagues gave him a round of applause as he blushed. "Doctor Spin," Stephanopoulos called him. "Neon Leon," said someone else. Panetta briefly explained that he thought his comments were overblown; he'd merely intended to assess the political landscape.

After the meeting, McLarty asked Panetta to stick around for a minute.

"Leon, what in the world?" McLarty asked him after the office cleared. "Either this is the most unintelligent thing you've ever done or we need to let you go."

Panetta responded he'd given essentially the same statements to another reporter a day or two before, and little had been made of it. He explained that expressions of frustration and candid assessments of congressional foot-dragging were second nature to him, but that he was sorry. McLarty said he understood. He relayed the explanation to Clinton, but encouraged the non-confrontational president to speak sternly to Panetta. They talked later in the day, but the White House said nothing about Clinton's taking Panetta "to the woodshed," as Reagan claimed to have done years before when his OMB director, David Stockman, spoke too frankly. "I just want to buck up his confidence," Clinton said.

All was forgiven among these generous men. Panetta was too valuable, credible, and likable to be fired, and this president was too warm and generous to fire anyone, much less Panetta, or to pretend he'd chewed him out when he hadn't.

In truth, Panetta had given the White House a reality check.

Then, on May 19, as if things weren't bad enough, the White House staff strode with blissful obliviousness into big trouble.

The staff made a public announcement that set off a two-month tempest that revealed its every foible and shortcoming, all benign but breathtaking. It revealed a smattering of Arkansans who mistook cronyism for good government; naivete throughout the West Wing, up to and including the president and his wife, about Washington's traditions and hot buttons; an absence of political sensitivity and institutional memory in its embattled counsel's office; an astonishing disregard for the rights of the accused; and a perfect bungling of its relationship with the national press corps.

The incident warrants recounting not for the comic value of amateur sleuths, office romances, breakdowns in communication, and occasional slapstick; in fact, it would contribute to a numbing personal tragedy that would beset the White House in mid-year. The significance is that it convinced Clinton, Hillary, and Mack McLarty that they needed someone in the White House who had a set of political antennae and a sensitivity to the ways of Washington and the media.

David Watkins had been a successful businessman in Little Rock, running an advertising agency that handled Clinton's gubernatorial campaigns through most of the 1980s. He invested in small-business enterprises on the side. He was one of the first half dozen employees of Clinton's presidential campaign, signing on full time to coordinate administrative operations.

One of his first tasks in the campaign was to set up a system for handling the national travel network of a presidential campaign. Watkins turned to his own travel agency, which happened to be Little

Rock's biggest and perhaps best: World Wide Travel. The occasional billing snafu notwithstanding, the agency did a creditable job and won good reviews in travel industry publications for its system of expedited billing of non-campaign travelers—the press, mainly—that contributed to keeping the campaign operative during a time of cash-flow problems in the summer of 1992. To work with the agency, Watkins assigned Catherine Cornelius, an Arkansan and distant cousin of the president himself.

In December, the rumor in the business community in Little Rock was that World Wide might soon expand its Washington operation and even set up an office in the White House. Apparently, Watkins already had designs on using the agency in the nation's capital.

In January 1993, Watkins became the assistant to the president for White House operations. He hired Cornelius as an assistant in his office, and soon she began to lobby for transfer to the travel office. Then in February, Mack McLarty announced that the White House would reduce its staff budget by 25 percent over the level of the Bush administration—trying to build support for raising taxes by demonstrating, or at least symbolizing, a willingness to cut spending itself—and assigned Watkins chief responsibility for getting it done.

Watkins already had his eye on the seven employees of the travel office whose primary responsibility was to book charter flights and make general travel arrangements for the scruffy White House press corps when the president was traveling.

The new Clinton team was suspicious of permanent White House employees, distrusting them because for the preceding twelve years they had served Republicans, and because the rumors flying around Washington about the Clintons' private behavior were believed to have emanated from inside the building.

In the first week of April, Watkins granted Cornelius her wish. She was assigned to the travel office to handle commercial travel arrangements for the president's staff.

A few days later, Harry Thomason, the president's Hollywood friend who had been given an office in the Old Executive Office Building to "consult on staging of presidential events," and who had the run of the White House, called Watkins. He related that a partner of his in an airplane leasing business based in Cincinnati had told him that the White House Travel Office had rebuffed his simple overture about whether the office ought to offer press charters for bidding, rather than using a single regular carrier, and that he suspected corruption. Watkins then asked Cornelius to assume a second assignment: keep her eyes and ears opened.

Her detective work was spotty. One day the copy machine jammed while she was seeking on the sly to reproduce some documents. Travel office employees, finding the jammed document, were understandably suspicious. Billy Dale, the veteran head of the office, thereafter locked the files. That inconvenienced Cornelius; she had a pile of documents at home and now she couldn't get them back into the file.

By May, Cornelius had a report for Watkins. The travel office was "pro-press," she said, as if that were an indictment and as if the office shouldn't appear pro-press when its job was to provide services for the press. Furthermore, she suspected kickbacks and had discovered a rather cavalier system for handling petty cash.

On May 12, Watkins took her report and Thomason's complaint to the man whose judgment was widely considered impeccable by people from Arkansas who had known him for years: Vince Foster, the chief deputy to Bernie Nussbaum, the White House counsel. Foster was a stoic, cautious, thorough, eminently successful corporate lawyer from the Rose firm in Little Rock, where he had been a senior partner and the best friend and confidant of Hillary. Foster called in his deputy, William Kennedy, another refugee from the Rose firm. One of Kennedy's jobs was to handle White House staff security, which entailed working with the FBI.

Watkins explained that the White House had no system of internal audit. Foster directed Kennedy to speak with someone at the FBI about the allegations to seek advice about how to proceed. The next morning, when Kennedy said he did not yet have a report, Foster told him to get back on it. Kennedy called the FBI, reported that his superiors were pressing him, declared that the interest in the matter extended to the highest levels of the White House, and remarked that if the FBI couldn't help him, he might call on the Internal Revenue Service. Kennedy would argue later that his end of the conversation sounded much worse in the recounting than it actually sounded at the time. He wasn't threatening or intimidating, but merely pressured and exasperated, he explained.

The FBI spoke with Cornelius and looked into a couple of the allegations, and reported to Kennedy that it saw a basis for a criminal investigation and would be happy to conduct it. Two FBI representatives briefed lawyers in the Justice Department, who raised no objection. Meanwhile, Watkins had reported to McLarty on the allegations and Hillary Clinton had asked her friend Foster what was going on, since Harry Thomason had mentioned his suspicions to her. She, lacking political sensitivity, was anxious to put "our own people" in the travel office. McLarty meanwhile mentioned the matter briefly to the president.

About that time, finally, a White House official raised a red flag. It was Foster, who questioned the appropriateness of an FBI investigation and suggested an independent management review or audit. He would later write a famous note saying the FBI "lied," apparently referring to the agency's implication that it was somehow pressured into conducting an investigation it thought potentially unwise or improper. His recollection was that the FBI was itching to do this favor for the White House, and that he had called off the agency. Foster blamed himself for asking Kennedy to get in touch with the FBI in the first place, and in time he would blame himself for having said anything to his friend Hillary, though she injected herself.

Watkins made arrangements for such a review with the Peat Marwick accounting firm. About that time he called his buddies at World Wide Travel in Little Rock and suggested they be on standby for at least a temporary White House job.

In a three-day review, Peat Marwick found "abysmal management" and such shoddy records that an actual audit couldn't be conducted.

Meantime, Cornelius had related her version of events to her boyfriend, Jeff Eller, who worked in the White House media relations office. Suddenly Eller began arguing to higher-ups for immediate dismissal of the seven employees.

Watkins decided on May 17 to fire all seven employees immediately, which he would get around to on May 19. He reported his decision to McLarty. Foster told Hillary about it. No one asked the obvious: Shouldn't these employees be given a chance to defend themselves? Are we perhaps acting a bit recklessly? The White House was awash in lawyers, and yet none of them seemed to recall the need to build a case.

Sometimes, a leading White House official would say months later, taking over the leadership of the world can turn you arrogant before you know it. McLarty, ever the organizational technician, would blame the absence of a clear flow of information.

On the morning of the immediate terminations, Watkins briefed Dee Dee Myers, the press secretary, to prepare her for the press statement.

She was to announce the firings on the basis of the independently determined abysmal management. She was to announce that World Wide Travel had taken over the travel office on an interim basis.

Watkins told Myers to tell the press that the review of the travel office was undertaken as part of the effort to achieve a 25 percent staff reduction, which was more or less true. He also told her to say that it was undertaken as part of Vice President Gore's National Performance Review to find new governmental efficiencies, which was not true. And he told Myers she could mention that the FBI had been advised of possible criminality.

Before Myers's daily briefing, the second red flag was raised—again by Vince Foster. He told Watkins to tell Myers that she should say nothing about the FBI or alleged criminality. When Watkins relayed that message to Myers, she said, essentially, "Oops." She'd already taken a press call and told the inquiring reporter about the FBI and possible criminality, which, naturally, left her with no recourse but to say it again at her briefing.

When she said it, the regular White House press corps was aghast, not to mention personally offended. The travel office employees were their longtime friends, who secured their charter flights, provided their meals, and got them through customs. In short order, memoranda from Cornelius and Thomason were leaked and allegations of cronyism led Watkins to ask his friends from World Wide Travel to vacate the travel office. Thomason and his wife, Linda Bloodworth, would go on national television to try to clear their names of suggested conflicts or improprieties, failing with sitcom-quality hilariousness when Bloodworth explained that she and her husband had so much money from television productions that they needn't worry about White House charter flights. Dee Dee Myers, the press secretary, asked the sitcom duo to please shut up and go back to Hollywood, which they did. Eventually they were asked to turn in their White House badges, though their personal friendships with the president and First Lady weren't affected. The four blamed the press for the inconvenience. Harry Thomason, a consummate nice guy, was probably telling the truth that he was motivated not by a desire for personal enrichment but by his interest in advising the White House of potential funny business. But, like so many with the run of the White House, he seemed to lack even a clue about political dangers in a town where politics is the company store. He was oblivious to the obvious appearance, which in Washington and in politics is as great a failing as corruption.

Republicans compared the fiasco to Watergate and Iran-contra and called for a special independent counsel to investigate. These were overstatements.

George Stephanopoulos's daily press briefings turned into circuses, with the travel office problems compounded by a media fascination with a hairstyling the president received from an exclusive, expensive Los Angeles hairdresser in Air Force One while the plane sat on a runway at Los Angeles International Airport.

Then one day Stephanopoulos mentioned that an FBI-written statement confirming the agency's determination of possible criminality in the travel office, and released by the White House, had in fact been compiled in the White House communication office as FBI officials met with several members of the president's staff, including chief counsel Bernie Nussbaum.

It was an astonishing revelation of what could only be stupidity. If it was intended abuse of power, why would Stephanopoulos, who had earned a reputation for genius at not saying anything, have revealed it?

Nussbaum had been the counsel to the House Judiciary Committee during the Nixon impeachment hearings in the early 1970s, but he raised no objection whatever to this collusion between the White House and a supposedly independent investigative branch of government on a public statement that tarnished the reputations of seven people who had never been given so much as a hearing with a supervisor.

Clinton, professing general ignorance of the travel office actions but taking ultimate responsibility, asked McLarty to conduct a complete review. In July, McLarty would release a lengthy report providing seemingly full detail, admitting a series of White House blunders (most of them analyzed as naivete), and specifically apologizing to the five non-supervisory employees, who were promised reassignments. McLarty stood before the press and took his lumps, occasionally trying to make a couple of points that, while valid, were almost irrelevant by now: The old travel office had indeed been mismanaged, and new arrangements were beginning to save money for the press, and do it with fewer employees.

Watkins, Kennedy, Cornelius, and Eller were given "reprimands," which essentially meant nothing. The White House got a bit of editorial praise for its candor, and the Republican clamor for a special investigation lost momentum.

Months later, McLarty, who loved football metaphors, would explain that the White House was doing better, picking up "first downs" and throwing fewer "incompletions." Three decades before, as a too-short but all-star quarterback for Hope High School, he had hoped to impress a scout from the University of Arkansas who had come to one of his games to check out a teammate of McLarty's. McLarty called a drop-back pass, which he proceeded to fire into the back of the helmet of his own center. Now, sitting in the West Wing, playfully spewing football metaphors, he said that the White House had fired only one pass into the back of its own head: on the travel office fiasco.

Late May brought retrenchment. Clinton added a new deputy chief of staff, Gore assistant Roy Neel, to ease the load on McLarty, who had emerged as a valuable liaison to moderate congressional Democrats, and to free the chief of staff to coordinate an effort to keep the oft-undisciplined president focused on passage of his economic plan. Neel would turn out to be one of the more valuable White House aides, coordinating meetings, taking control of scheduling, and actually listening and heeding advice and criticism.

Clinton called for Hillary and James Carville. They agreed on several things.

One was that the president needed a congressional victory to restore a sense of accomplishment, and nothing was as vital as passage of the budget reconciliation act. Losing it would be disastrous. McLarty began a series of three morning meetings each week to focus on passage.

A second was that the unveiling of Hillary's health care revolution would wait until June, at least, and that a campaign-style effort would be undertaken to sell it with television commercials, phone banks, mass mailings, maybe even a bus tour through the heartland around July 4.

Since the budget package had been recast in the minds of many voters as more tax-and-spend as usual, its congressional passage alone wouldn't rehabilitate the president. It might even hurt him. He needed to resume what he did best—traveling salesmanship. Clinton went to Cleveland, Chicago, and New York, where he announced what was mainly a gimmick soon to be disregarded: Money from tax increases would go into a trust fund dedicated only to deficit reduction, not new programs.

It also seemed a good idea to press campaign finance reform, to do battle as a seeming Washington outsider. Carville sternly told Clinton not to behave as a Washington insider, and advised him to portray his set-backs as the lamentable result of the hated inertia of politics-as-usual.

With European allies balking at the idea of military strikes in the former Yugoslavia, Clinton agreed to back away from the tough talk about such strikes. Gone was the moral strength of two weeks before, replaced by typical retreat, naivete, and a lack of clear purpose and resolve.

In his Cleveland speech in early May, Clinton talked publicly of his need to narrow his agenda. But then he rambled on for 45 minutes about his economic plan, health care, national service, and campaign finance reform. After his speech he took questions. The first was about gays in the military. The second about Bosnia. Retrenching, reloading, and refocusing were proving a little harder as president than as a candidate.

Stephanopoulos seemed less than impressed when I suggested to him a correlation: When Clinton didn't travel outside Washington, his approval numbers plummeted; when he got on the road for a speech or town meeting, showcasing his abilities to relate and sell, his popularity would shoot back up.

"I don't know. I think it's all circumstances," Stephanopoulos said, sounding a bit down.

Stephanopoulos, meantime, was about to be relieved of his duties as the White House's chief spokesman. On the evening of May 27, McLarty told him about his new White House colleague, David Gergen, a Republican spin doctor who had helped sell the nation on Reaganomics.

Meanwhile, Senator David Boren of Oklahoma, one of eleven Democrats composing an eleven-to-nine Democratic majority on the Senate Finance Committee that would consider Clinton's budget, announced he opposed Clinton's energy tax and couldn't support a budget that contained it. This was about two weeks after Boren had promised the White House he would stay hitched to the Democratic line so the bill could get out of committee. The oil industry had targeted Boren with inflammatory television advertising in Oklahoma. "I wouldn't want to be on a rowing team with David Boren," a Democratic Senate colleague said.

Clinton would now embark on his eminently predictable shift to the political center as his personal and messy work-in-progress continued. But the shift would be anything but smooth. Actually, the president's low point was yet to come as he tried to draw a distinction between the political center and his own.

CHAPTER 6

Gergen, Guinier, and Ginsburg

In the fine tradition of Bill Clinton, I will synthesize what I have sought to establish about the new president. And in the fine tradition of Bill Clinton, it will be a lengthy paragraph.

He is a work-in-progress and soft touch who aims to please. He lacks firm footing except in electoral politics, a volatile field that rewards slipperiness and provides his life's work and source of validation. He possesses an almost endearingly boyish belief that he is smart enough to transcend traditional political philosophies and make his beloved government a trusted source of social and economic progress through a "third way" that synthesizes liberal Democrats and the middle class by splitting their differences. But his presidency had begun with the vulnerability of a minority election. By its 130th day it was further beset by rampant blundering, miscalculation, and veering toward the liberal instincts of his soul that provided an unflattering public definition of him, which had been left unsettled in the campaign. In Arkansas and as a presidential candidate, he had demonstrated a remarkable resilience and a knack for midstream reinvention. He had begun his governorship on the activist left, and been defeated, and come back as a pragmatic centrist. He had begun his presidential campaign as the new pro-business centrist Democrat, then turned into the traditional Democrat—like Mondale against Hart in 1984—when a more credibly pro-business Paul Tsongas flanked him on the right, and he needed labor's support to win primaries in Illinois and Michigan.

I recount all this for a reason: It was about to manifest itself presidentially in a single personnel action.

On that 130th day, a Saturday morning, May 29, in the Rose Garden, there was an announcement of Clinton's hiring of the Republican spin doctor who had helped direct the message-control apparatus of the Reagan administration—the very administration whose legacy Clinton sought to undo—and who days before had asserted in his column in *U.S. News & World Report,* which he edited, that Clinton needed to show more backbone.

It had been a rascally Arkansas state senator named Nick Wilson who once marveled that during the two-year stretch when he gave Clinton grief, he won more favors from the governor than when he was handling his bills in the state legislature.

The hiring of David Gergen as "counselor to the president" made sense as long as one overlooked the essential partisan irony. What the White House lacked, Gergen provided. He had keen political antennae. He had been around Washington for decades. He had worked in the White House in three presidencies. He understood Republicans, who were killing Clinton. Though not registered as a Republican, his adult life had been spent as one, working for Presidents Nixon, Ford, and Reagan. He understood the Washington press establishment, which was helping to kill Clinton, since he was part of it. More than that, he was the prototype of Washington's emerging king of the jungle: the cross-pollinated pundit-political operative.

As a work-in-progress who needed rehabilitation if not reinvention, Clinton had figured out that he could use the services of a Washington insider with a centrist philosophy, maybe one a tad right of center, and a feel for the media and Republicans. He needed someone who had worked in the White House. By that job description, the pool was limited to centrist veterans of preceding Republican administrations who were parts of the punditocracy. It was, actually, a pool of one. Lynn Nofziger and Pat Buchanan were a little too far to the right.

As Republicans went, Gergen was moderate, thoughtful, sober, and solemn. Often as not, he found friendly common ground with left-leaning Mark Shields in their Friday commentaries on the MacNeil/Lehrer NewsHour. It wasn't as if Clinton had hired Robert Novak, who, appearing on CNN at the moment Gergen's prospective hiring was leaked, criticized Clinton's reaching out to this "jack-leg Republican."

This would not be Gergen's first political slide, though it would be his first bipartisan one. Back in 1980, he had agreed to be the issues man for George Bush's presidential campaign. But he didn't formally agree until Bush had won the Iowa caucuses. Then when Bush blew the New Hampshire primary and lost to Ronald Reagan, Gergen slid smoothly to the Gipper's campaign.

Gergen was an old acquaintance and casual friend of Clinton. They had gathered at the now-famous New Year's holiday "Renaissance Weekends" on Hilton Head Island, where politically oriented neo-thinkers gathered annually for the rejuvenating powers of pondering aloud about the complexities of life and politics, which to them were essentially the same. (Don Tyson, the poultry baron from Springdale, Arkansas, attended for the first time in 1993, a guest of his chief corporate counsel, Clinton friend Jim Blair. Tyson declared he would never go back. Those people were talkers, not doers, he pronounced.)

In January 1992, with his presidential hopes on the ropes in New Hampshire, Clinton had bared his soul to Gergen and sought and received the spinmaster's private counseling.

The old rules about journalistic objectivity and detachment did not apply in Gergen's league of cross-pollinated pundit pols.

On the summer morning in Atlanta in 1988 after Clinton's horrible speech to the Democratic National Convention, while I hammered out a half dozen articles for the *Arkansas Gazette* about the sudden demise of this once-rising political star, Gergen dropped off a note for the Arkansas governor at Clinton's hotel, the Embassy Suites in Marietta, urging him to keep his head up. "A lot of us think you're terrific," he wrote.

Now in the White House, Clinton had been thinking for weeks about the travails of Washington's nasty partisanship. In an Oval Office interview, David Broder had asked him why he declined to try to establish a bipartisan national government, applying those consensus-building skills he had displayed at National Governors' Conferences to broaden his base. As Broder recounted the interview in a column, the transparent Clinton came back to the question later without solicitation or reminder, analyzing the pros and cons, typically telegraphing his sensitivity. When Clinton senses that you're right about an element of criticism, he gets a faraway look in his eyes and then becomes preoccupied with analyzing what you have just said.

So when in mid-May chief of staff McLarty told Clinton that he thought they ought to try to hire Gergen—for all the aforementioned reasons and one other reason from McLarty's point of view, which was that McLarty wanted help tugging Clinton back toward the political center—Clinton's hopeful response was, "Do you think he'd do it?"

Sure he would. What prototypical pundit pol wouldn't accept an offer to save the presidency of a man he thought was terrific? Gergen made a great income giving speeches for big fees about Washington politics. After a couple of years in the White House salvaging a blundering president, he could double his fees.

All that was required was to create a job title and description for Gergen that fell somewhere between communications director, which he'd already held under Reagan, and chief of staff, which McLarty cared not to surrender and for which, truth be known, the disorganized Gergen would have been a disaster, especially in service to this personally undisciplined president. Gergen's work style is to rush harriedly from task to task, often running late. That was the last thing Clinton needed in a chief of staff.

Gergen wanted to do more than be the spin doctor; now he wanted policy influence. Hence we had a counselor to the president.

There was one other not insignificant step: running Gergen past Hillary's inspection. As a moderate of some intellectual repute with a basis of longtime casual friendship, Gergen survived. As previously explained, Hillary Rodham Clinton was no radical ideologue. She could practice the politics of inclusion as long as the one to be included had been a friendly admirer and if she could see a readily identifiable pragmatic benefit.

That McLarty would recruit a staffer who might overshadow him and get credit for whatever improvement might occur at the White House was proof that he was no typical modern-era chief of staff in the mold of John Sununu, Jim Baker, or Don Regan, clinging to turf and fancying himself as the deputy president or even the real one.

McLarty genuinely saw himself as the corporate-style chief executive officer. He saw his job as comparable in some ways to the last one he had held as chairman of an integrated *Fortune* 500 utility company with exploration and distribution operations. In the corporate world, it didn't diminish his role as corporate chairman to hire the best people he could find to run his divisions, an exploration man who knew much more than he about drilling and a distribution man who knew much more than he about pipelines. To the contrary, it enhanced it.

Essentially, Gergen would be the White House's assistant chief executive officer for political imagery, political antennae, and centrist policy advice.

McLarty was motivated by a great personal need not to fail. His

courteous demeanor belied a strong ego and healthy ambition. Whatever the factors, the debt-ridden, stock-plummeting difficulties encountered by Arkla under his stewardship were marks on his
professional reputation. Some in Arkansas had joked that they hoped
McLarty wouldn't do for the country what he had done for Arkla.
McLarty was willing to lose a battle of ego by hiring Gergen, but only
as a tactical matter designed to help him survive the bigger war, which
was about the success of the Clinton presidency.

McLarty had been politically ambitious as a young man. Now he
maintained an interest in someday seeking political office again in
Arkansas, perhaps when either Dale Bumpers or David Pryor left the
Senate. That helped explain his interest in not failing, as well as his
willingness to cooperate with an Arkansas political columnist writing
a book about Clinton's first presidential year.

It was after 9:00 P.M. on May 27 when George Stephanopoulos got
the word about Gergen. Clinton had just survived by a vote of 219 to
213 the first congressional roll call on his budget. It had occurred in
the House of Representatives after Clinton and McLarty made last-
minute promises of more spending cuts to moderate and conservative
Southern Democrats. To be more precise, McLarty, now more credible
among moderate and conservative Southern Democrats, assured the
dubious—Dave McCurdy of Oklahoma and Billy Tauzin of Louisiana,
primarily—that they could believe what he was telling them about the
president. Already the Congress sensed an ugly truth that the Arkansas
legislature had known: They couldn't always take this president at his
word; he was so inclined to oblige and so driven to succeed that he
sometimes said whatever was necessary.

That is not to suggest McLarty saved the day alone; it is to say that
when the roll was called, the holdout votes on a razor-thin margin
happened to be cast by Southern Democrats with whom McLarty shared
general beliefs and whom he knew personally through his days as a
utility executive doing business in their states.

But on a razor's margin, any Clinton administration official or House
leader who had won a single vote—and budget director Leon Panetta
had won plenty, as had Stephanopoulos, as had Majority Leader Richard
Gephardt—effectively saved the day.

After breathing a sigh of relief, McLarty took Stephanopoulos aside
and told him about Gergen.

For several weeks McLarty and Stephanopoulos had agreed on the
need for Stephanopoulos's reassignment. In his seemingly unending

sports metaphor, McLarty had deemed Stephanopoulos miscast as communications director and chief spokesman because the latter was a "defensive" position, designed to deflect the incursions of the media. He believed Stephanopoulos's campaign-related talents and his experience as an aide to House Majority Leader Gephardt were better suited for an "offensive" position as a strategic planner on policy and politics and as an adviser on dealing with the House. Stephanopoulos, who had tried to be both spokesman and policy political adviser, agreed that essentially he had bombed as spokesman. His reassignment as senior adviser to the president, with an office next to the Oval one and a role as Clinton's shadow with the responsibility of keeping the hyperactive president closer to his schedule and smartly focused on one well-chosen matter at a time, would be a promotion. But he knew his promotion would be perceived as the opposite, especially by the reporters, who would chortle—as they did—that they'd given arrogant young George his needed shot of humility.

Stephanopoulos was a bit taken aback by the specific arrangement, which was that Gergen would join the staff as a glorified communications director holding the title of "counselor to the president." He hadn't quite figured on that. It had been a draining day.

McLarty went to his home to meet with Gergen and put the finishing touches on their negotiations. They dined about midnight on leftovers. McLarty's wife, Donna, was in New York substituting for her husband at a function.

Meantime, McLarty wanted to shake up his chief of staff's operation and would reassign his lone deputy, Mark Gearan, a smiling former newspaperman, to be the communications director. Gearan was eminently more likable than Stephanopoulos, who agreed with Gergen that the new team's first action ought to be the reopening of the press offices to reporters. The moves would enable McLarty to make Roy Neel, Gore's longtime chief of staff and a Washington veteran respected for his thoroughness and ability to listen, his new deputy chief of staff.

Two days later, when Stephanopoulos stood to the side as Gergen's hiring was announced, young George had applied his talents for practical political analysis and accepted the purpose of the addition of Gergen. But he'd built his own fiefdom of youthful colleagues who were traditionally liberal, and those youngsters were irate and disillusioned that Stephanopoulos was made to appear the scapegoat and that they would now work with, even for, a Reaganite.

After the announcement, McLarty spent the weekend trying to soothe feelings and head off a small staff insurrection. Stephanopoulos helped calm feelings among some of his disciples. Gergen, after a week's vacation, eventually met with the communications staff to try to allay fears. The biggest problem was Dee Dee Myers, the press secretary. But she came around after a couple of days, assured of a more prominent role as the president's day-to-day spokesperson with greater access to Clinton.

Now Clinton's inner circle would be a symmetrical white-guy troika—Gergen on the right, Stephanopoulos on the left, and McLarty in the middle. It appeared to work smoothly. "David has a great touch, and he and George are finishing each other's sentences," McLarty said after a few weeks. The moderate Republican with an eye for political imagery was meeting in the middle the youthful eighties liberal Democrat with an eye for whatever compromises were necessary to accomplish the two objectives most important to Clinton politically: ending gridlock and appealing to mainstream voters.

Senator Daniel Patrick Moynihan, the colorfully cerebral New Yorker whose stature was greater than ever as chairman of the Senate Finance Committee, was quoted a few weeks later in *Vanity Fair* as saying that he'd found Gergen to be the real force in the White House and that McLarty was pleasantly irrelevant. For Moynihan's purposes, that might have been so. "I think Mack and the senator have a cultural disconnect," Stephanopoulos said. As is proper in Washington politics, Moynihan later went on "Meet the Press" on NBC and praised the fine and vital efforts of Mack McLarty. "I guess I'm just not a good interview," McLarty told me. "I don't spread rumors and I don't talk about people."

Younger White House staff members would in time make Moynihan-like assessments of McLarty—"Mack the Nice," they called him—in leaks to *The Washington Post*'s Ann Devroy. But the criticism lacked full context. McLarty saw his job as serving Clinton quietly, overseeing the pursuit of efficiency in the White House operation, and filling in the gaps where his relationships were helpful, mainly with the moderate-to-conservative Southern Democrats and businesspeople.

David Broder wrote that McLarty was "limited," as evidenced by the fact that he kept hiring deputies to compensate for his limitations. McLarty's strengths are organizational discipline, personal courtesy, bridge building, and a moderate, pro-business political philosophy. But he is not a great thinker or an articulate communicator, and he eschewed a high public profile in part because he wasn't comfortable with his competence to sit for an hour on "Meet the Press" taking shots from the toughest pundits. He appeared once in 1993 and for an hour offered nothing but exasperating platitudes.

But all of that was part of an intended role. Clinton did not want a typically strong chief of staff; he resisted supervision and he trusted his own political intelligence more than anyone else's.

"Washington will catch up with Mack's steady leadership," communications director Mark Gearan wrote to me during a period in which the *Post* had taken a couple of mild shots at the chief of staff.

But would Washington catch up in time? McLarty already had decided that eighteen months to two years of this would be plenty. It was, in fact, the average tenure of the modern-era chief of staff, the place where all blame goes.

Later in the year, in September, McLarty would take solace from an odd source. He told me about a handwritten note he had received from Richard Nixon, which, it turned out, was in response to a handwritten note that McLarty, an inveterate writer of brief personal missives, had sent.

This exchange of pleasantries had followed a personal meeting. One day Gergen told McLarty that Nixon was in town and that he was going over to see him to pick up some wisdom. He invited McLarty to come along, and McLarty found Nixon perfectly fascinating.

Nixon's note stated that he had determined that a president's chief of staff was most effective when he worked in quiet, unnoticed service to the president. Nixon told McLarty that he would know he was in trouble if he woke up one day to see a long profile of himself in the *Post* or the *Times*.

Of course, one of McLarty's problems with young and left-leaning staff members was that they didn't understand why a chief of staff to Bill Clinton would be chummy with a Reagan spin doctor and Richard Nixon.

Sometimes they wondered what the hell the election had been all about.

On the immediate agenda of this new White House team were the most defining events to date for the troubled presidency, events that showcased the good and the bad, the mangled process, the difficult synthesis of "left" and "center," of "old" and "new."

The first of these events would again reveal inept staff work in the office of the White House counsel. It would place a long-faced, clearly shaken Clinton in the press briefing room to abandon a friend and refer to his own "center."

Which was the real Bill Clinton, the one who had nominated Lani Guinier to head the civil rights division of the Justice Department, or the one who decided to abandon her nomination?

The answer is both. To know him is to understand how he could be for her early, and against her late. Her nomination was born of his liberal instincts and associations, as well as Clinton's lofty, self-inflicting rhetoric. Her abandonment was born of his Southern heritage as a moderate presenting himself as a pragmatic "new Democrat." Sometimes, try as he might, he couldn't be both.

He was a policy synthesizer, and policy is largely a product of personnel. As part of a whole, Lani Guinier could be an element of synthesis—just as Leon Panetta and Robert Reich could be quite different instruments for synthesis. But once the right-wingers set her apart to stand on her own— and the Republicans were brilliant at such things—she was only what she was: an African-American liberal who had written articles for law journals complaining that voting rights initiatives for minorities hadn't guaranteed the election and rise to power of sufficient numbers of minorities, and expressing ideas about how to solidify and enhance their electoral powers. Once set apart, she was certain to offend the pivotal white middle class, who resented entitlements for minorities and held the key to Clinton's hopes for a governing constituency and reelection.

Those closest to Clinton—McLarty and Stephanopoulos, principally—believed his eventual decision to abandon Guinier was his most personally courageous action as president. That wasn't mindless spin; publicly, the White House would confess error and take its lumps.

Their argument was that no easy political answer existed, and that abandoning Guinier was in many ways more politically devastating than sticking with her and seeing her nomination rejected by the Senate. They knew that withdrawing her nomination would appear a transparent manifestation of Clinton's calculated shift to the center that had begun two weeks before with Gergen's hiring. They believed that when faced with no good political solution, Clinton simply did the painfully right thing, and did it despite the fact that he would play into the hands of critics who said he had no sound principle to guide him.

"Say what you will about the President's foibles," McLarty told me sternly, "I'm going to stand behind him on Lani Guinier. I was never more proud of him."

McLarty, of course, had the advantage of knowing what he was: a moderate-to-conservative Democrat whose allies in Congress could not and would not go along with a federal civil rights lawyer who had written in those lengthy, plodding law review articles that perhaps minorities ought to be given something beyond the one-man, one-vote principle.

Clinton, the would-be synthesizer, with a more nuanced and inclusive philosophy, arrived more clumsily at his conclusion about where he stood. It was a strange situation. He had nominated as federal civil rights attorney a law school friend who had sued him. Yes, sued him. And won. One of Guinier's voting rights filings for the NAACP had been against a legislative redistricting plan drawn up in 1990 by the Arkansas Board of Apportionment, whose chairman was Governor Bill Clinton, thus a named defendant. That alone illustrates Clinton's diversity, if not his political schizophrenia. He was a friend of an Eastern civil rights lawyer who sued him because he was part of a white Southern political establishment that couldn't quite assure black people their due.

Clinton's Guinier problem began with what politicians call "podium policy," meaning policy initiatives established not by thoughtful processes, but by politicians in their often spontaneous, applause-seeking public pronouncements. Clinton, as a talented extemporaneous speaker who drew energy from his audiences, tended toward podium policy at times.

The best example was in 1986 at a dinner honoring all the living Arkansas governors, who spoke in order of their tenures, each succeeding speaker trying to outdo his predecessors in asserting cosmic progress. Clinton, as the sitting governor, went last. Others had spoken of racial progress, but Clinton trumped them all. By the time he left office, he said, he would have appointed a black person to every board and commission in the state. His staff members nearly choked on their chicken. His goal was noble and, in fact, his staff had been trying to achieve it. But now that he had publicly proclaimed the goal as a vow, they had no choice but to keep it under the watchful eye of the alerted news media. That's "podium policy," and it's not smart.

After his election as president, Clinton set podium policy by saying he would assemble an administration that "looked like America." Taken literally, he was promising an administration that had more women than men, one to two blacks among every ten appointments, and previously unreached numbers of Hispanics. Taken not so literally, it meant he had committed publicly that his cabinet and other political appointments would offer a previously unachieved level of participation by blacks, women, and Hispanics. Essentially, he had assigned himself a public goal that would be hard to meet because its definition would vary from person to person, and group to group.

As the Clinton administration labored mightily to appoint blacks and women, Guinier was ideal. She was loaded with credentials, educated at Harvard and Yale, a professor at Penn, an extensive writer on civil rights issues, and a litigator who had filed voting rights lawsuits on behalf of the NAACP. Civil rights activism had been squelched during the Reagan and Bush administrations; Guinier would sure be an agent for change. And she was a two-for-one: an African-American woman.

Another advantage was that she had gone to law school at Yale with Bill and Hillary, whom she counted as friends, and who counted her as a friend. Bill, actually, had known her better than Hillary. For weeks Clinton had been complaining as lists of recommended appointees came across his desk from his personnel director, Bruce Lindsey. "I don't know any of these people," he had said with frustration. His Rolodex wasn't sufficient to staff the government. But he knew Guinier. He liked and respected her. He wanted a genuine civil rights advocate in the Justice Department, and Guinier fit the bill.

But this is the important point: At that moment Lindsey had merely recommended Guinier, and Clinton had only tentatively approved her, pending an analysis of her background and confirmation prospects, called a "vetting," by the White House counsel's office.

What subsequently went awry was due to yet another manifestation of the political incompetence of Bernie Nussbaum, the White House chief counsel. He read Guinier's lengthy law review articles and determined them to be politically insignificant, and Clinton was never even briefed on them.

Nussbaum saw an eminently qualified black woman from academia, who had written esoteric articles in professional journals that made arguments that were to be expected from a black civil rights advocate from academia, and which were designed to stimulate thought and debate. His was an understandable assessment from one not politically seasoned, although a lawyer is supposed to consider worst-case scenarios. But his political assessment was naive and dead wrong, just as it had been on Zoe Baird and Kimba Wood.

This was "strike three" against Nussbaum, grumbled some of the young, mid-level White House aides. But as Bill Clinton's friend, only Lani Guinier would strike out.

Any conservative legal writer who read her articles would surely rush to the right-wing *Washington Times* or, as it turned out, *The Wall Street Journal,* which published a column labeling Guinier the "quota queen" and radicalizing her to the point that Republicans in the Senate were galvanized, and moderate Democrats scared to death about the prospect of having to vote for her.

"Why, with the budget bill and health care, are we fighting over this woman?" Senator David Pryor asked one evening of Clinton's former Arkansas chief of staff, Betsey Wright.

"Because, Senator, affirmative action is never easy," she said.

There, in one abrupt exchange, was the dilemma of Bill Clinton. Two key friends and advisers, one a pragmatic Southern senator and the other a left-of-center advocate of women and minorities, saw the Guinier matter through two sets of lenses: Pryor through common sense; Wright through the justice seeking of traditional liberalism. Bill Clinton fully agreed with both of his friends.

Clinton actually decided rather soon after that to abandon Guinier because the political complications were too great, but, typically, he waited and wavered. Attorney General Janet Reno, by contrast, stood by Guinier.

Clinton, as usual, was a rag doll for those who tugged from the left and those who tugged toward the center. He was torn by the contrast between his own personal instincts and his political instincts. He was torn by the honest internal debate of a soft-hearted original thinker who sees complex truth where others see the superficial reality of American politics. He always looked for that third option, but here were only two: stick with Guinier or dump her.

The main complication was Guinier herself. She would not go quietly. She declined to withdraw her nomination. She even went on a counterattack, defending her writings as academic dissertations not appropriate for the simplistic carvings of the political knife. She went on "Nightline" to defend herself quite eloquently. Clinton, susceptible to emotion and chronically vacillating, was tempted temporarily to let her stand and fight.

The political complications were intense. Clinton couldn't pass the developing conference report on his budget without the support of black Democrats in the House who would be livid and feel betrayed if Guinier was abandoned. But he couldn't pass his budget without the support of moderate Democrats in the House and Senate, either, and they had been the ones giving him the most trouble.

Stephanopoulos advised him of the political fallout; McLarty advised him to follow his heart, but made clear that Guinier was a problem for his moderate friends. Gergen advised him to confront the issue and get it settled one way or the other.

Finally, on a short airplane flight, Clinton read Guinier's articles. The general thrust of the controversy was Guinier's argument that it wasn't always fair for the majority to prevail exclusively and for the single winner to take all. She mentioned cumulative at-large voting for electoral districts: black voters could cast all their votes for one black candidate in a multi-member district, for example. The point, she argued, was to prompt a dialogue about assuring minority representation in the face of the threat of majority tyranny. After lengthy perusal, Clinton pronounced to aides, "I don't agree with this."

He really didn't. One of his genuinely moderate tendencies was a "new Democrat" belief that the next step in racial progress was a greater sense of responsibility among minorities, not another special privilege for them that would exacerbate white working-class resentment. But he could have accepted and defended Guinier's writings for what they were: academically advanced points for purpose of debate, not as disqualifying exhibitions of radicalism. The real problem was not the substance of what she had written, but the political image she carried.

The next evening Clinton met privately with Guinier for 75 minutes in the Oval Office. Only briefly were the old friends interrupted by staff. Guinier said later in interviews that Clinton talked of his distress mostly in a political context: the perception of her writings had become an out-of-control political problem. Clinton's aides said he talked of his distress in a substantive way and emphasized to Guinier that his decision wasn't political: if he didn't agree with her writings, how could he go to the wall for her?

The best explanation for the differing accounts is that all of us tend to hear what we want to hear.

Clinton did not tell Guinier at that meeting that he would jerk her nomination. He called her about an hour later, after the agonizing decision was made. All that was left was to announce it. A terse written statement might have been acceptable, but the Clinton White House was forever compensating for past criticisms. No one wanted Clinton to appear, as he had appeared during the Waco tragedy, to be cowering.

So he walked like a man to the press briefing room and announced his abandonment of Guinier.

He appeared a weary, beaten man, insisting that his action was not about the political center, but his own personal center. A consummate politician trying to distinguish his core belief from blatant political appearance will almost always look bad: conceding the need to draw the distinction is a sign of weakness. Like Richard Nixon saying, "I am not a crook," Clinton essentially insisted, "I am not a weakling."

"Nothing has taken a toll like that night," McLarty said a week later. It was, everyone believed, the worst night so far of Clinton's presidency.

The next day Guinier held a news conference at the Justice Department in a room provided by Janet Reno, who was not-so-subtly defying the president.

Then Guinier headed out of town. As she walked through Washington's Union Station to catch a train, shoppers and diners stopped and gave her applause.

"I did the right thing," Clinton told me two weeks later. "It was painful. She's a friend of mine. At least she was. I admire her very much. It also is true that we can be sharply criticized on that for not having the proper staff work. I put her through something I should not have put her through. We deserved to take a hit."

As had often been the case in Arkansas, I found myself sympathetic. In this matter I saw Clinton as more weak than strong, but mostly as a victim of himself and of circumstance. He was a victim of his own optimism that he could bridge gaps. He was a victim of the need to placate the competing wings of his own party. He was a victim of the career choice he'd made. "Viability within the system" had been his interest at the age of twenty-three. Now, five months into his presidency, "viability within the system" meant that Guinier had to go.

Still, if Nussbaum had possessed the needed political antennae, Guinier's nomination would have been stopped less conspicuously and with less damage. After the "vetting," and before a public announcement, the White House would have informed Guinier that they had decided on someone else. Another perfectly appropriate civil rights advocate, but less a lightning rod for criticism, would have been chosen.

One of the left-leaners in the White House surely would have leaked to the press the internal story of the advancement and eventual rejection of Guinier, trying to hold Clinton's feet to the fire. Guinier herself might have gone public. But the result of that would have been an analytical piece on an inside page of the *Post* or the *Times,* not a bold headline in the top right-hand corner of page one that helped provide a growing unflattering definition of this new president about whom the American people had reserved judgment. There were scores of stories like that of fully qualified friends of the president who didn't get nominations because of raw political considerations.

Like a late-night veto, Clinton always reserved the right to retrieve. But, thanks mostly to Bernie Nussbaum, Guinier had been advanced too far for quiet retrieval.

June's other defining event was the nomination of a new member of the United States Supreme Court. Nothing more vividly illustrated the difficulty Clinton was encountering in the job he had always wanted. What began as a glorious opportunity ended in his pitching a childish fit of pique.

Clinton's tendency for "podium policy" had given America an early frontrunner for the Supreme Court.

During the fall campaign of 1992, in his clever effort to use modern and innovative forums to connect with voters, Clinton had appeared on the Music Television Network, which in addition to serving as a venue for discussions about the future of constitutional law in America was the progenitor of the mindless animated epic "Beavis and Butthead."

Clinton stood before a roomful of youngsters and answered their questions, charming them and drawing energy from his ability to relate to them. One question was about the kind of person he might nominate for the Supreme Court. All he needed to do in response was toss out a few adjectives: smart, tough, compassionate, fair-minded. But the man who had spent much of his adult life in Arkansas evading questions with slick lawyer-speak answered this time with an extraordinary specificity that stunned aides.

He volunteered that New York Governor Mario Cuomo was the kind of person he'd like to see on the nation's high court. He explained that Cuomo was schooled in constitutional law, thoughtful, articulate, persuasive, committed to fairness, experienced as a courtroom attorney, and learned in politics, which might help him work with Reagan-Bush appointees. He said he would love to see the fiery, poetic Cuomo go man-to-man with Associate Justice Antonin Scalia, another cerebral and eloquent Italian-American, but a strict conservative nominated by Ronald Reagan.

It wasn't as if Clinton needed to say something nice about Cuomo to shore up his electoral chances in New York. He would win New York big. He had known that from the day he locked up the nomination.

What motivated Clinton was a purely personal desire to ingratiate himself with the New York governor.

In a taped telephone conversation less than a year before, Clinton had agreed with Gennifer Flowers—his "friendly acquaintance," as he described her to "60 Minutes"—that Cuomo had a certain Mafioso aura about him. Maybe Clinton was merely going along with the woman, who'd made the observation first. On the other hand, Cuomo had volunteered an assessment to New York friends that Clinton struck him as a yahoo who told people what they wanted to hear.

Three things had happened since then: Clinton won the Democratic nomination; Cuomo delivered a stirring nominating speech for Clinton at the Democratic National Convention; and Clinton, always motivated by a desire to gain the approval of those who don't readily extend it, and always able to put aside the criticisms of political battle, became a professed fan and admirer of the talent and intellect of the New York governor.

Clinton reached out to Cuomo when, in terms of rank, it should have been the other way around.

Then on Friday, March 19, 1993, Byron "Whizzer" White announced that he would retire from the Supreme Court. White's retirement was great news. Nominating a Supreme Court justice would be fun.

Clinton was a former teacher of constitutional law at the University of Arkansas and nothing excited him more than talking about Supreme Court nominations. He had been ebullient when Senator Joe Biden of Delaware, chairman of the Senate Judiciary Committee, called and invited him to come to Washington to testify against the confirmation of his old Yale law professor with whom he had often argued, Robert Bork. Now the law student would get to reverse the twelve-year Republican trend for conservative and anti-abortion justices. Now he could influence history in an extraordinary way, offsetting the developing right-wing majority on the Court and steering a course that would last long beyond his tenure as president. This was what running had been all about. And the opportunity had arisen only two months into his presidency, based on the resignation of a justice who was not the oldest or the frailest of the nine. In other words, Clinton might get two nominations in his first term as president. In four years Jimmy Carter hadn't gotten one. In fact, there had not been a Supreme Court nomination by a Democrat since LBJ. Whizzer White, who turned out to be conservative, was the only surviving Democratic nominee on the Court. He'd been nominated by John F. Kennedy.

Clinton declared publicly that he wanted to nominate someone whose selection would cause the American people to say, "Wow," perhaps because that's what he was saying to himself.

The day after White's announcement, a Saturday morning, Clinton gathered in the Oval Office with top advisers to discuss the process for nominating a new justice who would be in place for the October term. Mack McLarty. Bruce Lindsey, Vince Foster, and Al Gore were there. Janet Reno had been invited, but couldn't make it.

Since there were four people from Arkansas in the room (Clinton, McLarty, Lindsey, and Foster), there was brief discussion of Arkansas's most intellectual and celebrated judge: Richard S. Arnold, the chief judge of the 8th Circuit Court of Appeals at St. Louis. He'd be great, it was agreed, but the time wasn't right. In briefly considering him for Attorney General after the Baird debacle, the White House counsel's office—for once doing a good job—had come across his ruling, overturned by the Supreme Court, that the Jaycees of America could legally exclude women. Arnold might be the second nominee, or more likely the third. This nomination, being the first for a Democrat in three decades, would need to pass the muster of liberal constituencies. The nominee would need to be known to be pro-choice. Arnold probably was pro-choice, but as a judge's judge and acclaimed thinker, he was not always politically predictable.

The meeting was to establish a process for selecting a justice. Twenty-six names were put on a list. But Clinton, true to his MTV audience the year before, told his advisers that he had been serious about Cuomo. He said the New York governor would be an exciting and memorable choice, meeting the "wow" test. He and Hillary believed that Cuomo might be another Earl Warren, a big-state governor who applied his political skills to the Chief Justice's job to forge alliances to move the Supreme Court to legal, social, cultural, and political change.

Bruce Lindsey looked around at the roomful of Southern boys in the Oval Office and wondered which of them—maybe Gore, or perhaps McLarty—would speak the obvious. Who would rise to provide the service that the good ol' boys had provided for Clinton back in Arkansas, advising, "Mr. President, they might not go for that up in Yell County"?

Finally, Lindsey spoke. He said that after gays in the military, and with Republicans making points against the stimulus bill, the president ought to think twice about nominating a high-profile liberal to the Supreme Court.

"Mario's not a liberal," Clinton said.

Actually, Clinton was right, at least as far as conventional liberalism was concerned. Cuomo was an independent and sometimes innovative thinker on matters of constitutional law, sometimes distinguishable from knee-jerk liberals.

Here's an example: The American Civil Liberties Union supported the Fairness Doctrine that required the electronic media to provide equal time for differing points of view. That was the position of many establishment liberals, believing it necessary that those benefiting from government licenses to transmit through the air not be allowed to abuse that vast power for propaganda, advancement of a political agenda, or demagoguery. Cuomo argued that the Fairness Doctrine was an unconstitutional restriction on free speech and that any restriction on the First Amendment, such as this strange one on television and radio, was stifling and dangerous. Cuomo's position in fact was more purely liberal, or libertarian. But by the modern definition, he was off the liberal reservation.

Actually, except for the not insignificant matter of the death penalty, which Clinton favored and Cuomo opposed, Cuomo's record as governor of New York was no more liberal than Clinton's in Arkansas. Clinton had raised taxes time and again. He had reformed the system for distributing money to schools. Cuomo, confronted by the same need in New York, had stalled. Neither had pleased liberals in their states. Both were accused of not spending political capital.

Clinton's reaction to Lindsey's concern about Cuomo's reputation for liberalism confirmed the genuineness of the president's belief in a "third way" and his concern that superficial labeling was polarizing America needlessly.

(When he spoke with me in the Oval Office in June, Clinton seemed contemptuous of the liberal label that the issue of gays in the military had placed on him. He almost seemed to spit when he said "cultural left." His view was "libertarian," not "liberal," he insisted. Everyone around him was acknowledging that if they had it to do over again, they would have deferred the matter of gays in the military. But not Clinton. His postmortem was that he should have "brought Barry Goldwater in earlier." Goldwater had infuriated right-wingers by writing an Op-Ed piece supporting the lifting of the ban. Typically, while Clinton eschews political labeling, he once needed four words when pressed to put a label on himself: moderate mainstream pragmatic progressive.)

Clinton's reaction to Lindsey reflected his admirable analytical ability to see Cuomo as a free-thinking individual, not as a New York stereotype. But the point Lindsey then made was that most people aren't as analytical, insightful, or profound as Clinton. "They will not like this in the South," Lindsey warned.

Clinton said he thought the South might go for it. He countered that Cuomo had such star quality that the sheer excitement of his appointment would overpower geographic prejudice. He even mentioned that Cuomo was a former baseball player, as if that would mean anything to those boys around the bar back in Little Rock who once told me of their utter contempt for the man they called "Q-mo." They didn't really know anything about him except that he was an Italian-American from New York who opposed the death penalty. To them, the former ball player was out on three strikes.

Clinton had been gone from the South two months. Had he forgotten the place that quickly? He'd carried Georgia and Louisiana in November, in addition to his home state and Gore's. But if he had a Southern strategy now, it was starry-eyed.

As the meeting broke up, the conclusion was that the Clinton administration would embark on a process and look into twenty-six possible candidates, but that Cuomo was the early frontrunner.

Clinton and Cuomo failed a couple of times to make telephone connections, and the eminently unpredictable Cuomo announced after several days that if indeed the president was thinking of nominating him, he wished to be taken out of consideration. Lindsey's fears were allayed.

"Mario called me early," Clinton recalled in June. "So when he decided he didn't want to be considered, and since Justice White had given us six months, we could take about three months and still clearly get somebody confirmed to start the October term."

By June, when Clinton got back to the matter of nominating a justice, Gergen was on board and the slide to the center was under way. Now Clinton was less inclined to argue the fine points of philosophy against the broader points of superficial political appearances.

What ensued, blamed by Clinton on leaks by people who didn't know what he was thinking, was a messy series of reports of imminent appointments of moderates who were confirmable.

The first was Bruce Babbitt, the former governor of Arizona, who was widely praised for his work as Clinton's Interior Secretary. His few days as the apparent nominee led to a spate of articles in the Republican house organ, the *Washington Times,* about old and incredible charges of ties to organized crime. Commentators wrote that Clinton had abused Babbitt, hanging him out to face such charges, then turning to someone else.

Next was Stephen Breyer, an appeals court judge from Boston widely liked by Republicans, including the pivotal vice chairman of the Senate Judiciary Committee, Orrin Hatch of Utah. Breyer came to the White House for lunch with Clinton. The president, needing to feel a connection to people, didn't sense an especially strong one to Breyer. The next day the major newspapers reported that Breyer's nomination was in trouble because of the so-called Zoe Baird problem: he'd employed domestic help and not paid Social Security taxes.

Finally, Clinton named Ruth Bader Ginsburg, a highly respected member of the appeals court in Washington, D.C., who had been a pioneer in advancing women's legal and professional rights and whose cerebral moderation made one wonder why Clinton hadn't chosen her in the first place.

Senator Daniel Patrick Moynihan of New York had advocated her strongly. Gergen had been won over, as had Stephanopoulos. There was a bit of a "wow" to nominating a pioneer in women's rights and the Supreme Court's second woman.

"Do you remember when she came to Little Rock to speak out at UALR?" Clinton asked me on June 18. "I went to hear her, and I remembered thinking then that she was an extraordinary woman."

Ginsburg would be confirmed with stunning ease. She deflected every question that might identify her political philosophy except to make clear that she advocated women's rights and was pro-choice. She was the perfect selection, a worthy product after a mess of a process.

But the word in Washington was that Clinton had decided on Babbitt, then abandoned him as he had abandoned Lani Guinier, and then decided on Breyer before likewise giving him the Guinier treatment.

The word was wrong. Again, Clinton never decides until he decides, and then it's not final until it's announced and beyond the point of retrieval.

The messiness wasn't ended with Clinton's decision to choose Ginsburg, nor did it end with the irretrievable announcement.

On the day of her formal nomination in mid-June, announced on the South Lawn, Ginsburg delivered a touching tribute to her mother.

Clinton had tears in his eyes as he then stepped back to the microphone to take questions. The first came from Brit Hume of ABC, a politically conservative Washington native who prefaced his question by referring to the "zigs and zags" of Clinton's arrival at a decision. Clinton blew up and walked out of the news conference.

I saw Clinton four days later. Knowing better than to ask about zigs and zags, having encountered Clinton's pique six years before when I asked him about his indecisiveness, I asked instead for his analysis of why someone might get the idea that he had zigged and zagged. His face flushed for a second, and I thought I had made him mad anyway. But then he answered with this lengthy narrative:

"I think the problem here is different. I think the method I went through with the Supreme Court thing . . . I think the problem there is that, again, we didn't do our own leaking. I mean, this place leaks like a sieve. . . . They were simply giving out stories that simply weren't accurate.

"I'm going to tell you that I never made a decision on Babbitt or Breyer. I had seven people that I was really looking seriously at. . . . We looked at scores of people. Then we got it down to about forty people. I had seven people that I thought seriously ought to be considered, and three of them I thought I knew well enough, I didn't need to see personally. So then I wound up with the last three.

"I called Babbitt and told him that I thought we ought to have a non-judge in the finals. Some of our greatest courts had non-judges. So I called Babbitt. I told the truth. I said, 'I think you're the best-qualified non-judge, but I'm not sure I can take you out of the Interior Department because of what's going on in the Pacific Northwest [and] because of what we're doing on grazing fees. If you're willing to be considered, I'd still like to think about it—whether you could stay until at least we got through the Pacific Northwest issue.'

"The thing that was determining—really turned it for me in terms of deciding—was not all the calls I got, though I got a call from a governor out west saying, 'If you put him on the Court, I want to be Interior Secretary, but if you do it, you ought to have your head examined.' It became apparent to me through our legal staff here that if I nominated him, he'd have to resign immediately at Interior. He'd have to stop. The conclusion was that he could not reasonably make all these complex decisions at Interior while awaiting confirmation for the Supreme Court. He had thought that he could. When we first started talking, he said, 'At least I can—I mean, look how long it's going to take—I could announce this policy in the Northwest.' When it became clear that couldn't happen, the selection came down to Breyer and Ginsburg. They seemed to have the best combination of intellect, record, skills, esteem, and the ability to work with Reagan-Bush appointees. And the ability to work with mainstream progressive decisions.

"I wanted to see them, and I wanted to see them in some order. We should've done our own leaking, but, no, it came out that it was Breyer's to lose because he came here first. And the inference was that it was the Social Security problem, or did he have a bad interview? And the Social Security problem was clearly different from the Zoe Baird issue. We have nominated thirty people now, women and men, who have some sort of Social Security issue that has now been resolved. [Baird's big problem was that she had hired illegal aliens; Kimba Wood's big problem was that she wasn't forthcoming when asked if she had a "Zoe Baird problem."]

"So I just decided, after I met them both, that even though I liked him a lot, she was an astonishing person.

"The thing that bothered me about Brit's question, and bothered just about everyone else, was that after Ruth spoke, half the group was in tears. And the first question could have been—one, process or, B, getting back to her and her statement. I—it was a totally impulsive reaction. I just thought that moment, I truly thought, should have been hers."

After deciding on Ginsburg, Clinton had strolled into the office of Mack McLarty and said, "See, if I can feel it here," pointing to his stomach, "we do fine."

Hillary had always insisted that Clinton wasn't indecisive; she said it simply took him a long time to feel firm and right about a decision.

Clinton would get a second Supreme Court nonmination in 1994 with the retirement of Justice Harry Blackmun, a Nixon appointee who turned out to be a liberal, one of two or three on the court, depending on how Ginsburg was counted. Again Clinton would agonize over the decision, sending false signals to aides who would make leaks to reporters based on his latest private pronouncement. But these leakers weren't inside the president's head. At one point *The New York Times* reported that Clinton was 95 percent decided on Babbitt, who for the second time found himself considered strongly for the court—but eventually rejected. The *Times* was probably right, but with Clinton, a mind that is 5 percent unmade is a veritable Grand Canyon. Remember, he needs to feel it "here," meaning the pit of his stomach.

On May 13, 1994, Clinton settled on the runner-up from his first Supreme Court sweepstakes. He nominated Breyer, who by now had long since paid taxes on his domestic help, and who had such bipartisan support that Clinton knew that by appointing him he could avoid spending political capital to get him confirmed at a time he needed to preserve that capital for the health reform fight.

Clinton was in a buoyant mood the day he provided me with the preceding narrative. Ginsburg was a hit. His plan for a national service program for the nation's youth, though scaled back, was progressing nicely in Congress. He clearly seemed to think the worst was behind him and that he was getting his sea legs.

The day was June 18.

But in thirty-two days, a numbing personal tragedy would hit him and Hillary. The Clinton administration would have its first casualty. And as one of Washington's pundit pols put it to me: He hated to be political about everything, certainly a personal tragedy, but poor old Clinton just couldn't get a break. Just when things were starting to look better for him . . .

CHAPTER 7

A Casualty

Two days before Bill Clinton's inauguration as the nation's forty-second president, the friends and associates of his wife at the Rose Law Firm in Little Rock, the city's oldest and arguably most prestigious firm, gave a late-afternoon reception in her honor at the Mayflower Hotel in Washington.

Vincent Foster, Jr., a departing senior partner who had been the firm's resident star, a tall and almost patrician corporate litigator to whom all the firm's interns wanted to be assigned, arrived late. He had taken time off during the holidays to assist Clinton's transition to the presidency, but the firm's elder statesman, Phil Carroll, had not been prepared for the news that Foster gave him in early January: he was resigning to move to Washington to become chief deputy White House counsel. Carroll soon regretted declaring that he' wished George Bush had won the damnable election.

The Rose Law Firm, calling itself the "oldest law firm west of the Mississippi," already had a prestigious presence in Washington. In Statuary Hall in the U.S. Capitol, where statues memorialize two historic figures from each of the states, stands a remembrance of Judge Uriah M. Rose, who lent his name to the Rose firm and helped found the American Bar Association. He died in 1913.

Through the 1970s and the free-wheeling 1980s the firm had grown from thirteen lawyers to fifty-six. It had been led from 1965 until 1988 by a diminutive lawyer named Joseph Giroir, who left a job with the Securities and Exchange Commission to join the firm as Arkansas's pioneer securities lawyer and full-service corporate counselor. He provided counsel for private companies going public, eventually becoming managing partner and organizing the firm for the first time into sections with centralized management. He organized the first multi-bank holding company in Arkansas, and in 1979 became counsel to Stephens, Inc., the giant investment banking firm in Little Rock. He hired a young intern named Vince Foster, who had impressed him mightily, and a University of Arkansas football player named Webb Hubbell who had strong family recommendations. In 1977, Foster brought in a relative newcomer to the state whom he had befriended: Hillary Rodham was the wife of the young political phenom who was at that moment the state's thirty-year-old attorney general, fast on his way to the Governor's Mansion.

But in the late 1980s Giroir ran into financial trouble with freelance banking investments. He wound up in litigation against the Federal Savings and Loan Insurance Corporation, and he was getting plenty of negative publicity in Arkansas newspapers. In the spring of 1988 there was a palace coup: Vince Foster, Webb Hubbell, Hillary Rodham Clinton, and a young colleague named Bill Kennedy from a prominent banking family in nearby Pine Bluff, and another former University of Arkansas football player, persuaded a sufficient number of their partners that they needed to force Giroir out. From that point the staid old firm was led by a new generation, a managing quartet: Foster, Clinton, Hubbell, and Kennedy.

Now, in 1993, the leadership would be decimated. Foster would become chief deputy counsel in the White House. Hubbell would become associate attorney general, the third-ranking official in the Justice Department. Kennedy would become associate White House counsel, answering to Foster.

In a few weeks Carroll would apologize to Foster for his angry reaction. He would understand the rare opportunity presented the younger man for whom he had been a mentor. He would understand that Foster was at a point in his life, well off and with three children of college age or nearly there, at which he could make the move. But Carroll's initial reaction was understandable. Mack McLarty, a lifelong friend of Foster's from Hope, expressed surprise when Clinton told him that Foster would move to Washington. He was not surprised by Foster's willingness to serve his friends; he simply knew Foster as a firmly established corporate attorney whose career was the law and whose place was Arkansas.

On that afternoon at the Mayflower Hotel, the transition from the Rose Law Firm to the White House was taking place.

Max Brantley, editor of the weekly *Arkansas Times* and husband of an Arkansas judge, Ellen, who was a friend of Hillary, spotted Foster as he entered the reception. Brantley asked Foster if he was ready to go to work. Foster chuckled at the irony of the question. He said he'd been at work all day and would return to work in a few minutes after participating in the rather momentous occasion, paying his respects to his dear friend, the First Lady-to-be, and bidding his own farewell to the law firm that had been his life.

Six months later Brantley would recall sensing that Foster had come to Washington on a holy mission to lend his steady hand to serve his friends, the Clintons, his personal clients.

Hillary gave a brief speech at the reception in which she bade a sad farewell to her friends at the firm and declared a call to arms for the new administration in Washington. As Mrs. Clinton spoke, Brantley again turned to observe Foster. He saw tears. Foster, a man of widely reputed reserve and stoicism, was choked up. Seeing that Brantley had caught him in a display of emotion, Foster mouthed a few explanatory words. "I think it was, 'She's a remarkable woman,' or something like that," Brantley recalled.

W. H. L. Woodyard III of Little Rock, an insurance lawyer at a competing firm, the Mitchell firm, had been a close friend of Foster since the early 1960s when they met as high schoolers attending a state Key Club convention. When I sat in Woodyard's office ten months later and related the anecdote from the Mayflower Hotel, he expressed no surprise. He explained that surely Vince was tired; that he confronted at that reception the daunting life change he had chosen; and that the truth of the matter was that Foster's reputed stoicism was in some ways a learned and applied demeanor stemming from his professional and family obligations. Foster took those obligations with the utmost seriousness.

His friend, Woodyard explained, knew how to have a good time, but also was a sensitive and moody man.

On a weekend back in 1965, when Woodyard was in college at the University of Arkansas at Fayetteville and Foster was at Davidson in North Carolina, Foster invited his friend over. Foster had gotten Wood-yard a date. Let us just say, Woodyard said, that it was a weekend memorable for its fun and frivolity. That same year, Foster telephoned Woodyard to share his excitement: as social chairman for the Sigma

Alpha Epsilon fraternity at Davidson, Foster had just booked the greatest soul group he'd ever heard. It was called the Otis Redding Revue,
and Foster told Woodyard he could get the band for the Sigma Chi
fraternity at the University of Arkansas for $5,000. Woodyard explained
that his entertainment budget was maybe a fifth of that.

Foster carried a torch for Motown music into middle age, parlaying
it into a taste for progressive jazz. Music, wine, and making pasta were
his great avocational interests. Whenever Woodyard planned an important dinner party, he'd call Foster for advice on wine. "I knew my
California wines, but if I wanted to go foreign, I needed Vince," he
said.

On the day Woodyard's father died, Foster expressed frustration to
Woodyard's wife that he couldn't draw out his friend's emotions, and
he had tears in his eyes. Over the years the Fosters and the Woodyards
spent hundreds of hours together at dinners or lake houses. Sometimes
Foster would be "in one of his moods," as the others put it, meaning
he wanted to be left alone to read or watch television, and was obliged.
Woodyard did not speak of that as an omen of what was to come or
as a sign of something wrong. Surely we all have friends who are
moody; maybe we are the moody ones benefiting from close friends
who learn to accept our occasional retreat. It's one thing to accept that
a good friend sometimes goes into a shell. It's quite another to consider
that the friend would put a gun in his mouth and pull the trigger and
that you would be one of his pallbearers at a funeral on which the
nation's eyes would be fixed.

Having alluded to the closeness between Foster and Hillary, I should
say at this point that there were those in Arkansas who suspected a
romance between them over nearly twenty years of intimate friendship.
For my part, whenever I heard a charge implying that the Clintons
had a marriage of professional and political convenience—an "open
marriage," I suppose—I harked back to a time in the early 1980s when
I was on a campaign plane with them, trying to go to sleep. But my
eyes weren't quite closed, and I saw Hillary kiss her husband and
whisper that she loved him. They seemed to me to have the traditional
affections of a loving married couple, even if it was true that Bill was
a philanderer and seldom campaigned on a college campus or in a
Wal-Mart store when he didn't pop in the car afterward and carry on
in an adolescent manner about a good-looking coed or a tight-jeaned
country girl that he had seen. Foster clearly adored his wife, Lisa, and
his three kids, two boys and a girl. I rather agreed with this assessment

by a woman who was a friend of both Foster and Hillary: "They had such a strong friendship that to me it's totally irrelevant whether in the course of two decades they ever rubbed body parts."

Frankly, one of the more attractive things about Hillary was that she and Vince Foster were friends.

Foster and Hillary became close because they shared good brains, careers, general sensitivities, extraordinary responsibilities, generational interests, and the leadership of a proud law firm. When you are the governor and first lady of a small state, or when you are a serious-minded professional leading a staid and dignified law firm in that small state, there are few occasions when you can let your hair down. Together, Foster and the Clintons could sip wine, turn up Aretha Franklin's volume on the CD player, and splash into Foster's swimming pool in the affluent Heights section of Little Rock.

It's safe to say that no one except perhaps Chelsea was as close to both halves of the new First Couple. Foster, a year older than Clinton, had been the president's boyhood neighbor back in Hope. As an adult he was Hillary's best friend. He knew their joint privacies as their personal attorney. All the other close friends of the Clintons, with the possible exception of Betsey Wright, had an identifiably stronger bond with one than with the other. Hubbell, for example, was not as close to Hillary as was Vince, but he and Clinton were close friends.

Almost six months to the day after that tearful moment in the Mayflower Hotel, in the late afternoon of July 20, Foster was found dead. His body lay in the grass near a Civil War cannon on a secluded hill in the tiny, quiet Fort Marcy Park on the Virginia side of the Potomac River, which the mound overlooked. A .38-caliber revolver, with one bullet unused, hung from the thumb of his right hand. He had shot himself in the mouth. His coat and wallet had been left in the car in the nearby parking lot.

That day he had attended the announcement of the appointment of Louis Freeh to be director of the FBI. "We hit a home run today," his boss, chief counsel Bernie Nussbaum, told him, referring to Freeh. Foster had said only, "Yeah." Then he had taken lunch on a tray from the White House Mess to his office, where he ate alone, which was not unusual, and watched on television a bit of the opening of the confirmation hearings for Ruth Bader Ginsburg, the nominee for the Supreme Court—another home run. Around 1:00 P.M. he walked out of his office, told his secretary to take the package of M&M's off his tray before she carried the tray back to the mess, and to help herself to some. He said he would be back.

He got into his teen-aged daughter's Japanese sedan with an Arkansas license plate, which he had driven into the White House compound as usual about eight o'clock that morning, and which most likely contained the gun, and was gone. The automobiles of staff regulars with parking privileges inside the compound were not thoroughly checked; the routine was a quick sweep for a bomb and maybe popping open the trunk.

A couple of times that afternoon people in the White House mentioned that they hadn't seen him. Maybe he had a meeting.

A body was reported anonymously to the U.S. Park Police shortly after 6:00 P.M. It was about 8:45 P.M. when the Park Police, having completed the on-site investigation, placed a call to the White House chief of staff's office to report the discovery of a body bearing White House identification. At 9:00 P.M., Clinton went to the White House library to appear live for an hour on the Larry King show on CNN. He hadn't been told of the unnerving call. Mack McLarty and George Stephanopoulos went to the residential quarters to monitor the broadcast. Bill Burton, staff and policy director for McLarty, stayed in the chief of staff's office to take any additional calls from the Park Police. Burton, a lawyer, was the former editor of the *Hope Star,* the daily newspaper in the hometown of Bill Clinton, Mack McLarty, and Vince Foster.

About nine-fifteen, Burton took the call with the positive identification of the body. It was Vince Foster, a man Burton had greatly admired and a man from a prominent family to which Burton was indebted. Foster's late father, Vincent Sr., a businessman and raconteur, had raised money for the Burton family back in Hope when it had confronted oppressive medical bills. Vincent Sr., known as gregarious, was a fixture at the poker table at the Hope Country Club. Vince Jr. was more like his mother, soft-spoken and not given to conspicuousness. Then Burton had been a law clerk at the Rose Law Firm, where Vince Jr. was the idol of all young attorneys.

Burton went to the residential quarters to give the shocking news to McLarty, who immediately telephoned Hillary, who was back in Little Rock. McLarty chose not to interrupt the president until the show was completed. About 10:00 P.M., after Clinton had indicated a willingness to stay on King's program 30 minutes beyond the scheduled stopping point, and during a break in which the producer said he didn't think the unscheduled extension would be possible, McLarty asked Clinton to go with him to the president's private quarters. Burton came along in case Clinton had questions about the police report.

"What is it?" Clinton demanded as they walked. "It's not Hillary or Chelsea," McLarty told him. Then, standing in the private residence, McLarty gave the president the news, and Clinton cried out, "Oh, no."

Vince Foster was, according to everyone who professed to have known him well, the last person on earth who would lose control and take his own life. He was solid as a rock, the one to whom others went with their problems. Hubbell would declare that evening in a telephone call to Phil Carroll that if there was one thing he knew, it was that Vince Foster had not killed himself. Hubbell had relaxed with Vince two days before during a weekend getaway to the eastern shore of Maryland, the first recreational fun they had enjoyed since the Clinton presidency embarked.

Hubbell, in a state of shock and denial, was wrong. This was about as clear a case of suicide as you would ever see. But that made it no easier to accept or comprehend. People across the nation speculated ignorantly that surely Foster had been killed or had killed himself because of something sinister that he knew or feared. But in their ignorant suspicions they shared the doubts of some of Foster's closest friends.

If you had asked prominent insiders in Arkansas to assess candidly the people from their state who had descended on Washington to run the country, the composite opinion surely would have been that Vince Foster was the brightest and best.

Bill Clinton was widely admired for brains, a good heart, charisma, and political brilliance. But you could find people, even his friends, who would question whether he had sufficient commitment to his word and whether he had the ability to organize a two-car parade.

Hillary Rodham Clinton was widely admired for brains, toughness, and a commitment to children. But you could find people who would say that she was cold and calculating, and who would suggest that her attempts at public displays of warmth struck them as clumsy and transparently bogus.

Mack McLarty was extraordinarily popular and a man of impeccable manners whose word was bankable. But there were those who thought he had run the Arkansas Louisiana Gas Company into the ground and that his politeness and courtliness belied raw political ambition and compensated for a lack of competence. Arkla shareholders could be forgiven for their view.

Bruce Lindsey was seen as politically astute, hardworking, and admirably loyal to Clinton, but there were those who saw him essentially as a glorified "gofer" for the new president.

Webb Hubbell was seen as not quite the corporate litigator that Vince Foster was, and as a third wheel to the extraordinarily close professional and personal relationship of Foster and Hillary.

But Vince Foster? The consensus of people in the know back in Arkansas was that the Clinton White House would contain at least one person with the kind of impeccable professional and personal credentials who ought to be in government. He was seen as smart, clean, and tough.

Foster had ranked first in his law school class at the University of Arkansas at Fayetteville. He made the highest score on the state bar exam. He achieved partner at the Rose firm in two years. He regularly earned more than $200,000 a year as a corporate litigator, an elite income in Arkansas. He was respected by corporate clients. He was respected by the Arkansas media, partly because, with Phil Carroll, he represented legally many of the state's newspapers. He had three handsome children and a lovely wife. Other lawyers saw him as smooth and formidable; businesspeople saw him as focused, capable, and trustworthy; social liberals saw a good heart.

There weren't many big-time corporate litigators in Arkansas who donated their time in the late 1970s to establishing legal aid bureaus in the state. But Foster did.

Grif Stockley of Little Rock, a career legal aid lawyer and in recent years an author of fiction on the side, liked to tell this story: On an oppressively hot and humid summer day in 1977, he and Foster got into one of the Rose firm's company cars and Vince drove them 45 miles southeast to Pine Bluff, an Old South bastion and racially divided town. There they split up and went to the offices of the prominent white lawyers to try to sell them on the idea of supporting a Pine Bluff satellite office of the Legal Aid Bureau of Pulaski County back in Little Rock, where Stockley worked. Late in the afternoon they got back together, piled into the car for the ride back, and compared notes on the reaction they had received. "It was like we were from Mars or someplace," Stockley said. "Some of these guys were just dumbfounded at the idea that they would support free legal services for anybody. We had to laugh to keep from crying."

They were sweaty, especially Foster, since he was in his corporate lawyer's uniform, a black suit. About halfway back to Little Rock, the car ran out of gasoline. "There we were, stranded on the highway, hot as hell, going back to Little Rock with our tails tucked between our legs," Stockley said. "And I'll never forget: Vince didn't say a word. In that stoic way of his, he just got out of the car and started walking. I just sat there and watched those long legs take him down the side of the road. In a little while he came walking back, about the time the Rose firm sent a car to pick us up."

Associates at the Rose firm said Foster was different from the norm for corporate lawyers. He lined his pockets more effectively than most, but he appeared to have interests beyond writing briefs and making money. Nor was he the gregarious back-slapper that typified the Southern good ol' boy. He kept things to himself. Sometimes he ate lunch alone and read. One of the Rose firm's wives told me that Foster was the only person in the firm who seemed to show the least interest in anything she had to say about matters not bound up in the world of the law. While she dreaded the firm's annual Christmas party, she comforted herself that at least the kind and reserved Vince Foster would talk to her with seeming interest.

Knowing of Foster's combination of legal expertise, social progressivism, and reputed personal strength, I assigned credibility to what he had to say. As a political columnist, I'd run across him rarely in Arkansas. He eschewed a public role in politics. When I saw a political interest in him, it was not exactly naive, but earnestly altruistic.

His brother-in-law, Beryl Anthony, who was married to Foster's sister, Sheila, served for fourteen years as the Democratic congressman from southern Arkansas. He rose to prominence on the Ways and Means Committee and as chairman of the Democratic Congressional Campaign Committee. Anthony was quite the congressional insider, and that caught up with him in 1990 when he was defeated in his own primary by an irascible secretary of state who stole labor's support and benefited from the National Rifle Association's targeting Anthony for supporting the Brady Bill and a ban on assault weapons. Southern Arkansas is perhaps the deer-hunting capital of the world. It didn't help that Anthony had written a large number of checks drawn on insufficient funds at the House Bank.

After I wrote a column defending Anthony's progressive record and recounting some of the antics of his challenger, Foster sent a short note. "I was beginning to think that no one remembered anything about Beryl's opponent," he said.

Anthony lost the race although Clinton's presidential campaign in Little Rock lent him its telephone banks for a late push. It was highly irregular for a Democratic presidential candidate to inject himself into a Democratic congressional primary, but it made perfect sense to anyone knowing the relationship of the Clintons, the Fosters, and the Anthonys.

Later, Foster told me that during the campaign he had missed the *Arkansas Gazette,* a liberal institution that had been swallowed up the year before by its competition, the *Arkansas Democrat.* If only the *Gazette* had been alive, there would have been an institutional voice to stand up for his brother-in-law and competent progressivism, Foster thought.

I assigned considerable credibility to a note Foster sent to me early in the Clinton presidency after I had written a column suggesting that he and Hubbell were flirting with trouble over the Justice Department's injecting itself into jury selection for a criminal trial of U.S. Republican Harold Ford of Tennessee. Ford was black and was contesting an all-white jury on a change of venue from Memphis to Jackson, Tennessee. I stated in the column that Jesse Jackson had sent a letter in Ford's behalf to the White House, and that Foster had shipped it over to his buddy, Hubbell, at the Justice Department.

Foster sent this handwritten note: "I don't know if the witch-hunt is over, but just for your information, the letter was forwarded to acting Attorney General [Stewart] Gerson, stating merely, 'We are forwarding this to you for whatever action you deem appropriate.' I understand he didn't receive it even until after he made and announced his decision [of Justice Department intervention], and we never talked. Beware of the *Democrat*'s innuendo as a basis for concluding facts."

The reference was to reporting in the *Arkansas Democrat-Gazette,* a Republican-leaning newspaper born of the *Democrat*'s swallowing of the *Gazette.*

I accepted Foster's version of events, but was a little surprised at his sensitivity to an otherwise forgettable column published in his back-home daily newspaper about a fading issue. If that little column warranted his response, Washington and *The Wall Street Journal* would keep him very busy.

*   *   *

In the days and weeks after his suicide, much of Washington's punditocracy pondered aloud whether the city's cynical political games had killed Vince Foster, exposing him to mean-spirited public attacks for which his insulated background of uninterrupted success and admiration had not prepared him.

Associates in Little Rock scoffed. Joe Giroir, another of Foster's mentors, told me that although he had no explanation for Foster's suicide, he simply could not accept that a corporate litigator of Foster's experience and resolve would wilt under political heat. But if one thing should have become obvious in the Clinton administration's first fourteen months in Washington, it was that corporate law and big-time politics are entirely different things requiring entirely different skills. The law is largely a science; lawyers study the statutes and deal with questions narrowly, determining whether an action is permitted or prohibited. Politics is an art in which what people perceive is more important than what actually is. Imagine Ronald Reagan as a corporate litigator. Most likely you cannot; but he was a masterful politician. Consider the Clintons: he is a great politician and she is a solid lawyer; these are complementary and symmetrical strengths, but they are far from identical.

By the fourteenth month of Clinton's presidency, the corporate lawyer cabal with which Hillary surrounded herself—Bernie Nussbaum of New York City as chief White House counsel, Foster as chief deputy counsel, Hubbell as associate attorney general, and Kennedy as the third-ranking lawyer in the White House—would be even more decimated than the Rose Law Firm. Nussbaum would resign after a series of political blunders, including the final straw: his complicity in meetings between federal regulators and White House aides to give the Clintons a "heads-up" on a probe into a failed savings and loan association headed by a former business partner of the First Couple. Hubbell would resign after partners at the Rose firm discovered that he had stuck them with $100,000 or more in expenses stemming from a case he took on a contingency basis for his in-laws' parking meter company, and lost. Foster would be dead. Only Kennedy would remain, and after fourteen months his wife had left him and he had a formal reprimand on his record for his role in the travel office fiasco.

But Washington did not kill Foster; it merely gave him a crash course in the cynicism of partisan politics, to which he had previously been exposed only peripherally, and thus disillusioned him. Public error after an adulthood of private success did not kill him, either; it merely caused him frustration, embarrassment, and a feeling that he had let down the people for whom he'd come to Washington to serve with steady competence and a sense of moral purpose.

Whether that disillusionment, frustration, embarrassment, and a sense of failure triggered the mental illness, torment, and deranged state that led him to take his own life is a question best speculated on, if at all, by experts. Clinton himself probably had it right from the beginning: We'll never understand what kind of demon caused Foster's suicide.

The best explanation for an irrational act that defied explanation was that it was caused by clinical depression triggered by despair over failure or perceived failure, possibly by a specific incident or worry.

Foster had spent one recent Saturday working in his bed with the shades drawn, probably suffering depression. He had compiled and then torn into twenty-seven or twenty-eight pieces a note of exasperation that contained signs of paranoia, such as his charge that the White House's permanent staff was out to get Hillary and her decorator, Kaki Hockersmith of Little Rock. Two months before his death he had delivered a mostly lovely commencement address at the University of Arkansas Law School, but in the course of it made a comment that, in retrospect, might have signaled trouble: "I cannot make this point to you too strongly. There is no victory, no advantage, no fee, no favor which is worth even a blemish on your reputation for intellect and integrity. Nothing travels faster than an accusation that a lawyer's word is no good. A judge who catches you in a disingenuous argument or a mischaracterization of a case will turn hard of hearing when you next show up to argue. *Dents to the reputation in the legal profession are irreparable.*" (Emphasis added)

The general admonition was sound and valid, and no doubt something the young graduates needed to hear. But that last sentence simply was not true. Dents to the reputation in the legal profession are commonplace, not irreparable. Even if Foster referred to a lawyer's being censured by the Bar, his view was entirely too fatalistic. A person has no control over what others may choose to think of him, and one cannot despair over a personal Armageddon if his reputation is damaged. Instead, he must pick himself up from doom and despair and set about his personal rehabilitation. In the end Foster could not pick himself up from doom and despair.

Foster's friend Bill Clinton, a lawyer, was living proof of the fallacy of Foster's observation. Millions thought Clinton a philanderer, a liar, and a traitor. Yet he had managed to salvage enough of his reputation to become the President of the United States.

But Clinton was a career politician. He had chosen to spend his adulthood enduring the travails of seeking and holding office. Foster was a back-room lawyer who had never before been in the trenches of political warfare. In becoming the chief deputy counsel in the White House, he was going directly to the political big leagues without having faced minor-league pitching.

So while Washington didn't kill him, it did make him most unhappy, a condition exacerbated by his living conditions for the first five months he spent there. With his wife and son remaining in Little Rock until the end of a school term, Foster stayed in a tiny apartment near Georgetown. It was a far cry from his elegantly appointed home in Little Rock. At a reception at the Hotel Washington in the early spring, I asked him how he was faring in the city. He extended his arms outward as he explained that he could stand in the middle of his apartment and touch the walls on any side of him.

The sad irony was that Foster had not performed so poorly. He had made mistakes, most of them political, not legal. He quickly thought better of some of his errors, but the pace of events allowed no time for recovery.

He assigned a deputy to ask the FBI what to do about internal reports of mismanagement at the travel office. When the FBI indicated a willingness to barrel in head first with a criminal investigation, Foster sounded an alarm. A private audit would be more appropriate, he said. Then he had tried to get word to Dee Dee Myers not to make a public suggestion of criminality against the dismissed travel office employees, but he did so too late.

"I think Vince's problem with politics was the lack of control," Woodyard said months later. "In law, and at his firm, there were systems. But in politics, nothing ever ends, and at the White House level things can spin out of control before you know it. And Vince's frustration, I think, was that although he kept deciding on the proper things to do, like in the travel office, things kept happening that were just beyond his control."

Phil Carroll said months later that Foster was ever cool in tough litigation, but that the law usually offered a clear answer in a law book and a clear resolution with a judge's order. "You'll have to tell me if it's different from that in politics," he said. Surely he didn't need me to answer the question: In politics there is never a clear answer in a book, and there is only one interim resolution, that being an election. And there's always another election. Losers of elections don't go away. They keep sniping, and the press keeps quoting them.

Foster's other mistake was that he was part of a counsel's operation that erred on the political ramifications of matters affecting Zoe Baird, Kimba Wood, and Lani Guinier. As for strictly legal work, it was not surprising that Foster had prevailed in his defense of the privacy rights of Hillary's health care task force. What he hadn't counted on was being attacked for his line of defense on the editorial page of *The Wall Street Journal,* which in the Reagan era had supported the privacy privileges for the executive branch that it scolded Foster for advancing.

Foster's greatest regret surely was that he briefed his friend Hillary on the travel office developments and copied memoranda about them to her. Then when he insisted that the White House make a full disclosure of its errors in that incident, which was sound legal and political advice, it became necessary to mention the role of the First Lady. He thought he had let down this "remarkable woman." Actually, though, it was Hollywood's Harry Thomason who mentioned his suspicions to the First Lady. It was Hillary, then, who had the bad judgment to inquire about whether the house had been cleaned in the travel office and to ask Vince to keep her posted. Perhaps Foster thought that in his legal wisdom he should have recommended that he keep her out of it, which is indeed what he should have done.

When assistant White House counsel Steve Neuwirth went into Foster's office and turned Foster's briefcase upside down the week after the tragedy, out fell the pieces of a note. Put together, White House officials found a sentence in which Foster said he was not meant for the Washington life, another in which he said no one would ever believe the innocence of the Clintons, another in which he said he had not intentionally violated any law or ethical standard, and, finally, the famous one: "Here ruining people is considered sport."

That was a slight overstatement. In Washington, ruining people is considered to be for a higher purpose than winning a ball game. If the Republicans can ruin the Democrats, or vice versa, then the winners can lead the nation on the political and policy path they deem best. The assumption is that those who enter the political arena accept the rules. Sometimes the byplay can be so trivial as to be gratuitous and mean, such as the editorial in *The Wall Street Journal* that poked fun at the White House for not sending it a picture of Foster to illustrate an editorial. Actually, the photograph had been sent by the time the editorial was published.

Foster's ripped note also made the point that the editors of the *Journal,* which he had read irregularly back in Little Rock, but without much regard for the Reaganesque editorials, "lied without consequence." That was quite true. Editorial pages devoted to knee-jerk partisanship are filled with lies. No one can be strictly partisan and tell the whole truth. The Democratic president isn't always right, nor is he always wrong. Editorials predetermined by partisan advocacy routinely lie by omission or commission. The truth in politics, if there is any, would have to begin from a non-partisan premise that sometimes Democrats could be right and sometimes Republicans could be right.

Anyway, the central *Wall Street Journal* editorial about Foster—"Who is Vince Foster?"—hardly qualified as an attack. It was widely deemed too silly for that. The *Journal* seemed more amused in an ironic sense than angry that Foster had pursued an argument defending the privacy of Hillary Clinton's health care task force that sought to exempt it from federal laws for open government. The tone, substance, and blind partisanship made the editorial eminently dismissable. By his statements at the White House, Foster appeared to dismiss it. By his actions, he couldn't quite.

All of that is hardly unique to Washington. It's the story of politics and journalism, including politics and journalism as they are played back in Arkansas.

The day after the text of Foster's reassembled note was released to the media, *The New York Times* published an editorial saying, "Mr. Foster's lament says more about the insularity of political life in Little Rock than it does about Washington."

No, Mr. Foster's lament said more about the seriousness with which he had come to Washington and his lack of personal political experience than it did about any place on the map, be it Washington or Little Rock.

Had he jumped into the political arena back in Little Rock, Foster would have encountered the kind of sleaze that had toughened Clinton's skin for the 1992 presidential campaign. Here are a few of the recent "insular" niceties of Arkansas politics:

- In 1986, Clinton was accused of snorting cocaine and cavorting with an investment banker who was under investigation, and eventually indicted, for cocaine trafficking.

- In 1990, he was accused of fathering out-of-wedlock children and carrying on affairs with aides, beauty queens, and media starlets.

- That same year he benefited greatly from the exposure of a pattern of expense account fraud by the state attorney general, who had decided to run against him in the primary and who had treated girlfriends to champagne and liqueur by inventing dining guests and business purposes on his credit-card record. Then a Republican gubernatorial candidate saw his congressional medical records leaked to the press, showing that he'd had a pint-a-day Bourbon habit. That was spattered across the top of the front page of a daily newspaper's Sunday edition.

- In the fall of 1992, *The New York Times* dispatched a reporter to Little Rock to do an article on the state's opinion columnists. The angle was that never before had a serious presidential contender been treated so harshly by his local media.

Clearly, Vince Foster did not kill himself because Little Rock was a serene and civil hamlet that didn't prepare anyone for combative politics on a national level. I must take up for Little Rock here. My hometown can be a hateful place.

A better explanation is that Foster simply wasn't personally prepared to accept with his supposed stoicism—which turned out to be a veneer—the unfair exploitation inherent in the partisan battle, which he had found distasteful from the sidelines in Little Rock, but which he experienced directly on a compounding basis in Washington. Errors of inexperience and bad judgment were being portrayed as evil conspiracies. Foster told the Anthonys he thought he might need a lawyer to defend him in the travel office matter. It is said that Foster would read the newspapers in Washington and mutter, "No. No. That's not right." Of course, countless others surely did the same thing. Bill Clinton once screamed at George Stephanopoulos that the *Washington Times* was the sorriest excuse for a newspaper he had ever seen. (It may be the most partisanly Republican, even on the front page. Liberal newspapers are more subtle, usually.)

Foster couldn't adjust to Washington because he'd never played the political game; because he'd come to this city of partisan game playing with probably naive intentions to do good and protect his friends from trouble; and because he made mistakes that, for the first time ever in his life, were readily available for public consumption.

If the insularity of Foster's Arkansas culture was a factor, it probably was that even in tough litigation in Little Rock, a lawyer is likely to meet his opponent at a charity function or the repertory theater. That can temper the tendency toward cutthroat, bridge-burning tactics.

So Foster despaired, became ill, and died.

Naturally, Foster's suicide led to frenzied innuendo, speculation, and gossip by the major elements of Washington's one-industry and small-town mentality: partisan opponents and the media. They suggested that he fell on his sword to save the Clintons from embarrassment on some legal or financial matter. They cited discrepancies and blunders in the White House account and handling of events.

Had Foster shown signs of depression? Clinton initially said no, then White House aides confirmed a press report that Clinton had called Foster two nights before his death to try to cheer him up.

The explanation was rather simple. The way things had been going in the White House, a lot of people seemed down. But in the frenetic pace no one had given the least thought to the idea that Foster might be suffering clinical depression and teetering on the verge of suicide. Foster was a quiet, internalizing person. A few days before his death, he had sought a prescription for anti-depressant medication from a Little Rock doctor. But he didn't feel obliged to make an announcement and no one had any reason to think that Foster was any more blue than, say, Bruce Lindsey, who was inundated with résumés in the personnel office as Hillary breathed down his neck over the slow pace of appointments, and as the press said it was his fault because he didn't stop Clinton from getting a haircut as Air Force One parked on a runway at Los Angeles International. Clinton had tried to cheer up Bruce Lindsey, telling him to try to have some fun, but that didn't mean that Clinton should have expected Lindsey to commit suicide.

Beryl Anthony, Foster's Washington-wise brother-in-law, told me: "Sure, we talked to him about how things work in this town; how the Republicans do what Republicans do, and how the press does what the press does, and you just go on. But those kinds of discussions were going on with a lot of people in the White House."

Yes, the White House erred in not immediately sealing Foster's office.

The night of his suicide, Maggie Williams, the chief of staff for Hillary Clinton, and Patsy Thomasson, an administrative aide in the White House from Little Rock, went into the office. They should not have done so, and what they were doing there remained a mystery for months. It was noteworthy that Hillary's chief of staff was there, and it is equally noteworthy that months later Hillary would resist openness on the Clintons' personal financial matters, some of which Foster had handled.

Days later, Bernie Nussbaum kept police investigators at a distance as he denied them access to certain of Foster's papers that he deemed personal and to be covered by the Clinton-Foster attorney-client privilege, including papers about a bungled land development project called Whitewater.

But, remember, Bernie Nussbaum had seldom done anything right all year as the White House's chief lawyer. He had ample evidence to support a defense of political incompetence against suggestions of impropriety. To the end Nussbaum saw his job as service to the Clintons rather than to the country, and he never looked beyond the precisely legal questions to the larger political ones.

"There's just *nothing* there," Mack McLarty told me in early August after William Safire had written a column for *The New York Times* suggesting something—a cover-up, an unsolved mystery—because a small piece was missing from the Foster note that was reassembled from twenty-seven pieces. That missing triangle was at the very bottom of the page, far below the rest of the text. It could have been a doodle. It could have been a drawing of a hand extending the index finger. Or it could have been blank, and simply floated away when Foster ripped up the note.

But as time passed, even White House aides began to wonder whether there might have been another trigger—a worry of something to come—for Foster's suicide. Friends of Foster began to hedge their pronouncements.

A top White House official told me in early 1994—as speculation about Foster was rekindled—that he was 85 to 90 percent certain that the tragic story of Foster's suicide was as I have told it here and that rumors of intrigue involving the First Couple or the Rose firm were just rumors advanced by conspiracy theorists. But put another way, he assigned a 10 to 15 percent chance that there might indeed be some matter of intrigue.

That's not an insignificant percentage, either as a chance of rain or as a reflection of a White House insider's uneasiness and uncertainty about what drove Vince Foster to suicide. No one seemed certain what Foster had meant in his note when he wrote that no one would ever believe the innocence of the Clintons, and that he had not violated knowingly any law or professional ethical standard.

Most likely, those were the paranoid overreactions of a man suffering depression triggered by failures and criticism. But might he have known a politically damaging secret? Had he discovered that he might have some appearance of complicity in an action that might be judged illegal or unethical?

Never considered anything other than smart and thorough, Foster might have seen coming the firestorm of political and legal problems stemming from matters back in Little Rock—and he might have seen the coming embarrassment for his beloved law firm. On the other hand, his death turned out to be the sustaining element for intense interests in those matters.

Still, a chance of one in ten, or thereabouts, was enough to keep the interest alive. But it was illogical to suggest Foster had learned something disillusioning about the Clintons and taken his life because they had let him down; after all, his note asserted their innocence.

If indeed there was something else, it was bound to come out. The Foster suicide had intrigued a nation already hooked on John Grisham novels about lawyers, law firms, politicians, and mysterious deaths. Robert Fiske, a Manhattan lawyer assigned in January 1993 as a special prosecutor looking into the Clintons' involvement in Whitewater and more peripheral involvement with a wheeling-dealing savings and loan association, signaled in February that he was at least as interested in Foster's suicide as in the land deal or the S&L matter.

That Washington is a gossipy and insular town was evident in the issue of *Newsweek* magazine the week after Foster's death. An article declared that on the very afternoon that Foster shot himself, his wife, Lisa, had sat in the restaurant of the Four Seasons Hotel in Georgetown with Mack McLarty's wife, Donna, and expressed her great concern about her husband's state of mind.

Donna McLarty was flabbergasted to read it.

That day she and Lisa had gone together to a luncheon planning meeting for the Ambassadors Ball to benefit the fight against multiple sclerosis. They got in the car intending to go see the Dead Sea Scrolls, but changed their minds. They wanted merely to sit and visit, and they chose the large, breezy restaurant at Georgetown's Four Seasons, an exclusive spot frequented for Sunday brunch by administration insiders.

A woman of McLarty's acquaintance stopped by, said hello, and was introduced to Lisa Foster. Then the woman sat down fully across the large room. For about an hour, from 1:30 to 2:30 P.M., the two White House wives and old friends from Arkansas talked. Lisa Foster said that Vince seemed a little more chipper and that they had thoroughly enjoyed their weekend on the eastern shore, where they had played tennis.

"I'm not from such a small town that I don't understand table talk," Donna McLarty said months later. "But, honestly, we had an upbeat conversation. We talked about our sons and their college plans. And there was no one—*no one*—around to hear us. And then we drove back to Lisa's house so we could each take a car and drive between our homes so we could tell our sons how to get back and forth to visit each other."

Two months later, the woman who had introduced herself and sat down across the restaurant that day telephoned Donna McLarty. Embarrassed, she said she wanted to apologize. On the evening after seeing Donna and Lisa Foster in the restaurant, she had been at a party when the news came that Vince Foster had been found dead of an apparently self-inflicted gunshot wound. The woman admitted that she had exclaimed that she had met Foster's wife just that day, and that, well, she might have speculated about what Mrs. Foster and Mrs. McLarty were talking about. That, she was certain, had led to the *Newsweek* item.

There was a time quite recently when the mainstream news weeklies were vital sources of information, lending new insight and perspective to news events. But with the advent of talk radio, 24-hour television news, home computer news services, and nationally distributed newspapers, sometimes those news weeklies, in frantic efforts to produce some new angle about a juicy story, resemble supermarket tabloids.

Bill and Hillary Clinton took two lessons from the tragedy. One was to keep in closer touch with their friends. At the cemetery after Foster's burial, Hillary hugged Little Rock friends and said she needed to have them to the White House for a party soon. For her forty-seventh birthday, in October, she would have such a party: a combination birthday-Halloween costume bash. The other lesson was to reach out to Republicans for support on the developing health care program. They already had intended to do so as a tactical ploy, but now the president, who was a soft touch anyway, wanted to bridge some of the gaps that stymied progress in Washington and caused one of the best men he'd ever known to become disillusioned.

On the night after Foster's suicide, Clinton went to the Fosters' home north of Georgetown, where he and other friends comforted Lisa, shared their grief, and remembered their friend with what they later described as a combination of tears and laughter. Close to midnight, someone mentioned to Clinton that Foster's neighbor was Senator Richard Shelby of Alabama, a conservative Democrat who had voted against every significant White House initiative and then thumbed his nose at the Clinton administration's attempts to punish him.

Shelby had embarrassed Al Gore by calling publicly for more spending cuts and fewer taxes when he and the vice president appeared together before a television camera. Then when the White House got the idea to punish Shelby by taking a few NASA-related jobs out of Alabama and denying him extra tickets for friends and constituents when Alabama's national championship football team was honored at the White House, Shelby expressed his condescending amusement and won plaudits from his constituents, who didn't care much for Clinton in the first place.

But on that night of numbing personal tragedy, the President of the United States went next door, asked Richard Shelby if he could come in, and, over a couple of glasses of wine, poured out his heart to a man of his own party who had snubbed him at every turn.

Shelby boasted about the visit the next day on Capitol Hill.

En route to Foster's funeral, Dale Bumpers of Arkansas told Clinton that one of his aides was angry to hear that the president had been so friendly and solicitous to a political Neanderthal like Shelby. Clinton was absolutely mystified that anyone would find fault with his willingness to be friendly to a foe.

That story tells as much about Clinton as any other. He genuinely likes nearly everyone; he wants everyone to like him; he has been in politics all his life and, with a few exceptions, easily dismisses the nasty things said and thought in the heat of electoral or legislative battle.

Alabama's Richard Shelby, it should be added, still voted against the president's budget when it came through the Senate in August, needing literally every vote it could get.

CHAPTER 8

"We Don't Have the Votes"

"You know, the Republicans are great at gaining six inches and claiming a yard. And we're just as great at gaining a yard and claiming six inches."—Bill Burton, staff director for the White House chief of staff, quoting a "senior White House official" from a staff meeting.

"But the thing was," Burton added, "nobody slapped their knees or laughed. Everybody just kinda said, 'Yeah, that's the way it is.' "

On the evening of Friday, August 6, 1993, Congress completed passage of Bill Clinton's five-year budget plan.

Seldom had a president looked as pitiable in triumph. Seldom had the messiness of a process so obscured the worthiness of a product. In the football metaphor so prevalent and favored in Mack McLarty's White House, Clinton had scored a touchdown only to receive boos from his own fans because he'd staggered across the goal line and landed with his face buried deep in mud. It's hard to do a little dance and spike the ball when you can't get up from the muck and mire.

In the end Clinton won not because he was strong, but because he had become so weak that a hair's-breadth majority of Democrats in Congress felt a proprietary need to save him from utter failure and maybe destruction not seven months into the first Democratic presidency in a dozen years.

I recalled a day in the fall of 1982 when Clinton unbuckled his seat belt to step off an airplane for another stop in the brutally negative campaign that put him back in the Arkansas governor's office. He said to me, without prompting or any real context, "I may win this thing, but I'm going to be a walking sore before it's over." And he laughed as he stepped down to the asphalt for another round of handshakes. It requires a tough, gritty politician even to conjure such imagery, much less enjoy it as humor.

Clinton had lost that sense of black humor a few times as his budget made its death-defying highwire trip through Congress.

Vice President Al Gore, never as vital in the U.S. Senate when he actually worked there, took a mid-evening limousine ride along Pennsylvania Avenue from the White House to the Capitol to cast the tie-breaking vote, his second such journey in six weeks. By the 51-to-50 margin he provided, the federal government had a new five-year budget plan that reflected a verifiable and responsibly paced reduction in the federal deficit, something on the order of $450 billion to $500 billion cumulatively over five years. It would get the red ink down to $200 billion by 1998, when it would have been well over $300 billion if nothing had been done.

The Republicans said that Clinton hadn't cut spending enough and that he had taxed too much, or should not have taxed at all. Some Democrats said much the same thing. Some administration officials privately tended to agree. Nearly everyone decreed that Clinton had oversold the grand virtue of his budget and then shown weakness by retreating too readily. Public opinion had turned against him. He was routed in the rhetorical war, not only by Republicans but by his erstwhile "new Democrat" colleagues as well.

My only complaint was that Clinton hadn't resisted the consummate politician's tendency toward sleight-of-hand. He talked about sacrifice when in fact he proposed a budget that hardly asked for sacrifice from the pampered middle class. He preached deficit reduction and austerity while he made government bigger.

In his heart, the president believed too much in government's service to people to downsize it significantly or unnecessarily. In his heart, he believed too much in his own political viability to offend the group on whom his fortunes hinged: the middle class.

It was ironic that a spender such as Clinton, who had doubled the meager Arkansas budget over a decade, became president in the anti-spend era. As a fish out of water, he was doing the best he could.

A "new Democrat," remember, is a Democrat with novel ideas for government programs, which cost money. It is not the same as a conservative Democrat or a deficit hawk.

Since Clinton had lost the rhetorical war anyway and triumphed only on an unbecoming plea for Democrats to keep him on life support for the balance of his presidency, he may as well have told the truth about what he proposed and why.

He was right all along in the essence of his program, if not the packaging. He chose to reduce the deficit incrementally and as a percentage of the gross domestic product, from 4.6 percent in the winter of 1993 to 2.9 percent in 1998, by best estimates, while reserving the right to avoid the severe political risks, and likely political failure, of proposing significantly slashed entitlement programs. He also wanted to raise and transfer money to start a few new programs designed to promote urban jobs, schools, job training, national service, childhood health and immunizations, and, in time, health reform and welfare reform. Altogether, that charted a wiser course than eliminating the budget arbitrarily or precipitously, damaging the economy, and leaving government with no ability to meet needs. And $100 billion-plus, a very conservative estimate of the fifth-year reduction in the projected annual shortfall, was a lot of money even in the federal government. Extracting higher taxes from the well off and granting income-tax credits to child-rearing people who worked, but drew wages in the vicinity of the poverty level, was a noble initiative that blended the "old Democrat" idea of transferring wealth with the "new Democrat" idea of rewarding poor folks who worked and stayed off welfare.

All it would cost the middle class would be 4.3 cents on a gallon of gasoline; that hardly warranted worry in the view of one who spent time in 1993 in Washington, paying more than $1.25 for a gallon of gasoline, and Little Rock, where he paid about $1.10. The natural price fluctuations would readily obscure 4.3 cents a gallon.

Even so, Senator David Pryor of Arkansas, one of Clinton's common-sense advisers, had in the end advised him to get rid of the minuscule gasoline tax altogether because he might not pass anything otherwise. Key Democrats from Western states were balking: it was unfair to their constituents, they said, to raise the gasoline tax. Out west, geography and the culture require the use of a personal motor vehicle to get anywhere, especially a job. Somehow Western Democrats decided 4.3 cents per gallon was acceptable, while a nickel or 6 cents wasn't.

It was true that Congress had done much the same thing in 1990, when George Bush acquiesced to a Democratic plan to get the deficit down by an estimated $490 billion over five years, only to see a recession, fluctuating interest rates, and rising unemployment turn the econometric models upside down. But this was significantly different on a couple of key points, one of which was that Clinton didn't acquiesce. He actually took the lead.

His budget was based on credible numbers and his own initiative and personal recommendations for specific tax increases and spending cuts. He eschewed gimmicks, except for his brief flirtation with a "deficit-reduction trust fund," which meant nothing real. Otherwise he rejected illusory generalities like constitutional amendments to balance the budget and generic "caps" on spending that ignored the real issue of who would take responsibility for the pain or inconvenience.

His plan may not have been enough for some. It may have been too much for a few. It may have taxed now and cut later. In fact, it did precisely that. It may have been smoke-and-mirrors in terms of packaging and marketing. It relied very little on actual spending reductions, but on the reductions in the rate of spending growth in what are known as "out years." But at least it was an exercise in responsibility and initiative, and a pragmatic, credible, finely synthesized step in the right direction.

Clinton's budget was such an amalgam of increments, so much a collection of a little of this and a little of that, that it seemed to defy supportive passion and fervor. Instead, as a middle ground, it invited opposing passion and fervor from all directions. It was just bold enough to frighten easily pressured Southern Democrats such as David Boren of Oklahoma, who yielded to a television advertising campaign in his state against the BTU tax paid for by the oil industry. It was just timid enough to allow Republicans and deficit-hawk Democrats to criticize it as too little, though Republicans managed to have things both ways: they said the spending reductions were insufficient, but they opposed the biggest real one in the defense budget.

Then as the program began to unravel through congressional changes and Clinton's retreats, Senate Majority Leader George Mitchell and Senator Daniel Patrick Moynihan of New York, chairman of the Senate Finance Committee, had to rescue it, both in terms of making the program add up and then finessing the product through the congressional minefield. Things had changed since the first week of Clinton's presidency when an unidentified White House staffer, obviously heady with inaugural excitement, was quoted in *Time* magazine as saying that if the independent and unpredictable Moynihan wouldn't go along, the White House would roll over him. That had sent Clinton scurrying to the telephone to apologize to the senator, and good relations had been slow in developing. But finally they did.

One day in June, as the budget was tied up in the Senate Finance Committee, by Moynihan, and as the BTU tax had been declared dead and awaited a less-bold replacement, Moynihan called Mack McLarty, the chief of staff with whom he couldn't quite connect, to say he was preparing to go on a network news program. Moynihan wondered if he should refer on the program to a gasoline tax or a broad-based energy tax as the replacement for the BTU tax. He would say either one; he merely awaited orders. McLarty suggested he refer to a broad-based energy tax, and he did. But what was worked out a few days later was only a gasoline tax, and it was Moynihan who did the trench-work. He could have answered his question better than McLarty.

The White House, by then appearing almost Reaganesque in its detachment, participated in the late stages of the conference committee work only by listing four or five principles to which it wanted adherence. The cumulative five-year deficit reduction had to top $490 billion, for example, to exceed the amount in the plan Bush acquiesced to in 1990, and there had to be some kind of energy tax. Months later, senior White House aide Bruce Lindsey would complain that the White House kept publicly setting thresholds to define its own success, giving opponents a fat target.

To achieve the budget reduction it demanded, the White House had no option but to make income-tax-rate increases for high-income taxpayers retroactive to January 1, 1993, a thoroughly unpopular idea that put Clinton in the position of taxing dead people and being defenseless against the rhetorical lambasting by Republicans. Weeks before, White House economic czar Robert Rubin, a Wall Street multi-millionaire, had appeared on "This Week with David Brinkley" on ABC and performed miserably when Sam Donaldson pressed him on the retroactivity. Rubin called it a "minor point" that the Congress could deal with "in its wisdom." But it was not a minor point to those paying, though it might have seemed so to a Wall Street mogul, and the public had no great confidence in the wisdom of Congress. Rubin didn't appear on many national television interviews for a while.

The effect of all this was that Clinton got no credit, only ignominy, for what should have been declared on balance a worthy exercise in presidential responsibility and leadership.

I found few people who believed as strongly as I did that despite the false packaging, tactical blunders, weak retreats, and rhetorical lapses, Clinton deserved respect for pursuing and adhering to the wise, balanced, and responsible course that America needed.

Most of those who advocated cutting spending more deeply enjoyed freedom to say so without bearing responsibility. Deeper cuts in subsidies or entitlement programs carried compensatory prices somewhere else, maybe at the grocery store or on hospital bills. Simply taking the government out of the subsidizing business wouldn't lower costs; it would merely transfer the costs to consumers, and thus amount to a hidden tax increase.

It certainly was true that Clinton could have tried to kill the expensive NASA space station program or the super-conducting super-collider research project, both based in Texas. But there were political realities to consider: he had promised a vital friend and Democratic colleague, Texas Governor Ann Richards, that he wouldn't do so. And he needed to try to help Bob Krueger, the Democrat who had been appointed to take Treasury Secretary Lloyd Bentsen's seat in the Senate. In the end, Krueger was beaten horribly in a special election; Clinton trimmed the space station's costs, and the House of Representatives killed the super-collider for him.

Tunnel-visioned deficit hawks in the Congress and elsewhere wouldn't have to answer the White House switchboard and face the wrath of retirees, middle-income taxpayers, farmers, and consumers if they proposed honest-to-goodness budget cutters such as means-testing Medicare, eliminating cost-of-living raises for Social Security retirees, raising the retirement age, putting a ceiling on the deductibility of mortgage interest, doing away with myriad agriculture subsidies, or, as Ross Perot had advocated in a previous life, putting 50 cents, not 4.3 cents, in additional taxes on a gallon of gasoline.

And, naturally, Clinton looked to a synthesis of ideas so that he could actually pass a bill. He understood that the one thing people wanted most was an end to gridlock. He understood that a 43 percent president must win congressional votes and public support; that he can't order them up on the power of his mandate.

Critics said that Clinton should have been tougher on Congress. At times he should have been. He could have chosen either firm moral leadership or clever synthesis, but it's hard to be a moral leader when you have a 43 percent pulpit. The first thing you must try is to make your pulpit larger. That's what Clinton tried to do. If Congress wouldn't go along with a tax on BTUs or eliminating the honeybee subsidy, what were the odds of Clinton's ramming something really bold down any-one's throat? The only thing his one vain attempt at great moral lead-ership had netted him—when he stood for the principle of not discriminating against gays—was his hat in his hand.

The irony was that Clinton had shown courage by choosing a wisely moderate course while nearly everyone else advocated one reckless or politically unachievable extreme or another. In Washington, simple rhetoric from Congress can seem so exciting and refreshing in contrast to the pronouncements of a minority president saddled with respon-sibility, debt, and the necessity of building a bigger consensus.

A couple of months after the budget vote, I said all of this to Bruce Lindsey, by then winding down his massive assignment as White House personnel director and taking a more comfortable role as senior adviser and Clinton's aide-de-camp. He merely looked at me and chuckled. Maybe he was taken aback to hear something good about Clinton's budget. Maybe he was thinking that at least the chapter on the budget plan would be friendly. Finally he quoted an old column I'd written in which I said that when I began agreeing with Clinton, the president was in a world of political trouble.

That happened to be the interview in which Lindsey tried to explain away some of Clinton's early problems adjusting to Washington by saying, "We weren't the favored candidate of Democrats in Washington; Bob Kerrey was."

While that may have been true of the ten-mile square called the District of Columbia, an insular place of pundits and politicos where predictions often are as wrong as the after-the-fact analyses are pithily omniscient, Clinton was the favored candidate of the rest of the Dem-ocratic establishment. He raised more money than Kerrey. He had a better campaign apparatus. He landed the Democratic establishment's celebrity strategist, James Carville, and celebrity fund-raiser, Bob Farmer. He had the backing of the Democratic Leadership Council and most of the Democratic governors and all of the leading moderate Southern blacks—Mike Espy of Mississippi, John Lewis of Georgia, and William J. Jefferson of Louisiana.

He had something else that Kerrey lacked: a coherent message and the ability to articulate it with fresh appeal.

It was strange, then, and somewhat unfair, that on the night of August 6, 1993, when Clinton's budget edged into law, the spotlight was stolen by that same Bob Kerrey, the Vietnam War hero and iconoclastic Democratic senator from Nebraska.

As a presidential candidate Kerrey had advocated national health insurance and had been in lockstep with Clinton on the sop to the middle class: a financially irresponsible tax cut that might buy with the government's charge card some of the middle-class votes that had gone Republican through the 1980s.

But now Kerrey preached courage, boldness, sacrifice by the middle class, deep spending cuts, and deficit reduction. He was Paul Tsongas reincarnated, but with matinée appeal.

Kerrey said that Clinton's budget-cutting efforts were too little and too timid, and that the president hadn't displayed sufficient leadership. This from a man whose national health insurance plan would have been expensive; whose support for a middle-class tax cut would have exacerbated the deficit for the purpose of voter pandering; and who only weeks before had declared in *The New Republic* that Clinton's proposed tax on BTUs, which would have asked a slightly greater sacrifice than the simple gasoline tax that the Senate replaced it with, was so academically complex as to be suspect. Now he was saying that Clinton had been on the right track with the BTU tax, and shouldn't have backed away from it.

The White House was in no position to make an issue of Kerrey's contradictions or accuse him of hollow grandstanding. It could only listen. On the day of the vote in the Senate, the White House could count 49 votes for the president's budget after frenzied dealmaking and unabashed appeals to tepid Democratic supporters to vote to save the president. It could count 50 certain "no" votes. Gore would break the tie on a 50-to-50 vote, but Kerrey had to vote "yes" to give Gore that chance.

Until the evening of August 6, Kerrey pondered, evaded, and soaked up the media's fascination. He was interviewed on the afternoon of the vote by a gaggle of reporters in the hallway of his office building, and his meandering analysis of the effect of voting either way was stupefying.

He couldn't beat Clinton in the Democratic presidential race, but now he could save or ruin him, or so the pundits declared, and he kept the president hanging.

Clinton and Kerrey were friends, and still are. They jog together. Kerrey had spoken up for Clinton on the issue of gays in the military, lending his credibility as a winner of the Congressional Medal of Honor. They had at least two candid personal visits, one quite heated, during the intensive White House courtship of Kerrey's vote. They had generational and political bonds.

Clinton had seriously considered Kerrey as his running mate, to the point of sneaking him into Little Rock for a late-night visit at the Governor's Mansion, but settled in the end on Gore, the Southerner with a moderate reputation and a large and handsome family. Gore had a wife who didn't like dirty song lyrics. Kerrey was divorced and had shacked up in the Nebraska Governor's Mansion with Debra Winger, the actress.

It was interesting to consider the twists of fate. If Clinton had picked Kerrey, might it have been Kerrey casting the tie-breaking vote and Gore holding out to the last minute, appearing the thoughtful statesman, devoted to the end to bold and courageous leadership?

Others in the White House lobbied Kerrey exhaustively and found him ever affable. No one seemed to resent him. White House officials enjoyed Kerrey's charisma and wit. Kerrey told White House lobbyists at one point that considering the pressure he was under, or had put himself under, he felt like John Wayne Bobbitt.

Four days before the vote, Kerrey agreed to meet for lunch with David Gergen, Mack McLarty, and Howard Paster. Kerrey went to the American Cafe near the Capitol; Gergen took McLarty and Paster to the American Cafe on Fourteenth Street Northwest near the White House. They finally made connections by phone, and Gergen, McLarty, and Paster went to Kerrey.

"I thought you were supposed to know Washington," McLarty said to Gergen as they scrambled to get to the right restaurant. This was the odd couple: McLarty was short, a stickler for courtesy and detail, and a Washington novice; Gergen was tall, chronically late for appointments, disorganized, and a consummate Washington insider. But there they were—the president's Mutt and Jeff—attending Bob Kerrey's court.

Throughout Kerrey's Hamlet routine, Washington insiders assumed that Clinton would prevail. They had assumed as much on each of the three narrow preceding votes on the budget: the first in the House on May 27 when it passed by 219 to 213; then in the Senate on June 25 when it passed by 50 to 49 on Gore's vote; then by a single vote in the House August 5, on the conference committee report to reconcile differences between the original House and Senate versions.

Each time the insiders had been right—but barely. They were right that Clinton surely could garner party loyalty or cash in a chit or make a deal to put himself over the top. On each occasion the White House had a very tenuous couple of votes that it probably—*probably*—could have called on.

So it was with Bob Kerrey. "Surely" he would vote in the end to salvage Clinton. "Probably" he could be counted on. He had put himself in a situation to decide Clinton's fate; now, ruining his friendly adversary would cause him more problems than saving him. And, posturing aside, he was more friend than foe of the White House.

Into the early evening of August 6, Kerrey was lobbied by everyone from Bob Dole to Clinton to Moynihan. The New York senator was a friend of Kerrey; he had, in fact, been a major backer of Kerrey's poorly executed presidential campaign. Finally, late that day, Kerrey let the White House know that he would vote to save the president.

Other members of Congress had extracted all kinds of concessions for such votes. But Kerrey aimed for statesmanship. In exchange for his "yes" vote he wanted two things—more spending cuts later, and to take the Senate floor before the eyes of C-SPAN, CNN, and the world and call his friendly adversary a weak man.

At that point, Clinton would take it in a trice. He would pressure Al Gore to come up with expedited savings on the project undertaken by a group he headed to "reinvent government" through efficiencies and modernization. What Kerrey meant was something bigger, but Clinton knew that any real savings he might find would be needed first for health care reform, then for welfare reform. He would promise more cuts now and worry about delivery when he crossed the bridge. Back in Arkansas, legislators and lobbyists had learned that Clinton didn't always deliver.

Predictably, when Kerrey argued for more spending cuts in November, the White House opposed him, though it did appoint him to a special task force assigned to find ways to cut the growth in spending for federal entitlement programs like Social Security, Medicare, and Medicaid. That was another of Clinton's favored tactics from Arkansas when confronted with a promise he couldn't keep: appoint a task force, put your loudest critics on it, and ask for a report.

As for being called weak, Clinton wasn't at all unaccustomed to that. He'd reconciled himself years before to winning while resembling a "walking sore," and winning ugly had carried him all the way to the White House. Hearing a condescending nationally televised lecture from a likable man he had defeated was a simple enough price to pay for getting the damnable budget—"the bone in the throat," he called it—behind him.

In mid-evening, past the normal dinner hour, Kerrey took the floor of the Senate for his spotlight dance. The Washington punditocracy declared his speech candid and extraordinary, and, in truth, it wasn't bad. Had he given such a speech as a candidate, he might be the president, some of the pundits said. I'd heard the same thing for years about any number of post-defeat speeches given by failed presidential candidates. All it meant was that rhetoric was easier than reality, and that pundits fall in love with political also-rans as they grow tired of critiquing the winners.

Kerrey's appeal for sacrifice by the middle class bore no resemblance whatever to what he had promised as a short-time presidential candidate. And suddenly he seemed positively enamored of that ominously academic BTU tax.

This is what he said:

"Mr. President, I've taken too long, I'm afraid, to make this decision. My head aches with all this thinking, but my heart aches with the conclusion that I will vote yes for a bill that challenges America too little because I do not trust what my colleagues on the other side of the aisle will do if I say no.

"Individually, the Republicans in this body are fine and able people— patriots, parents, God-fearing citizens who came here to serve their country as every other member of this body. Collectively, however, you have locked yourselves into the idea of opposition—opposition not to an idea, but to a man, a man who came to this town green and inexperienced in our ways. And he wants America to do better, to be better, and to continue to believe in the invincibility of ideas, of courage, and action.

"Oh, you say this plan doesn't have enough cuts; you say it is too heavy on taxes. One by one, you have approached, however, individuals and groups to tell them the price of this program is too high. Oh, how I wish this evening that I could trust you. But the truth, Mr. President, is in fact that the price of this proposal is too low. It's too little to match the greatness needed from Americans now at this critical moment in this world's history.

"This is not to say we are free from blame on this side of the aisle [Democrats]. When the challenge came from someone who didn't want to pay or didn't want to accept less from their government, we unfortunately all too often ran, too. We ran when opposition arose to the BTU tax. We ran when some seniors said they didn't want to pay higher taxes. We ran, Mr. President, when the program-getters, the salary-seekers, the pay raise–hunters, the COLA-receivers [cost-of-living adjustments on Social Security], and other solicitors begged us to leave them alone.

"So I vote yes, Mr. President. . . .

"President Clinton, if you are watching now, as I suspect you are, I tell you this: I could not and should not cast the vote that brings down your presidency. You have made mistakes and know it far better than I. But you do not deserve and America cannot afford to have you spend the next sixty days quibbling over whether or not we should have this cut or this tax increase.

"America also cannot afford, Mr. President, to have you take the low road of the too-easy compromise, of the too-early collapse. You have gotten where you are today because you are strong, not because you are weak. Get back on the high road, Mr. President, where you were at your best. . . .

"What do we achieve by our actions, Mr. President? Unfortunately it is disdain, distrust, and disillusionment. Shared sacrifice, Mr. President, is our highest ideal, and the only way we will build the moral consensus needed to end this nightmare of borrowing from our children. Get back on the high road, Mr. President. On February 17 [the date of Clinton's State of the Union speech] you told America that our tax system must encourage us to save rather than consume. Savings, Mr. President, is just as difficult as shared sacrifice. To save, I must say no to something that I want now because I believe deeply that the dollar I save today will be worth more tomorrow. You have the right idea, Mr. President, with the BTU tax, and when we came after you with both barrels blazing, threatening to walk if you did not yield, you should have let us walk. You should have said to us that at least we'd be exercising something other than our mouths. Instead we find ourselves with a bill that asks Americans to pay 4.3 cents a gallon more. If they notice, I'll be surprised. If they complain, I will be ashamed. . . ."

Kerrey cast the fiftieth vote. Gore cast the fifty-first. And they breathed a sigh of relief in the White House. It was better to look bad and win than to look bad and lose.

* * *

That final Senate vote was no more dramatic or death-defying than the preceding three—the first go-rounds in the House and Senate and then the conference committee vote in the House.

In fact, the very first vote, the opener in the House on May 27 when the bill passed by a tally of 219 to 213, thought to be the easiest of all, may have been the most frightening. It sent the president into a tizzy.

On that afternoon Clinton and George Stephanopoulos were holed up in the Oval Office poring over the roster of House membership and working the telephones. Stephanopoulos, still the communications director at the time—for a few hours, as it turned out—was doing dual service as spokesman and right-hand man. His experience as a top aide to Representative Richard Gephardt, the House majority leader, made him valuable in sizing up the House.

Stephanopoulos is notoriously pessimistic and fatalistic, and frequently takes on a kind of hang-dog, beaten-down demeanor. Mack McLarty walked in to see how things were going, and Stephanopoulos despaired. "We don't have the votes," he said. It wasn't the first or last time he would say it. This was George's lament.

McLarty had been busy all day working on his new best friend, Senator John Breaux of Louisiana, who mixed a laid-back Southern style with a dry wit and clever political instincts and was Clinton's successor as chairman of the "new Democrat" Democratic Leadership Council. Breaux, being from an energy-producing state, had decided that the BTU tax had to go.

It mattered what John Breaux thought because he was one of the Democrats composing an eleven-to-nine majority on the Senate Finance Committee, which would consider the president's budget when, and if, it got out of the House. Since David Boren of Oklahoma, a Democrat and Finance Committee member, apparently was jumping ship, Breaux's public opposition would be devastating.

McLarty knew, and Clinton was by now in the process of accepting, that when the budget got to the Senate, the BTU tax would die. But scores of liberal Democrats in the House supported the BTU tax and were prepared to vote for it that night. The White House needed those votes before Breaux announced his apparently decisive opinion of the BTU tax. A dozen or more moderate-to-conservative Democrats would bail out risking a vote for the president's budget as it was proposed that day if they knew that their Senate soulmate, John Breaux, would provide pivotal opposition in the Senate.

McLarty's assignment was to convince Breaux to stay on the ship—
that is, keep mum in public about his opinions and intentions to fight
the BTU tax until after the House voted. Breaux agreed to oblige. He
liked McLarty. He liked the president. He wanted to be helpful; there
was a kind of Southern brotherhood there. Breaux, McLarty, and the
president had gotten together for a special satellite showing in the
White House of the big Arkansas-LSU basketball game, and they had
had a fine time.

Now, with Breaux under control, McLarty asked Stephanopoulos
what he could do to help secure the House votes. It turned out that
there were about six conservative Democrats from Oklahoma, Texas,
and Louisiana who were wavering or opposed. These were McLarty's
people. His gas company had done business in those three states; he'd
contributed heavily to the Democratic Leadership Council, partly because he believed himself a "new Democrat" and partly because it
ingratiated him with his company's congressmen. And, not insignifi-
cantly, as an old gas company chairman McLarty hadn't thought much
of the BTU tax in the first place.

So McLarty called Breaux again. He needed another favor. Would
Breaux take three of those congressmen? McLarty would take the other
three. They needed to land at least half of the six to be safe.

Breaux called back in a few minutes to joke that he had won the
race: he'd already picked up two of his three. McLarty later secured
two commitments. Then, later in the day, he picked up an insurance
third: Dave McCurdy of Oklahoma, another DLC regular who was in
line to succeed Breaux as head of the organization and who had been
strongly considered by Clinton to head the CIA or the Defense
Department.

McCurdy was in such agony that McLarty thought at one point that
the Oklahoman was about to cry. He wanted to back the president,
but the Oklahoma pressure was severe. He couldn't go along with the
BTU tax and there simply weren't enough spending cuts.

McLarty laid it out for him: John Breaux would kill the BTU tax in
the Senate, replacing it with something smaller that would require a
proportionate increase in spending cuts to get the president to his
stated $490-500 billion five-year goal. But, McLarty explained, the
president couldn't come out and declare that as his intent; it would
throw the House into disarray on the day of the vote. But he could
say this much: The BTU tax would be "looked at" in the Senate, and
the president was resigned to the necessity of producing more cuts in

spending with, at the least, tighter restrictions on the projected growth in entitlement spending.

McCurdy asked if he could really trust the president. "He gets it now," McLarty assured him, meaning that Clinton now understood, essentially, that he was a little heavy on taxes, a little light on spending cuts, and a little left of the political center. McCurdy said he would vote with the president, but would reserve the right to explain the background to his local press the next day. Fine, said McLarty, who was desperate.

So as the vote began that evening, Clinton, Al Gore, Stephanopoulos, and McLarty assembled in the president's study off the Oval Office and watched the mounting tally on C-SPAN. Right away the two congress-men whom Breaux thought he had recruited voted "no." Howard Paster, the White House's congressional liaison who was close to the liberals but not the DLC types, called in with the news. "Mack, our strategy isn't working," he said.

McLarty recalled that Clinton turned whiter than he'd ever seen him, except for that night in November 1980 when Clinton realized he had lost his bid for a second gubernatorial term in Arkansas.

"I think we're still all right," McLarty said, listing the three votes he was counting on, including McCurdy's, which would provide a margin of one vote over the 218 needed for a majority.

Then Clinton went into panic. Tired and scared, with his presidency on the line, he became addled when he suddenly thought about the fact that two seats in the House were vacant.

"We didn't think of those," Clinton said frantically. "We're two votes short. We've lost." McLarty thought Clinton might be right.

Stephanopoulos and Gore knew better. They were still trying to convince Clinton that of course they had considered those vacancies, and not quite succeeding in reassuring or calming him, when the final tally rolled on the screen: 219 for, 213 against.

Clinton settled down, then went out to the Rose Garden to make a statement praising the House for its courage.

The highwire presidency, indeed.

The first vote in the Senate on June 25, with the BTU tax out thanks to Breaux, wasn't quite as death-defying. Two senators were absent due to illness: Patty Murray of Washington, who favored the president, and Arlen Specter of Pennsylvania, who didn't. Both sides contemplated hauling their infirm selves to the floor, but then realized it would be needless considering that they'd cancel each other.

Otherwise, the White House had 49 certain votes in favor. That assured a 49-to-49 tie, and Gore would cast the tie-breaker.

Actually, Senator Bennett Johnston of Louisiana told the White House he would vote for the budget if he had to do it, though he would prefer not. So Clinton had a choice: Call in Johnston's chit and win 50 to 48, or let Johnston vote as he preferred and win with Gore. He chose the latter, expecting to save Johnston's support for later.

On the Senate floor, Johnston awaited a hand signal from David Pryor of Arkansas: "up" meant he would be needed to vote "yes"; "down" meant he could vote "no." He got the "down" signal.

What happened, though, was that word got out that Johnston was prepared to vote for the plan if necessary, depriving him of any credibility for his "no" vote with Louisiana constituents. Johnston didn't appreciate that the word leaked. The effect was that he was an absolute and unequivocal "no" for the second vote when it looked for a while that his support would be vital. But then Bob Kerrey came around.

Then when the conference report of the bill came back to the House on August 5, Clinton's own Democratic congressman from Little Rock, one-time friend Ray Thornton, voted against him.

It was an extraordinary thing. In February, I had attended a dinner in Crystal City, Virginia, of chamber of commerce officials from Arkansas at which Thornton was positively giddy about the greatness of Bill Clinton and the success he would gladly help him achieve. Now, less than six months later, Thornton, a chronically nervous man who in 1974 had been the last Democrat on the House Judiciary Committee to make the agonizing decision to vote an article of impeachment against Richard Nixon, jumped ship.

Thornton, a notorious political wind-tester, decided that Clinton's plan had become so politically unpopular even in his home district that he couldn't safely vote for it. He had told the White House of his opposition, but his friends there neither believed nor accepted it

With time expiring on the vote, two more votes were needed for passage and three votes were still uncast. The stragglers were Thornton; Pat Williams of Montana; and a freshman Democrat from a Republican district of Pennsylvania, Marjorie Margolies-Mezvinsky.

The three gathered near the well of the House and looked at each other. Thornton, in seeming agony, shook his head and prepared to fill out his card voting "no." That meant both Williams and Margolies-Mezvinsky had to vote "yes" to save the president. They did so.

Mezvinsky had promised the president she would vote for him if necessary, and now her Democratic colleagues were breathing down her neck as Republicans chanted, "Good-bye, Marjorie." In a daze, she cast the decisive vote for the president's budget, having secured only minutes before Clinton's hurried commitment to come to her district and speak at a conference on entitlement spending. At that point she probably could have been conveyed the deed to the White House.

Thornton, a veteran congressman from a safe district where his reelection was virtually assured, rushed off the floor as members of the House leadership cursed him behind his back for his cowardice, for betraying his own president, and for forcing a green and vulnerable freshman to save the day.

Thornton stopped to tell an Arkansas reporter that his vote was based on the gasoline tax, which he called unfair to his home state, where people drive their motor vehicles more miles per capita than motorists in forty-one other states.

That made little sense. Thornton had been a staunch advocate of the BTU tax, and had voted for it in the first House vote in May. It contained a gasoline tax about 3 cents more per gallon than the one he had just voted against on the contention that it was unfair to his home state.

His vote had to do not with the fluctuation of the gasoline tax but with the fluctuation of the president's popularity.

Would he have voted for Clinton's budget had his vote been necessary? "I would have voted my conscience," Thornton said.

And just what did his conscience tell him? Well, that same night Thornton telephoned an understandably cool Mack McLarty at the White House, where he'd been a helpful insider for months.

"Mack," he said, according to two of McLarty's aides, "you know I was there for you if you had needed me."

Thornton was not a White House insider after that.

He went home to Arkansas to explain to constituents that the Senate had made the budget bill worse by filibustering against it. That wasn't true by any remote stretch of the facts. The budget reconciliation bill could not be filibustered under the rules. Instead, the filibuster had taken place on the $16 billion stimulus bill. All the Senate had done to the budget was lessen the size of the tax that Thornton called unfair to his constituents, one he had supported when it was larger.

"It was an interesting vote. That's all I'm going to say," McLarty told me days later.

I remembered the day in December 1992 in Little Rock when McLarty was announced as Clinton's surprise choice for chief of staff. McLarty mentioned his good friends in Congress, David Pryor and Ray Thornton. He would be counting on their help and counsel, he said.

The Washington pundits decreed Clinton weak because he couldn't win the support of his own congressmen. *The Washington Post* wrote a puff piece on Thornton—"A Thornton in Clinton's Side"—describing him as a man of brave conscience.

Sometimes the Washington pundits could get things wrong. It was true that Thornton's vacillation and betrayal reflected the demise of the popularity of Clinton's program, even the Clinton presidency. But to call Thornton brave and conscientious on the matter of the budget while calling Clinton weak was to have things approximately backward.

With the bone cleared from his throat, Clinton was ready to rest, reassess, then soar in the fall. He had big plans. He also had big problems. As James Carville put it, "People don't know what Clinton-ism is."

More than that, they still didn't know who Bill Clinton was.

They had formed a premature and mostly unflattering judgment, but, like a late-night veto, Clinton's bad image was not yet beyond retrieval.

Chapter 9

What's Our Slogan?

Bill Clinton needed a vacation. The young president known as voracious, energetic, and brimming with optimism and confidence ran low in mid-August.

Clinton had performed with tactical and strategic ineptness; as a clever political analyst and quick study he knew his errors as thoroughly as anyone did. He had been severely bruised by the Washington establishment, which often treats the politics of governing as a contest of will and cleverness, one that Clinton had lost on both counts to the Republicans and the media.

He hadn't dealt with strong Republican opposition in Arkansas, where the legislature met in regular session less than three months every other year. A mere tenth of it was Republican. Nor had Clinton dealt with an unrelenting media. We in the Arkansas press could be fairly tough, or so he thought, but we lacked the Washington press corps' ability or willingness to keep a story alive after the first or second telling.

For example: We would write an article in which an accuser said the governor had improperly interfered to get a state contract for a friend in the advertising business, complete with the governor's denial. We would follow up seeking further information, if not truth. If no one kept talking, we moved on to something else. In Washington, a hint of such inappropriateness by the president would not be abandoned after a two-day hunt.

Clinton had lost a treasured friend and confidant to shocking, numbing suicide, which he suspected would not have happened if his friend hadn't followed him to Washington. He needed to rest, retrench, reflect, ponder, and apply his exceptional analytical and political skills to determining what he had done wrong and what he could henceforth do right.

Alas, he had nowhere to go. He didn't enjoy the seclusion of Camp David, where his chronic allergies, which were severe enough to puff up his face and impair his breathing, were irritated. The quiet bothered him, too. Clinton is not proficient at being alone; if nothing else he'll pick up a telephone.

He'd spent most of the year in Washington, taking no significant break from the messy processes of his governing. As a career politician with little experience outside of election to jobs that provided housing, he was a man without substantial means. He had no San Clemente, no Kennebunkport, no Johnson Ranch, no Hyannis Port, no peanut farm. His mother had a modest lakeside home in Hot Springs and his mother-in-law a modest condominium in midtown Little Rock. Neither offered the size or seclusion preferred by the Secret Service. Bill Clinton was the homeless president. He needed to get away, but possessed no getaway, which seemed to further his image as a pedestrian president. Washington can imprison a president, especially one who seldom gets out of town.

White House reporters, anxious to make their travel arrangements and accustomed to following Reagan and Bush to the lush environs of California or the Maine coast, were led to believe one day that Clinton might vacation at one place at a certain time, then led to believe something a bit different the next day. They joked that this president couldn't even get a vacation right. One day Mark Gearan devoted nearly half his daily briefing to questions about vacation specifics. Since their familiar travel agents were now gone from the White House, the reporters were unusually restless about where and how they would spend this president's vacation.

At the last minute Clinton decreed that he didn't think he would take a vacation at all. According to *Time* magazine, Paul Begala told the president that if he didn't take a vacation the American people would think he was weird, and Clinton replied, "I *am* weird."

Finally he took a vacation, and, typically, the president's late-August getaway turned out to be a worthy product after a messy process. He spent a couple of days in Vail golfing with former President Gerald Ford and Jack Nicklaus, the latter enthralling the president with a subtle tip about how to get up and out of a sand trap. Clinton loves learning; one of his charms is that he goes through life as a bright-eyed schoolboy. Then he went home to Arkansas, to the northwestern corner, where he spent several days reading, relaxing, and pondering his presidency at the lakeside home of his dear friends, Jim and Diane Blair. He golfed with a quartet of old friends. In a cart ride along a fairway with David Matthews, the lawyer and former state legislator who had risen to his defense in New Hampshire in the winter of 1992, Clinton remarked, "I think the American people know that I'm working hard." Matthews laughed. No one, not even the most unreasonably harsh critic, could accuse this president of not working hard.

Later Clinton showed Matthews how to get up and out of a sand trap. "He is incredibly competitive," Matthews said. "He couldn't wait to show someone the tip that Jack Nicklaus had shown him." Clinton loves to expound instructively, whether on the intricacies of the welfare system, the history of the modern presidency, the full-court pressure defense tactics of his beloved University of Arkansas basketball team, or something he just learned about hitting a golf ball.

Then Clinton headed to Martha's Vineyard, the quaint and exclusive New England getaway, where he stayed in the vacation home of Robert McNamara, the Defense Secretary of the Kennedy-Johnson era. The arrangement had been mostly the handiwork of Vernon Jordan, the stately Washington insider who was one of Clinton's best establishment friends. "The Vineyard" was just what Clinton needed: a combination of quiet time and stimulation. He could think, golf, and read, and then he could dine with authors, actors, and other notables. There was enough stimulation to keep him from becoming bored with private thought. There even was a yacht trip with Jackie Onassis and family, which had to be an extraordinary experience for a middle-class man from Arkansas who had idolized and emulated John F. Kennedy. Mack McLarty attended another Onassis-Kennedy function on the Vineyard that week. He was the guest of U.S. Representative Joe Kennedy, a good friend, and McLarty was amused at the seeming irony when Joe advised him ahead of time, "There may be some highbrows there."

As an optimist who practices spin doctoring without even trying, Clinton determined in his reflection that his presidency had been a smashing substantive success and a failure only in style. He believed that the problem was that the American people hadn't fully considered all that had been accomplished.

First there was the enactment of the bill providing family and medical leave from employment. True, it was worthy social progress, but the fact was that it wasn't Clinton's program. The Democratic Congress had passed it the year before and George Bush had vetoed it. Clinton's only role was to sign it.

Second was the enactment of the motor vehicle bill to facilitate voter registration. That was the same story: an existing Democratic initiative that Clinton merely signed.

Clinton had no pride of authorship in either regard. Those weren't initiatives that were identified with him or were particularly reflective of his campaign.

Then there was national service, the touted program to provide college and other post-secondary educations to youths who volunteered to do two years of public service. But it had been so watered down because of fiscal restraints that it would have no great impact on the college-going population. There was a new, streamlined college-loan program designed to appeal to the middle class, but it was a program that people would appreciate only as they learned of it.

And what about the earned-income-tax credit, which would provide tax breaks to low-income workers supporting families? It had been lost in the budget madness because it was in a legislative package that the Republicans had defined as tax-and-spend. (In fact, early in 1994's tax season, Clinton would actually plead with eligible taxpayers to take advantage of it.)

Clinton's legislative batting average was quite good, and he hadn't vetoed a bill. Gridlock had been eased in actuality, though it appeared entrenched in rhetoric.

Then there was the budget itself. It was, in fact, a great victory: For the first time in a dozen years, a president had proposed a credible deficit-reduction plan that the Congress didn't reject out of hand, but passed in a significantly altered yet still recognizable form. Clinton's presidency had hung in the balance of the budget vote; he had survived. Now he was sustained; he could move on. But it was such an ugly victory, and he had suffered such rhetorical damage through Republican portrayals of him as a tax-and-spend liberal, that the substance of what he had accomplished was dwarfed by the seeming ineptness with which he had accomplished it.

Clinton's analysis, then, was that he needed to keep doing what he was doing, but do so more cleverly and sell himself better. He also knew he had to reassert himself as a "new Democrat." Presented a birthday cake at the White House, he joked as he cut it that he would start on the left and work to the center.

He knew too that he needed to define himself more clearly. In Arkansas, he had grabbed in 1983 the motto of better schools and held to it for a decade as the single issue with which voters instinctively associated him. After seven months in Washington, "taxes" and "gays" were the issues associated with him. It had not been possible as president to seize one issue as a defining and popular cloak.

James Carville, though drippingly contemptuous of Ronald Reagan, said that Reagan's political advantage had been that people thought they knew what he was all about: lower taxes and a tougher defense, the former supposedly to stimulate the economy and the latter supposedly to win the Cold War. Carville said the nuances and complexities of the post–Cold War era, and of Clinton's expansive agenda and synthesized policy initiatives, left people pretty much without a clue as to the essence of the man and his presidency.

As Clinton returned from vacation for his autumn agenda, he had made these decisions and therefore confronted these circumstances:

- He had decided to adhere to an activist agenda because the American people wanted action. That meant he would push a massive reform of the nation's health care system, partly because it would put his government in the position of trying to help the middle class.

- He had no choice but to decide what to do about the North American Free Trade Agreement (NAFTA), since the deadline for congressional ratification of the treaty negotiated by the Bush administration was nigh. As an avowed free trader who had committed as a candidate to an essentially unassailable position—he favored NAFTA, but with new side agreements—he knew he had to go forward with it. He also believed in it.

- He already had dispatched Vice President Gore to lead a task force on one of his favored modern concepts—"reinventing government"—to apply the efficiencies of technology and the leaner-is-better philosophy of corporate America to government. Since he was under attack for not having cut spending enough in his budget, he would accelerate that project to try to claim "new Democrat" spending cuts.

- Polls showed Americans more fearful than ever of violent crime, which they perceived to be growing out of control although, in truth, the incidence of violent crime was down slightly from recent years in some of the urban areas, such as Washington, D.C. But with front-page accounts of drive-by shootings and stray bullets from gang members striking young children on public playgrounds, Clinton instinctively sensed that Americans wanted him to show toughness on crime. If he could embrace a law-and-order position, he could reposition himself on the philosophical spectrum. If he could fashion a law-and-order image while favoring the Brady Bill and bans on some so-called assault weapons, the kind of finesse and synthesis I had seen him accomplish in Arkansas, he would show himself a politician for the ages.

So this was the plan: Work to give Americans security in their health care, support NAFTA to appear presidential, and embrace "reinventing government" and crime to try to position himself as a "new Democrat" and the first Democrat in a generation or more to try to take a couple of defining domestic issues away from Republicans: smaller government and law and order.

How, then, could he blend those seemingly disconnected initiatives into a seemingly connected theme so that Americans could get an idea what Clintonism was—beyond, that is, an attempted clever synthesis to fashion a reelection equation? How could he appear to the American people to be doing one thing generally, rather than too many things specifically?

James Carville gave that assignment a try with a guest column on the Op-Ed page of *The Washington Post* seeking to connect health care reform and NAFTA. But what he wrote was the partisan positioning of an unreconstructed political operative. He said Republicans should not be allowed to get away with serving their corporate constituents by supporting the president on NAFTA while not serving the interests of businesses and their employees on the need to overhaul the health insurance system.

Such attempted policy synthesis was not Carville's forte. His forte was slogans; hence, "The economy, stupid." His was an instinct for connecting with middle America, which, as he liked to put it, spent its time scouring outlet malls in a diligent search for bargains. He liked to say that the most popular tourist spot in history-rich Virginia was not Mount Vernon, Monticello, or Colonial Williamsburg, but the Potomac Mills outlet mall.

Yet in September when I spoke with him briefly to inquire about the political ramifications of Clinton's support for NAFTA, and as Carville endeavored to explain that NAFTA's political ramifications could not be considered separately from the other autumn initiatives, the best he could do for a possible slogan to define Clintonism was: "Work hard, work smart."

Yes, governing was proving harder than campaigning. Carville meant that the essence of Clinton's initiatives was that America needed to work harder and smarter to keep its population affordably healthy, streamline its government to attack debt and profligacy, and encourage its business and industry to modernize to compete in the new global economy with the twenty-first century on the horizon. But "Work hard, work smart" sounded like an admonition to the president himself. I never heard any more about it except when I was teased by Mack McLarty about having suggested in a newspaper column that it might be the emerging motto of the Clinton administration.

Essentially Clinton returned to the White House with two general objectives: Push a massive health care reform system that would extend irrevocable health insurance to every American; and appear more a centrist and "new Democrat" than he had appeared previously because of gays in the military and a budget containing tax increases.

Typically, these objectives competed. Clinton's health care reform proposal, designed by his wife and a vast task force, was an attempted synthesis much as his budget had been an attempted synthesis. It was a hybrid plan somewhere left of the center and somewhere right of the left—in no-man's-land. It was an attempt to split the difference between the traditional liberal view for a single-payer, Canadian-style health care and the DLC model requiring additional personal responsibility and steering clear of mandates on business.

Three factors led him to such a proposal.

First, the president's sense of history and his reading of the public's mandate for change convinced him that extending health care to all Americans was the great social need of his generation. He couldn't credibly extend health insurance without paying for it, thus he proposed the mandate that employers pay into purchasing pools on behalf of all their employees—which amounted to a tax, according to the Congressional Budget Office.

Second, his pollster, Stanley Greenberg, was a supposed "new Democrat," but one who veered from the DLC on the issue of health care. Greenberg's polls convinced the president that middle-class people did not object to entitlement programs altogether, but only to entitlement programs that cost them money and to which they weren't entitled. About 70 percent of Americans desired the permanent security of universal health insurance that would not be denied by unemployment, sickness, or job change. Therefore, Clinton thought the route to a "new Democrat" appeal to the middle class would be to give the middle class an entitlement. On the contrary, the DLC thought the route to a middle-class connection was to hold costs down through managed competition and ask shared responsibility among the middle class, primarily by limiting the full deduction allowed employers on their group health insurance contributions.

Third, Hillary Clinton, whose ability to focus on a complex issue and master it was greatly admired by her husband, convinced the president that unlike more politically palatable plans, hers actually would work to the desired end—universal health coverage with generous benefits for a reasonable amount of money and an eventual restraining of health care cost increases. She was confident that her task force had designed a thorough proposal. One of the problems with American health insurance was that people couldn't change jobs without risking the loss of it; she would change that. Another was that people with medical conditions couldn't get affordable insurance and therefore relied on public health services subsidized by taxpayers; she would change that. Another was that vibrant young people with good jobs who thought they would live forever simply declined to buy health insurance, raising the costs for everyone else; she would require those people to pay 20 percent of their health insurance costs through their workplaces. And too many employers relied on part-time or temporary employees and provided no employment benefits to them; Rodham Clinton would require a partial payment into a health care plan by all employers for all part-time and temporary employees.

To address the spiraling cost of health premiums, a spiral that actually abated in 1993, she would impose premium caps. Americans fearful of losing the right to choose their doctor would be allowed to steer clear of health maintenance organizations and go to their preferred doctor, though it might cost them extra. Cigarette smokers took health risks that caused cancer; she would charge them for their habit. In lawyerly fashion, she had assessed every problem and proposed a narrow solution. But on the whole, her program scared conservatives, and it eventually began to scare the decisive middle class, because it certainly put government more into the business of health care than it was already. The danger was that the health plan would meet the same fate in 1994 that the budget met in 1993: it was a responsible plan that would probably reap desired benefits, but it risked definition as tired and failed liberalism.

Outside of his daughter, I doubt there are any two people more important to Bill Clinton than his wife and his pollster. The political complication was that his wife and pollster were tugging him toward the left on health care at the very time he was determined to reclaim the political center on NAFTA, crime, and "reinventing government"— at the very time, in fact, that he needed to show Americans a clear, central, uncontradicted identity and appear a "new Democrat" truer to the Democratic Leadership Council heritage.

A year before, at the annual dinner of the DLC, President-elect Clinton had delivered a triumphant address. A black-tie, job-seeking crowd filled the main floor of Washington's sprawling Union Station, overflowing to hallways and anterooms where big-screen televisions were set up for closed-circuit viewings of this "new Democrat," the favored son of the DLC, who was now ready to run the country on the principles of centrist, neo-activist thinkers once dubbed by Jesse Jackson as "Democrats for the Leisure Class."

The conversation that evening centered on the contrast with DLC functions in the past, which sometimes filled only partitioned sections of hotel ballrooms. The toast of the evening was Al From, a veteran Washington staffer and a rotund fireplug of a fellow. He was the president and driving force of the DLC. He had declared for years that someday the "new Democrats" would emerge; that only a "new Democrat" could win back "Reagan Democrats" and regain the White House; and that the governor down in Arkansas by the name of Bill Clinton was the likeliest agent.

At the time From was on loan to the Clinton transition team as domestic policy adviser. It was not a job he had wanted in the administration; he would return to the DLC and lead the organization that, with its sister think tank, the Progressive Policy Institute, would be to Clinton what the Heritage Foundation had been to Reagan: the powerful, in-vogue house of modern political thought.

Clinton had been a two-year chairman of the DLC, and From told friends that no other chairman of the group—not Chuck Robb, Dick Gephardt, Sam Nunn, or John Breaux—had done as well in comprehending the "new Democrat" message and articulating it. From believed that the political strategists such as Carville and Stephanopoulos had been given entirely too much credit for Clinton's election as president. It was Clinton himself, From believed, who went from stage to stage, by bus and plane, articulating a vision that the DLC embraced and which appealed to swing voters who had left the Democratic Party in the 1980s. One of From's theories was that the political operatives could err during the campaign and skirt exposure because Clinton covered for them since the focus was on his daily performance, but that once Clinton was elected, staff errors came to the forefront because Clinton wasn't on the road selling.

In public throughout 1993, From gave Clinton credit for "new Democrat" initiatives such as national service for college youth, an improved college-loan program, and NAFTA, and for advancing such ideas as welfare reform, a school-to-work program blending education and job training, apprenticeships, and reform of the government's myriad and bureaucracy-laden job-training programs. In those areas where Clinton had veered to the left—on gays in the military, the budget, and health care—From and his DLC friends tended to blame the people around the president, mainly Hillary, Gore, Stephanopoulos, and the labor-friendly chief congressional liaison, Howard Paster.

From explained publicly that history had made Clinton a Democratic president at a time of transition for the party from the traditional left to the modern center on economic and social issues. Because of that, he said, Clinton had to behave as a "bridge" between the declining old and the emerging new.

But in private From and his allies spent much of the year fuming as Clinton seemed most influenced by Greenberg's poll-driven definition of a "new Democrat" with middle-class appeal. From peppered the White House with memoranda on political and policy strategy for adhering to the safe, pragmatic political center. Clinton even joked about it, saying that From reminded him of Tom Watson, the golfing great and Ryder Cup team captain who, when visiting the White House, counseled Clinton on his golf swing, advising him how to balance the left hand and the right to keep the ball straight.

From and the DLC advocated stimulating competition to drive health care costs down, and asking people to take a measure of personal responsibility, which they would exercise by taking affirmative action to join a health plan and surrendering the benefits of the full deduction of health insurance costs enjoyed by employers. The DLC did not advocate universal coverage as an automatic entitlement; it advocated making coverage universally accessible, not universally guaranteed. The DLC asked: Why force businesspeople to pay more because some people were too individually irresponsible to get health insurance? Greenberg, on the other hand, advocated government's granting middle-class people something they deserved: automatic health insurance that would go with them from job to job and could never be taken away. Health care would fill in where Clinton's promised middle-class tax cut had been abandoned.

Not to be forgotten was the traditional left and its affection for a single-payer, Canadian-style system in which government would take over health care and pay the bills. It was supported by a formidable bloc important to Clinton, but it was not passable, nor was it acceptable to the middle class.

Clinton, armed with Greenberg's polls and influenced by Hillary, believed he saw the clever blend he always seeks. He would set up a system of large regional purchasing alliances to provide for so-called managed competition in health insurance plans. Through the leverage of their size and buying power, these alliances would stimulate price competition and greater reliance on alternative insurance plans such as health maintenance organizations (HMOs). But Clinton also would build quite an extensive government apparatus to assure and regulate Greenberg's middle-class entitlement program. Any state so liberal as to desire a single-payer system would be authorized to establish one.

This was the failed formula of Clinton's budget plan—a little something for everyone, a dose of liberalism and a dose of centrism.

Earlier in the year, From's view of health reform—stimulate competition to cut costs and get the deficit down, extend the availability of insurance by preaching personal responsibility without guaranteeing coverage by government entitlement or regulating it by heavy bureaucracy, or paying for it by mandated payments on business—seemed to be carrying the day at the White House.

In the spring, Senator David Pryor, whose work on drug pricing and other health issues as chairman of the Senate Aging Committee made him a natural ally of his friends in the White House on health care reform, told me that the White House agreed with him that no new health care system could be sold to Congress or the American people if it was portrayed and defined as either a tax proposal or a social program. It must be sold as deficit reduction.

But by fall, the White House knew it couldn't get away with misleading the American people—health care reform would cost more in the short term. Greenberg and his polls had carried the day on the selling point. No longer would the thrust be cost control or deficit reduction; it would be "security," designed and marketed as the greatest social program since Social Security itself.

When Clinton declared himself flexible on all points except universal coverage, Pryor gulped. But, typically, Clinton left himself room for rhetoric. On universal coverage, he didn't say when and he didn't say how.

Still, the very tactic that David Pryor had said in the spring would not work was the tactic eventually embraced at the White House by the fall.

The DLC torch was carried, meanwhile, by Representative Jim Cooper of Tennessee and Mack McLarty's good buddy, Senator John Breaux of Louisiana, who had been instrumental at pulling Clinton toward the center on the budget battle. Their plan was hotter than Clinton's on Capitol Hill at year's end, yet Hillary and Greenberg assured Clinton that the Cooper-Breaux bill would not hold up to scrutiny. It was a pragmatic political approach, but a fatally flawed policy approach.

"Some sausage is going to be inevitable here," Mack McLarty said, referring to the adage that the American legislative process resembles sausage making: it's better to enjoy the finished product than watch the ugly process. McLarty expressed confidence that a health care compromise could be achieved so long as a friend like Breaux was on the opposing side. He expected essentially a reprise of the budget battle—a death-defying walk along the highwire ending in a narrow victory for an altered proposal that, in time, would prove itself sound and effective policy.

There was a certain smugness at the White House, where it was believed that Republicans did not want to face the mid-term elections having blocked any reform of health insurance. The smugness was based on a belief, not ill-founded, that Clinton and his wife had so effectively seized health reform as their issue that they would get the lion's share of credit for whatever eventually was enacted.

Political fortunes in America turn on the superficial assessments of working-class people who don't have the time to follow the intricacies of government, but who know what they want. What they wanted in the fall of 1993 was affordable, irrevocable health insurance, jobs, a more efficient government, and a war on crime. Bill Clinton was prepared to give them all that, and, at last, he thought he had a slogan: "Security."

That was what the body of research had shown as American's greatest interest. Though the reference was to health care, the White House decided to embrace the word and the concept and apply it to all the policy initiatives in an attempt to connect them to an understandable theme.

"Security," for these purposes, meant not only health care, but a deficit-reduction plan to lessen the long-term threat of mounting public debt. It also meant preparing America for the perils of the modern global economy, and thus it applied to Clinton's embracing NAFTA. Of course it applied to fighting crime by making people feel more secure in their homes and on the streets. And, in the end, "security" was what foreign policy was all about.

Clinton gave a couple of speeches developing the theme of "security," but mostly the press reported his transparent effort to find a theme and a slogan, not the points he made. That's the danger in a presidential tactic: the Washington press corps, always pursuing an inside story rather than an outside one, will report and analyze the tactic rather than the points made in the course of trying the tactic.

The brilliance of Clinton's campaign had been based on well-articulated themes and simple slogans. But Clinton the candidate and Clinton the officeholder were different people doing entirely different jobs. Unless one is as simplistic and fortunate as Reagan, a president can't easily define himself and his philosophy in a few understandable words and phrases. The problem is that the pace of events forces a president to confront unexpected problems.

For example: At the very time Clinton talked about "security," his foreign policy appeared to offer anything but. His Achilles heel was exposed. Clinton had hoped to coast through foreign policy for his first year. The world wouldn't let him.

In a nine-day span in early October as he endeavored to redefine himself and give his ambitious domestic agenda a cogent central message of "security," eighteen American servicemen under U.N. supervision were killed in Somalia; Boris Yeltsin routed right-wing insurgents who were trying to take over his government in Russia; and a ship loaded with lightly armed American soldiers on a mission to provide technical assistance to assist the return of ousted Haitian President Jean-Bertrand Aristide turned back because of armed thugs awaiting it in Port-au-Prince.

Congress went into a near panic about the confused state of American international strategies and its lack of confidence in the new president and his foreign policy team.

Many in the Clinton administration became defensive and contentious at the mention of Clinton's desire to coast through foreign policy in the beginning. Yet it wasn't criticism; it was sound observation. While it implied detachment, there were good political and policy reasons for Clinton to try to keep foreign policy in the background. There also was prominent precedent.

Ronald Reagan had hoped to coast through foreign policy in his first year, and mostly he succeeded. In his first year Reagan chewed out a State Department official because an international issue had shown up on the front page of *The New York Times*. He wanted nothing to distract from his tax-cut proposal and his so-called New Federalism. Yes, it implied detachment. By his second term, Reagan would plead innocence to a scandal in his own White House over the Iran-contra affair by invoking that very detachment from foreign policy detail.

Clinton encountered different circumstances in a different era.

He was the first president elected since the end of the Cold War. He had defeated a foreign policy specialist who had led America to a gloriously triumphant war not two years before. Clinton had promised to focus on the economy and to extend health care. When he talked of foreign policy in the campaign, he did so with the easy rhetoric of an outsider and a challenger. He talked tough about removing China's most-favored-nation status if it did not change its ways in violating human rights and suppressing its people, but that was an irresponsible, self-penalizing idea from which he not-so-subtly retreated once elected. He talked with great moral leadership about using America's military might to combat inhumanity in the world's complex new hot spots, such as Bosnia, and to promote democracy and market economies.

Once he was elected, the issues became tougher, with military advisers questioning the clarity of the objective and invoking the idea of another Vietnam, while the polls showed Americans to be too uninformed, confused, or apathetic to support a military role in Bosnia that, even if limited to air strikes, would put American youths in harm's way. He spoke in the campaign of U.S. participation in multinational alliances through the United Nations to make or keep peace and promote human rights and democracy. But in Somalia, the slain American soldiers were under the ultimate supervision of a U.N. commander, yet their role was never altogether clear—as least to the people who mattered politically, American voters.

Despite all that, Clinton's ability was not as limited and his performance in foreign policy hadn't been as bad as many critics charged:

- America's biggest foreign policy challenge was still Russia. Clinton had acted decisively to support Yeltsin unequivocally, which was his only viable option in a vast country so unsettled that no comfortable path existed.

- The problems in Bosnia and Somalia were inherited from a supposed master of foreign policy, George Bush, and Clinton essentially tried to maintain the policies he inherited in those trouble spots.

- Clinton had studied international relations as a collegiate undergraduate at Georgetown, had traveled extensively, and possessed the kind of analytical mind that was properly suited for a new world that presented a president with myriad diverse hot spots, not one prevailing problem, meaning the Cold War. In a strange way, Clinton, by being indecisive and inclined toward a disorganized process of decision making, was better suited for this new world than he would have been for the Cold War.

- In the new international economy, trade was as vital to foreign relations as defense. Clinton was strong on the international economy, well versed on trade, and uncannily effective—owing to his personal warmth, charm, and policy command—at summits of world leaders considering economic issues. Just as he'd always been a bright star among American governors convening for their annual conferences, he stood out at the summit of leaders of the G-7 nations.

His problems on foreign policy were these: He lacked stature and credibility because of his background; he was indecisive by nature, as evidenced by his optimism and then retreat on Bosnia; and, as a tactical matter, he was detached from foreign policy because he had been elected on a domestic agenda in a new era.

What he needed, then, was a strong set of foreign policy advisers around him who would compensate for his background, indecisiveness, and detachment. While he would centralize domestic policy in the Oval Office, he sought to decentralize foreign policy with a strong, stable, experienced Secretary of State, which is what he expected Warren Christopher to be; an innovative thinker with military credibility as his Secretary of Defense, which he expected Les Aspin to be; and an effective presenter of credible options as national security adviser in the White House, which is what he expected Anthony Lake to be.

In each case he was let down.

Christopher, a quietly capable negotiator, turned out to be too bland to act as a surrogate American president for foreign affairs. Clinton needed a Democratic Kissinger; what he got in Christopher was a Milquetoast who sometimes fell asleep in public.

Christopher, known to friends as "Chris," was a successful corporate lawyer who had been an effective deputy Secretary of State to Cyrus Vance during the Carter administration. But Christopher was a latecomer to Clinton's inner circle, and in more ways than one he owed his rise to prominence in that circle largely to Mickey Kantor, the Clintons' longtime Los Angeles friend who chaired the campaign in 1992 and became U.S. trade representative in 1993.

Kantor had touted Christopher, his fellow Californian, in mid-1992 when Clinton began to devise a process for looking for a running mate. Clinton wanted respected, discreet Democratic veterans to coordinate his search by establishing procedures, locating prospects, and conducting preliminary screening and interviews. He knew that his friend Vernon Jordan would be one of the coordinators. He took Kantor's advice and selected Christopher to join Jordan. The selection process was a smashing success: Al Gore enhanced Clinton dramatically, even inordinately. Jordan and Christopher got credit, although Clinton made the decision to choose Gore with only his closest aide-de-camp, Bruce Lindsey, in the room. But Clinton appreciated the thorough, quiet search that Jordan and Christopher had conducted. He developed trust.

Then, after Clinton's election, Christopher became chairman of the "transition board" because Kantor, who wanted the job, had fallen into disfavor during the general election campaign.

Although Kantor carried the title of campaign chairman and had behaved as one during the primary, the real stars of Clinton's campaigns were the strategists and political operatives: James Carville, George Stephanopoulos, campaign manager David Wilhelm, pollster Stanley Greenberg, and media specialist Mandy Grunwald. Kantor was widely deemed detached and a bit territorial; in fact, for the last few weeks of the campaign, with victory likely, he worked quietly on setting up a transition operation. He expected to parlay that assignment into chairmanship of the transition team, and that into the job of White House chief of staff.

But as soon as he was elected, Clinton was advised by key campaign staff, such as Stephanopoulos, that Kantor was assuming a prominent role for himself and that they objected to Kantor's style and presumption. Clinton's mind was made up when Hillary agreed with him to deny Kantor the transition chairmanship and give him a mere seat on the transition board. Hillary had met Kantor first, in the 1970s, when she and Kantor served together on the board of the Legal Services Corporation.

Clinton's first reaction was to ask Mack McLarty to head the transition board and then become White House chief of staff. But McLarty wasn't yet certain that he wanted to go to Washington; he suspected he would go, but he didn't want to commit by taking the transition helm in early November. So Christopher was the logical choice, and as head of Clinton's transition, he could have the job of Secretary of State for the asking. In addition to earning the president's trust, Christopher had a solid reputation from his days at the State Department in the Carter administration. But there was not a deep reservoir of intimacy between the new president and the man to whom he would delegate foreign policy.

Christopher would not be the weakest link in the foreign policy team. A capable politician, he weathered the disasters of Bosnia, Somalia, and Haiti by rehabilitating himself and being flexible to White House–dictated changes, such as accepting Clinton's old Oxford roommate, former *Time* columnist Strobe Talbott, as his top deputy.

Les Aspin had seemed in the beginning to be everything Clinton needed in a Defense Secretary. He had been a "whiz kid" under Robert McNamara in the 1960s, then a college professor. After being elected to Congress he rose to prominence as a thoughtfully hawkish chairman of the House Armed Services Committee. Clinton needed someone with military credibility, an innovative thinker who could redefine and redesign the Pentagon for the post–Cold War era. Aspin had been conspicuous among Democrats in supporting the Persian Gulf War, and he had distinguished himself for leadership in a so-called bottom-up review of the Defense Department to restructure it for downsizing. He had shared his views with Clinton's campaign, and the candidate had embraced them in his rhetoric and position papers.

But Aspin turned out to be too much like the president—professorially verbose about options, and indecisive. He talked too much in private without coming to a strong conclusion, and he talked too much in public: in the first week of the Clinton administration, he acknowledged publicly that the administration was operating from a position of weakness on gays in the military because the Joint Chiefs and the Senate could stop it.

In private Aspin never connected with the Arkansas forces in the White House. Two of those Arkansas forces talked one day about their inability to make a connection with Aspin. They decided it must have had something to do with people from Wisconsin: they couldn't connect with Ann Devroy, the tough White House correspondent for *The Washington Post,* either. She is from Green Bay.

Aspin would eventually lose his job, a fate that became obvious when, in an appearance on "Meet the Press" on November 7, 1993, on NBC, Clinton declined to stand up for him. That fate actually had been sealed a month before. The day after the Somalia disaster, Congress was nearly in a panic. The White House dispatched Christopher and Aspin to conduct a briefing. Neither of them had much to say, but Aspin looked weaker because he actually admitted the administration's uncertainty by asking the congressmen what they thought the administration should do.

It wasn't altogether Aspin's fault that the administration had an uncertain policy. It was mostly Clinton's, and Christopher was as seemingly clueless as Aspin. But the Defense Secretary was the easiest sacrificial lamb, largely because he was the kind of person who would signal indecisiveness to Congress at the precise moment Congress least wanted to see it.

Lake, meanwhile, was performing his job as national security adviser as it had been designed . . . weakly.

But for all the slogan searching and foreign policy hand-wringing, Clinton would soon be rehabilitated not on a slogan, but on an issue, and a foreign policy one at that. Trade was a foreign policy issue, remember. NAFTA would be Bill Clinton's miracle cure.

CHAPTER 10

The Damp Leg

J. Bill Becker grew up in Chicago in the 1930s and 1940s, the son of garment workers. He came south as a labor organizer in 1949, stopping off in Kentucky before winding up in Arkansas with the Amalgamated Clothing Workers. In 1964 he was elected president of the Arkansas State AFL-CIO, a job he has held since.

He is a diminutive, scowling, irreverent, bitingly articulate and bitterly combative man. Perhaps his hostility could be forgiven considering his lot in life, which for years had him alternately pitied and kidded by labor colleagues around the country.

An ice hockey player would be only slightly more of an oddity than a labor leader in Arkansas, where "right to work" is treated more as part of the Bill of Rights than what it actually is: a ban on closed union workplaces and a euphemism for low wages and an absence of labor trouble for employers in a place of dogged personal independence and near feudalism where nearly all the money is in the hands of a few.

My permanent image of Becker is of him dragging himself with obvious fatigue and disdain over the marbled hallways of the Arkansas State Capitol during sessions of the state legislature, which was filled with good ol' boys for whom "good guvment" meant anything that was "good for bidness." Becker's perpetual battle was the protection of the very ideas of collective bargaining and workers' compensation.

It was in the spring of 1990, amid a Democratic gubernatorial primary in Arkansas that had Bill Clinton opposed from the left by a lawyer and think-tank veteran named Tom McRae, that Becker decided he was fed up with labor's decade-long game of love-hate with the chameleon governor, whom he saw as a silk-suiter and a liar who took labor's endorsement for granted during campaigns and then made his bed with the corporate CEOs when the balloting was done.

In Arkansas, a group of the state's wealthy and storied businessmen— the late Sam Walton, Don Tyson, even White House chief of staff Mack McLarty—had formed a group called the "Arkansas Business Council," which I nicknamed the "Good Suit Club." Clinton embraced the group's joint effort to influence public policy, and happily participated in the formal announcement of the group's formation. True, it was extraordinary that top businessmen were preparing to advocate higher taxes on themselves for education. But then the group's first action, taken with Clinton's acquiescence, was to rewrite the state corporate code to strengthen management's powers over minority stockholders.

Becker, I suspect, hated Bill Clinton, seeing hypocrisy and hollow expediency where Clinton saw bridge building and new ideas for a new age in which a politician needn't choose a polarized side with either business or labor, but try to be a friend to both. Over the years I, too, had resented Clinton's sometimes successful attempts to have things both ways. But by 1993 I had begun to consider the possible truth and merit of the idea that old political alliances were passé, and that if a politician could simultaneously ingratiate himself with traditionally polarized foes, it might not only be good politics but helpful in effecting policy. To give one example, Clinton passed NAFTA one week, pleasing business and displeasing labor, then the next he prodded American Airlines to agree to renewed discussions to end a strike by flight attendants.

But on that spring morning in 1990 at the state labor convention in Little Rock to consider endorsements, Becker stood before the delegates and vented his resentment in one memorable, prophetic, and absolutely on-target metaphorical line: "Bill Clinton is the kind of man who'll pat you on the back and piss on your leg."

(Or, as I once put it in a column in 1992, Clinton was the one Democrat with the splendid dexterity to urinate on Jesse Jackson's leg while hugging him.)

Becker was pleading with his delegates not to give themselves to Clinton one more time with an endorsement he would take for granted as usual. McRae, a gangly blue-blood who had the political skills of a brick, couldn't take the endorsement away. But at least labor could have the self-respect to remain neutral, or so Becker implored.

The disdain for Clinton was based on four issues, primarily.

- In 1983, when Becker helped him pass a seminal sales tax increase for education, Clinton promised to return the favor by helping labor get a rebate for low-income people from the additional tax. Arkansas applies the sales tax to groceries, making it even more regressive (inordinately burdensome to low-income people) than it was already. The deal was that if Becker would help Clinton with a few pro-labor legislators to get the emergency clause adopted, meaning the money would be collected immediately, Clinton would help Becker get the poor people's rebate. Two days later, Clinton had his emergency clause but Becker didn't have a rebate. Clinton told the press that his arrangement with Becker had been only a "24-hour commitment." Clinton professed great concern for the unfairness of the sales tax as applied, but it was the easiest way to raise money in Arkansas.

  Clinton continued to profess concern when he raised the sales tax again, by half a cent, in 1991, when it still applied to groceries. Exempting groceries would cost too much in such a low-budget state, and key legislators were adamantly opposed, Clinton explained. The prevailing attitude in Arkansas was that the sales tax was the fairest tax of all because everyone paid the same amount. Such illogic was what Bill Becker was up against. Why, in the 1980s the federal government had to force Arkansas to exempt food stamp purchases from the sales tax.

- In 1989, the United Auto Workers went on strike at a small plant northwest of Little Rock called Morrilton Plastics. Clinton's Arkansas Industrial Development Commission, an agency devoted to job development, guaranteed a loan to the company so it could shore up its inventory against the strike—a loan on which the company eventually defaulted. The plant was minority-owned, and Clinton, as a professed "new Democrat," was more committed to empowering black people with opportunity and responsibility than to a traditional, pro-labor, old Democrat principle.

- In 1990, the Arkansas Industrial Development Commission published a brochure touting Arkansas as a kind of Mexico to the north—a "right to work" state with lower-than-average labor costs. After a newspaper article about the sales pitch, Clinton publicly professed to have been unaware of it and ordered the brochures changed.

• Then there was the matter of Clinton's keeping the job of state labor commissioner vacant for more than a year because, as a consensus builder, he couldn't get labor factions to agree. He finally picked the person Becker didn't want.

Becker carried the day that Saturday. No endorsement was made. But over the next two weeks, individual unions and locals led by friends of Clinton issued a steady trickle of news releases announcing their solidarity-breaking, ad hoc endorsements of the incumbent. On balance, Clinton was labor's good friend; he was doing all that could be expected of him, or so these releases said. Privately the word was that Becker carried a personal grudge. Bill Clinton, the persuasive "new Democrat," had split the pitiably small labor movement in Arkansas.

During the Democratic presidential primary in 1992, Becker berated Clinton in every interview he was asked to give. He prepared a report on Clinton's "abysmal" labor record and sent it to the national office, where Lane Kirkland, the national president, ordered it kept in a desk drawer. After Clinton locked up the Democratic nomination, Becker was ordered by his bosses to forever hold his peace. The best shot in twelve years of getting the Republicans out of the White House would not be ruined or inconvenienced by the rantings of the leader of the inconsequential labor movement down in Arkansas.

In November 1993, just before Thanksgiving, Clinton won passage of the North American Free Trade Agreement, which labor feared and opposed heavy-handedly because it was a fundamental change in attitudes toward the economy and employment. Becker called the national labor office from a hospital bed in Little Rock, where he was being treated for intestinal problems. "Lane Kirkland's leg is wet now. Not mine," he told Rex Hardesty, the AFL-CIO's public relations director.

"At least Clinton's consistent," Becker told me.

Bill Clinton, meanwhile, was rehabilitated, almost magically and essentially overnight, by passage of this forward-looking, new-world trade agreement. He showed he could work with Republicans. He showed himself a leader who could transcend partisan battles. He appeared principled. He showed himself a man who could build a single-issue campaign as president just as he could perform a tenacious electoral campaign as a candidate.

The man who had been the "education governor" in Arkansas and then had promised to "focus like a laser beam on the economy" as president began instead by the end of his first year in the White House to appear the "trade president."

Becker's assessment of Clinton—that he was a silk-suiter and a liar—was only about 40 percent right. Clinton was no silk-suiter, and the full thrust of the word "liar" bothers me as applied to a man who means no harm with his chronic tendency to finesse and waffle out of commitments.

I'll gladly call him weak, over-promising, and dissembling, but then, maybe I'm merely clinging to softened euphemism whereas Becker tends toward the brutally candid.

The fact is—and there is no reason for euphemism here—that America's forty-second president had a history of failing to place sufficient value on his own word. My best explanation is that he was influenced in formative years by a doting mother, devoid of a strong paternal influence, and blessed by a series of rapid, too-easy, early-adult successes that had people complimenting him and pandering to him. Somewhere along the way there was a gap in his personal development.

Consider this case of classic Clinton: In August 1992, after formally securing the Democratic presidential nomination, Clinton had a telephone conversation with Lane Kirkland, who was worried above all else about NAFTA. Not to fear, Clinton told him. He supported NAFTA, but only with a new side agreement on labor issues that would satisfy Kirkland's concerns. His position on the labor issues was essentially the same as that of Richard Gephardt of Missouri, a NAFTA opponent, Clinton assured Kirkland. Straightaway Kirkland sent a message to state labor presidents reporting that the Democratic nominee was fine on NAFTA and to feel free to proceed with formal endorsements of the Democrat's candidacy. But a year later, Clinton could secure only a side agreement on labor issues that fell far short of addressing all of Kirkland's concerns or of aligning his position with that of Gephardt, who remained a staunch NAFTA foe. Clinton argued that he secured the best side agreements possible and had made a good faith effort. Kirkland, like Becker before him, felt he had been betrayed.

As always, Clinton's sin was the too-easy promise of campaigning rather than the responsibility of governing. He could have told Kirkland that he was committed to NAFTA and to getting the best side agreement on labor issues that he could negotiate. But he typically overstated, because of his frenzied desire for victory.

The conversation with Kirkland aside, Clinton appeared to the American people, more importantly, to be a man of honor on NAFTA. He said as a candidate that he would support it; he did so. He said as a candidate that he would negotiate side agreements to address labor and environmental issues; he produced side agreements. He insisted he genuinely supported NAFTA and was not pretending; he proved it.

As for being a silk-suiter, Clinton could more fairly be described as a new thinker.

He came from modest beginnings and cared about the working person. But as a student of trends who genuinely believed that a Democrat needed to be "new" because the world was changing, he believed Americans should be weaned from the anachronistic ideas of one-job lifetimes and the supposed sufficiency of an insular American economy. It was one of the surest and clearest elements of Clinton's economic philosophy.

This was Clinton's view, a long-held one about which he'd given speeches for seven years and one that genuinely identified him as the "new Democrat" he longed to be. The economy was now a global one in which America was a lagging competitor, not a dominator; the driving force of the national economy was foreign trade; one of the paramount objectives was to form new international partnerships to compete with the Japanese and the Europeans in the world marketplace; the best new jobs in the United States would be skilled jobs in small companies, probably without union representation and requiring good schooling and training. Since America had lost jobs to foreign competition, anyway, it would be foolhardy to decline to participate in the world economy because of a fear of jobs lost to cheaper wages when that had happened already. Clinton wanted to increase markets and get Americans ready for the vanguard of modern production and distribution, which would encompass, but not be limited to, the basic educational and technical skills of the Information Age. Education, job training and retraining, and opened markets worldwide—that is Clintonism at its clearest and best.

Remember that throughout the early 1980s low-skilled manufacturing jobs in Clinton's Arkansas were lost to Mexico, South Korea,

and elsewhere. The state rallied over a decade in retailing, data processing, electronics, trucking, and through general entrepreneurial leadership that had very little to do with Clinton, but the worth of which
he came to understand. "Work hard, work smart" is how James Carville
had put it.

Inherent in all of this was the intimation that the labor movement
was irrelevant, or becoming so; but as a Democrat determined to synthesize old constituencies with new middle-class appeal, Clinton
wouldn't admit that. For electoral purposes he wanted to apply the
Arkansas formula: Give labor enough, and make enough friends there,
to remain eminently preferable to Republicans even as he shafted labor
on one or two seemingly essential points that appealed to the middle
class by sending a signal he was no hostage of the tired old liberals.
He wanted to have it both ways, in other words. Frankly, there was
no reason he shouldn't.

On those points Clinton was not dishonest. He genuinely believed
in NAFTA, and he stood for principle and won. He genuinely believed
that on balance he was as good a friend as labor could reasonably
expect in the White House in the 1990s, and I suspect he was right.
He genuinely believed that it was fair, not to mention smart politics,
to send a signal of independence to middle-class voters when in fact
he was behaving with the honest independence of a typical Democratic
constituency, and I suspect it was fair. I know it was good politics,
just as it was good politics to pick a fight with the NEA over teacher
testing in Arkansas in 1983.

In regard to NAFTA, it also was good policy. Clinton's view of the
global economy was the right one. Nearly every reputable economist
agreed with him. It was widely believed that if not for labor's hold on
certain Democratic congressmen, NAFTA, as an issue of merit, could
have sailed through the House of Representatives. Becker had spent
an adulthood as an oddity in Arkansas; now he and his labor brethren
nationwide were becoming out of date. Rather than having what Clinton
called "the courage to change," they adhered in the NAFTA battle to
old economic rules and old political styles. And they lost, as they should
have.

Clinton's labor record in Arkansas was not so much anti-labor as it
was something that, for lack of a better word, I call "neo-pragmatic."
He was able to increase taxes for education while trying to lure jobs
to a poor state with the sales pitch of a tax burden that remained one
of the lowest in the country, counting state and local taxes. In a populist,

anti-tax state, he relied on a regressive tax because it was more acceptable to the legislature and the people, and because, owing to a crazy quirk in the state constitution, it required fewer votes to raise. As for guaranteeing a loan to a firm being struck, he weighed support for a minority enterprise with a traditional pro-labor position and chose support for a minority enterprise. It was all eminently sensible, and, as he liked to say, he resisted efforts to make "the perfect the enemy of the good."

But Becker was right, of course, that Clinton couldn't be counted on to keep his word. That was relevant considering the number of deals the president cut with members of the House of Representatives to bring NAFTA back from the dead and pass it by a reasonably comfortable margin.

Rahm Emmanuel, the widely disliked young Chicagoan who was kicked out of his job as White House political director in the summer and then rehabilitated by the autumn as a key operative in the NAFTA "war room" in the Old Executive Office Building, was asked one day at a staff meeting what the NAFTA strategy was. "It's the Lamaze method: breathe and push, breathe and push," he said. Later, as Clinton acceded to congressional requests for projects and programs in exchange for NAFTA votes, which is what congressional politics is all about, Emmanuel announced that he had the solution: It was to send a catalogue up to Capitol Hill offering gifts and an order form saying, "Just call 1-800-PANETTA."

Leon Panetta was the director of the Office of Management and Budget, the deficit hawk who had to figure out how to pay for Clinton's promises while keeping the lid on the budget.

Back in Arkansas, Clinton had been famous for horse trading—"inside baseball," he called it—with members of the legislature. He had admitted in Arkansas to having overdone it from time to time.

Arkansas has by its constitution a relatively weak governorship, but Clinton strengthened it largely by proposing tax increases and promising funding to capital improvement projects that would be contingent on the enactment of the taxes. He also promised appointments to state boards and commissions. He didn't always deliver and frequently he was accused of double-crosses because he lacked a knack for saying no.

"When you ask him for something and he just looks at you without saying anything, that means no," said Chris Burrow, who lobbied the Arkansas legislature for Clinton for a decade. Percy Malone, a businessman who also lobbied the legislature for Clinton, told this story: One day he went in to Clinton to tell him that a certain state representative would vote for one of the governor's bills if a friend would be let out of prison. Clinton responded, "Dammit, I'm not lettin' anyone out of jail. I've given these guys everything they've asked for, but that's where I draw the line."

Betsey Wright had said since May, "He'll figure it out. He always does." Anyone familiar with Clinton's pattern over more than a decade would have wagered a few dollars on his presidential rehabilitation.

But no one could have fully foreseen the miraculously rehabilitating powers of passing NAFTA—unless, perhaps, it was Clinton himself—partly because for the longest time no one could be sure he would get it passed. Any contemplation of what he would gain by passage was long overshadowed by contemplation of the high stakes he would lose by failure.

There would be no rehabilitating powers in embracing a concept alien to labor and many congressional Democrats and then getting beat on it. Clinton had won the budget by looking like a miserable loser; the last thing he needed was to lose again.

Still, some of the Clinton's most trusted outside political advisers—James Carville, Mandy Grunwald, and Stanley Greenberg, all of whom had ties to labor or sympathy for labor—encouraged Clinton to put NAFTA to a vote but not really extend political capital on it.

George Stephanopoulos wavered between their view and the one of the centrists in the White House—Mack McLarty and David Gergen—who consistently encouraged Clinton to go to the mat on NAFTA because it was the right thing to do and would enhance his presidency.

When I asked Stephanopoulos in September about the politics of Clinton's decision to push for NAFTA, specifically whether it would provide the rehabilitating and "new Democrat" kick the president needed, Stephanopoulos said, "It's two different things: if we get it and if we don't get it."

What that meant was that once Clinton decided to go for NAFTA, he had to go all the way. Supporting it alone would be no virtue. Beltway thinking that Clinton was pretending to support NAFTA to effect an image while expecting labor to beat it was based on the inane premise that transparent trickery and defeat would somehow accrue

to his benefit. Transparent trickery and defeat—on the budget bill—
were what had saddled him with unprecedented early disapproval
ratings in public opinion polls in the first place.

The political complexities of NAFTA were evident in the divergence
of opinion from two of Clinton's common-sense advisers from Arkansas: Senator David Pryor and chief of staff McLarty, who were dear
friends.

"Bill Clinton didn't get elected on NAFTA," Pryor told me three days
before the vote in the House. "He's gonna get it, and the only people
who will care will be a bunch of corporate CEOs who are gonna vote
Republican anyway."

But McLarty said, "I don't agree with that. I think it's important in
the message it sends about the President and the presidency." As a
corporate-style linear thinker, McLarty believed it was important and
probably vital that Clinton pass NAFTA, then go to the long-scheduled
trade summit with Asian leaders with a strong hand and enhanced
stature. As McLarty knew from governors' conferences, Clinton
always performed well at such meetings. But he could perform much
better—he could, in fact, deliver a bravura performance—if he appeared a rehabilitated and strong president on the cutting edge of global
trends.

Pryor may have been right that only corporate CEOs wanting to do
business in Mexico celebrated, and that they'll vote Republican anyway.
But McLarty was right about the enhanced stature, which Clinton
needed desperately. He had appeared a blundering and pedestrian
president. Now suddenly he appeared "presidential"—a word you can't
define, but a quality you know when you see it—by embracing a
proposal favored by the political establishment, surrounding himself
with former presidents and former secretaries of state, and then winning
by relying mostly on the Republicans with whom he had been polarized
three months before on the budget.

The best way to analyze the rehabilitative powers of NAFTA for
Clinton would be to accept that presidencies are defined by images
resulting from two or three actions or issues, and then to contrast the
defining images of NAFTA with the defining images of Clinton's first-
month presidential debacle: gays in the military.

John F. Kennedy was defined by the Cuban missile crisis and his
assassination; Lyndon B. Johnson by the Great Society and Vietnam;
Richard Nixon by opening doors to China and Watergate; Gerald Ford
by pardoning Nixon and appearing physically clumsy; Jimmy Carter

by a so-called misery index and hostages in Iran; Ronald Reagan by cutting taxes and building up the nation's military hardware; and George Bush by the Persian Gulf War and vomiting in Japan.

Clinton's first year as president was defined by gays in the military and NAFTA, the first signaling cultural liberalism and naivete, the second signaling principled bipartisan policy, new economic and political thinking, and salesmanship. Together, they represented Clinton's improvement—the learning curve I'd watched in Arkansas.

Let's return to the four questions I proposed at the start as determining the political and policy success of the Clinton presidency. By embracing NAFTA and getting it passed, Clinton provided favorable answers to three of them—and inevitably to the fourth as well:

Q: Would he show himself somehow verifiably different from the stereotype that the white middle class, both blue collar and white collar, had come to apply through the 1980s to Democrats— that they were anachronistic adherents of failed economic and social policy?

A: Yes, unequivocally. Most Democrats in the Congress were living up to that stereotype, siding with the antiquated view of a traditional constituency, labor, out of concern for their reelections. But Clinton took on labor, worked with Republicans, and embraced a modern economic principle that defied stereotyping and the usual labeling.

Q: Would Clinton have enough credibility, as a president and a man, to lead?

A: Yes, unequivocally. As president, he had the credibility to take a dormant issue and raise it from the dead to the point of comfortable victory. As a man, he took a position and adhered to it unwaveringly in the face of stiff odds.

Q: Could Clinton end gridlock and get anything accomplished?

A: Why, yes, he could. He tore down the partisan dividing wall that had plagued Washington through the Reagan-Bush years and beset Clinton on his budget battle in August 1993. Again, he took a dormant policy proposal and passed it in defiance of rampant predictions that he could not. Americans love a winner. It's that simple.

Q: Would the country enjoy peace and prosperity?

A: There was no immediate effect. But nearly all economists said NAFTA's long-term effect was clearly beneficial to the American economy. Quite pleasurably, if coincidentally, the economic indicators began to chart a significantly perked-up economy in the final quarter of 1993.

In other words, Clinton's position and performance on NAFTA were fresh, bipartisan, principled, and strong. It should have been no wonder that he was reborn. Until NAFTA, Clinton had appeared stale, partisan, unprincipled, and weak. NAFTA fixed what was broken.

The dramatic come-from-behind trade agreement victory was not his personal victory, Clinton told the Democratic Leadership Council in December. "Someday," he said, "the full story will be told" about the many-faceted and refreshingly bipartisan effort.

He didn't choose to tell that story, but it was true that there were many heroes and players whose roles were as vital as the president's.

Vice President Al Gore was given the risky but potentially choice assignment of doing the one thing that Representative Newt Gingrich, the right-wing Republican leader, had told the White House was essential to embolden members of his party's freshman class to vote for NAFTA. He said that something or someone had to discredit or neutralize Ross Perot, who opposed NAFTA and whose appeal scared these Washington novices and whose vocal opposition to NAFTA seemed to have frozen them.

Perot's popularity had been in steady decline since April, when he tormented Clinton and pulled even with him in at least one poll. It's difficult to sustain high popularity during prolonged periods of high visibility in modern American politics, as Clinton knew all too well. Perot was beginning to grate on nerves and to be seen for what he was: a blowhard who could rail against anything without offering any positive solution.

Three months before the NAFTA stretch run, Perot had appeared on "Meet the Press" on NBC. Tim Russert, the host, had pressed him on the budget plan his campaign had presented. *The Washington Post* had suggested in an analysis that it didn't add up and that Perot's boasts of fiscal responsibility and deficit elimination were bogus even with the 50-cent-per-gallon tax increase he had proposed and seemingly forgotten.

Perot became flustered, defensive, even angry. He said he hadn't brought his charts. Had he known he would be asked about his budget proposals, he would have brought the charts, he declared.

It was comical for a supposedly credible political figure to say he couldn't talk about his own policies without his charts. They were chortling the next day at the White House. Clinton himself was smugly amused that the press, which had badgered him mercilessly with detailed questions, had asked a few specifics of Perot. Most important, the White House had noticed something interesting. As one staffer told me, "That guy [Perot] can't play defense."

Like many monstrously successful businessmen, Perot spent his life equating his own intelligence and charm with his level of business success. He lived a life in which he dominated his own environment and was surrounded if not by sycophants, then certainly by people with the good grace not to suggest he was less than magnificent. But politics is no place for a person without training in the fine art of thickening one's skin against insult and degradation.

Gore's assignment, should he choose to accept it, would be to accept Perot's call for a debate on NAFTA, then get in the billionaire's face and force him to play the game he couldn't play: defense. Gore gladly accepted this vital assignment, one that had the objective of bursting the Perot balloon, lessening his public appeal, and breaking his hammerlock on timid members of Congress.

Many pundits questioned the wisdom of the move, finding it a desperation tactic that might backfire. Gore was notoriously stiff and Perot was a sound-bite machine. But Clinton had distinguished himself for years as an unconventional risk taker: He went on the "Tonight Show" to poke fun at himself after his debacle at the Democratic National Convention and he went on the Arsenio Hall Show and MTV to appeal to young voters during the 1992 campaign. Back in Arkansas in 1982, he had begun his political comeback not with a formal announcement of his candidacy to win back the governor's office he'd lost two years before, but with an unexpected television commercial in which he popped up on the screen during the local television news programs to announce he would be a candidate and wanted a "second chance."

There was one other thing the White House knew—one thing, that is, beyond the fact that Perot couldn't play defense: It was that Al Gore, at least in private, had a feisty combativeness and charm. At times he behaved as the clown of the West Wing, believe it or not; at other times he showed more spark and spunk than anyone. If he could get comfortable and be more the person he was away from the camera than he usually became before it, he could handle Perot.

The White House decided to accept Perot's challenge of a debate, and to do it with Gore on the Larry King Live show on CNN, where Gore had performed comfortably in the past. They knew Perot's ego would not allow him to decline.

The only thing that went wrong was that Clinton announced the challenge prematurely. In Kentucky one day to give a speech about NAFTA and jobs, Clinton responded to a reporter's shouted question about Perot by spinning around from a handshake line to announce the challenge. Back at the White House they groaned. The message-control agenda had provided for Clinton to make headlines for the speech that day, then come back with the debate challenge the next.

"I stepped on my story, didn't I?" Clinton said, for the second time in a year, as he got into the car after the Kentucky appearance.

By every conceivable standard, Gore proceeded to rout Perot in the debate. He confronted, rattled, bothered, frustrated, and angered the Texas billionaire, who looked petulant, demagogic, hypercritical, and pitifully ill-informed. Perot made absolutely no sense. His argument seemed to be that American jobs would speed to Mexico because people lived without indoor plumbing down there. When Gore turned to him politely and remarked that he knew of no corporation that had lobbied Congress more exhaustively over the years than Perot's, it was over.

No other single event contributed so heavily to the NAFTA turn-around. From that moment forward, Perot seemed less scary, even less relevant, to House members who suddenly felt more at ease about casting the vote they knew to be right and responsible. Like the Reagan White House, the Clinton White House had played an outside media game to effect an inside victory in Congress.

Al Gore had emerged as the Most Valuable Player of the Clinton administration. He had broken the tie on the president's budget, and now he had broken Ross Perot.

Another hero, most unlikely, was Newt Gingrich, the bombastic Georgia Republican known for extreme conservatism and transparent partisanship, a man who would have been detested by the White House at any other time on any other issue. But on NAFTA—a pro-corporate idea that Republicans embraced—Gingrich tackled the issue and never wavered, despite White House distrust that the GOP might position itself as pro-NAFTA and then leave the vulnerable president out to dry. "We just have to hope there's no Republican funny business," William Daley, the Chicagoan named to head the NAFTA campaign by Clinton, told me one day about a month before the vote.

There wasn't any funny business. In the last week of the NAFTA fight, Skip Rutherford, a Little Rock political operative who had come to Washington to assist his friend Mack McLarty, looked down a hall of the West Wing and saw George Stephanopoulos huddled plotting House vote-getting strategy with a leading aide to Newt Gingrich. He would not have believed it if he had not seen it.

Republicans genuinely believed in NAFTA, did not want to be obstructionist, and wanted to reserve the right to say that they—not Clinton—had shown leadership and passed NAFTA.

In the end Republicans got little more from the White House than Clinton's assurance that he would defend them on NAFTA against attacks from Democratic challengers to their reelections. It was an easy assurance to grant: Clinton could defend them on NAFTA in a form letter while he criticized them on everything else and warmly endorsed their Democratic opponents. But it was basically moot: Clinton had no coattails. He had yet to demonstrate an ability to help anyone in a local race. So far he had been nothing but a hindrance.

Others deserving credit included Mack McLarty, the chief of staff, for his behind-the-scenes work in securing Mexico's support for side agreements through the burgeoning friendship with key people on President Carlos Salinas's staff and for his work as liaison to businesspeople lending credibility to Clinton's position. McLarty also was vital in another regard: When the White House got the idea to bring former presidents to the White House first for the Israeli-PLO accord and then for a pro-NAFTA joint appearance, it was McLarty who worked mostly with James Baker to get George Bush beyond his hesitance.

Trade Representative Mickey Kantor, the Californian and old friend of Bill and Hillary who had thought he might be chief of staff, rose to the occasion with exhaustive work on the details and the selling of the trade agreement. His earnest and relentless style paid off.

Rahm Emmanuel, his brightness and energy overcoming his abrasiveness, worked feverishly and smartly in the NAFTA "war room," where he was under the supervision of an old friend from Chicago,

Bill Daley. With the Democratic majority leader, Gephardt, against NAFTA, Emmanuel had almost daily strategy discussions with Tony Coelho, the former House majority leader, who had such intimate relations with the White House that whenever anyone got the idea that McLarty needed to be replaced as chief of staff with a seasoned political operative, Coelho's name came up.

And Bill Daley of Chicago, son of the former mayor, brother of the current one, was helpful through his appointed role as "NAFTA czar."

On the day Clinton announced his appointment, Daley spoke one short sentence and impressed absolutely no one. But back in Chicago he was known as a quietly effective behind-the-scenes operator.

"It will take a dual effort," Daley told me about a month before the vote, when few people gave NAFTA much chance. "It'll have to be an inside game to get the votes in Congress, but it'll also have to be an outside game to build grass-roots support. And it all has to be done accepting that labor is entrenched against us."

He helped pull off both. Newspaper people around the country began getting personalized letters from Daley arguing the case for NAFTA and, if appropriate, noting their interest in the issue as evidenced by their columns or editorials that he had supposedly read. Editorial writers and columnists around the country picked up the phone over those weeks to hear that Bill Daley was calling from the White House. After a pause, he'd get on the line to explain their importance to public understanding of the issue.

This was a massive, methodical public relations campaign, augmenting the work on Capitol Hill; by the time the House voted, a decisive number of members had been persuaded to vote "yes" because they perceived from editorials back home that the climate was right.

In the end some tried to dismiss the significance of the NAFTA victory. With the entire political establishment and the entire corporate lobbying community behind the treaty, it was certain to pass, some said.

That simply wasn't the case. The political establishment was not especially respected in a new Congress with a heavy dose of new members, all elected by running against politics-as-usual. The corporate lobbying community was at its best in the hallways and meeting rooms, behind closed doors during conference committee meetings. NAFTA was an up-or-down vote on an issue described as life or death by labor, demagogued by Ross Perot, and defined for the longest time by Perot's "giant sucking sound."

It was a worthy and dramatic victory, and Bill Clinton was back, inevitably. Only organized labor's leg was damp.

"I think, in the end, there was a sense of being on the right side of history," Clinton would tell me six months later.

So, by Thanksgiving, after the fourth-quarter rally of Bill Clinton's first presidential year, Republicans confronted an animal they had not seen in a quarter century: A politically savvy Democrat in the White House who signaled that he might be able to transcend traditional tax-and-spend labeling—even rearrange the national political landscape, perhaps for a generation—and appeal to pivotal swing voters in the middle class.

Clinton was personally rehabilitated by NAFTA. He had taken the rhetorical lead on crime and violence. The economy clearly was recovering, with interest rates still low, unemployment down, and inflation not appearing a problem. On health care, that seventh of the American economy, Clinton had positioned himself smartly: Republicans knew that the public would be angry if Congress failed to address health care in some fashion in 1994; so, even if the particulars of Clinton's plan were systematically chopped away, as seemed likely, Clinton could take the full load of credit for whatever bill survived and whatever benefits might accrue to the middle class. Health care was his issue, and his wife's, and the Republicans found themselves having to play on the president's home court.

This new animal scared Republicans, who had in the modern era dominated the White House.

But Clinton remained personally vulnerable. The American people had elected him by a minority, yet reserved judgment. They didn't widely trust him as a man of strong character, integrity, and commitment to his sales pitches.

By the end of the year, Clinton would be hit where he was weakest. The right-wing attack machine would polish and resubmit to the American public the image of an arrogant snake-oil salesman from Arkansas who philandered and practiced hayseed ethics.

CHAPTER 11

Backwater, Whitewater

As everyone knows by now, Arkansas is profoundly different from Washington, for which residents of both places surely are grateful.

Arkansas is small, slow-paced, relatively poor, underdeveloped, unsophisticated, and about as far from the centers of media, government, and commerce as any non-Alaskan place in America. Generally, Arkansas eschews intellectual and cultural stimulation and pursuit. Outside influences are scarce, and I refer to interstate, much less international, ones. People like things the way they are, and in Arkansas you can go all month without hearing any language other than drawled English. The dominant institutions are Fundamentalist churches and Saturday-night honky-tonks; there is evidence of those seemingly conflicting influences in the style and persona of Bill Clinton, part preacher and part entertainer. People of Arkansas pride themselves on common sense and a disdain for affectation, and they wonder why anyone would want to live in Washington, D.C., though relatively few have been there to see the blazing cherry trees in spring. Remember, the very idea that Bill Clinton carried presidential ambition caused resentment in Arkansas.

Despite all that, Arkansas seems a breeding ground for political and business genius. In the same year that Bill Clinton became president, Wal-Mart, based in Bentonville, Arkansas, displaced Sears as the nation's largest retailer. Stephens, Inc., in Little Rock was the second-largest off–Wall Street investment banking firm in America. Tyson

Foods of Springdale was nearly three times as large as the second-largest poultry processor. *The Washington Post* had proclaimed Arkansas "the little state that conquered America," and described a certain Arkansas style: stealthy, sneaky smartness. The economic range—from some of the world's richest people to the intense poverty among blacks in eastern Arkansas—gives the state a political environment, economic structure, and culture that strikes some outsiders as comparable to the Third World.

Washington, on the other hand, is high-income, high-paced, and high-stress, an educational and professional showcase of credentials, talent, and workaholism, the governmental center of the world, now truly an international and ethnically diverse city, home to storied museums, breathtaking historic monuments, and so many media standouts that they spend much of their time interviewing each other while some of the people in the backwoods listen for insight and wisdom.

Some Washingtonians like to say that their city is more Southern than Northern, but they are wrong. If Little Rock had a subway system—it barely supports a bus system—people wouldn't sit stonily with their faces in newspapers or books. They would say to each other, "Hey, how're you doin? Howz the famly? Let's ride back together this evenin'."

In Arkansas many people grow teeming vegetable gardens for food. In Washington many people tend glorious and sculpted flower gardens because, with government an endless process in which productivity is hard to measure at the end of the day, they need something productive to show for their labors.

Not that there aren't striking similarities. In Little Rock the white people live north and west of Markham Street and the black people south and east. In Washington the white people live north and west of 16th Street Northwest and the black people south and east. In both places, the concentration of violent crime is black-on-black in the south and east. Both towns have troubled and majority black public school systems, though the First Couple didn't find Little Rock's quite so bad that it was unworthy of their daughter. In fairness, the difference may not have been the quality of the schools but the dangers of being the president's daughter in a new town as compared to the lesser conspicuousness of being the governor's daughter in a familiar town. Politics is rough-and-tumble in both places, providing entertainment and sport. Both places offer former mean-spirited celebrity newspaper columnists; it was Paul Greenberg, the editorial-page editor of the *Arkansas*

Democrat-Gazette, a Pulitzer Prize–winning phrasemaker and a confounding blend of civil libertarianism and doctrinaire Republicanism, who coined "Slick Willie" to define the political artfulness of Bill Clinton and, as best I can determine, was the first to use "Fornigate" as a dismissive term for charges leveled by two state troopers about Clinton's voracious sexual appetite.

The latter was something that, for heaven's sake, we'd widely suspected for years in Arkansas. It was such commonly accepted speculation among insiders that the Bar Association in Little Rock, in its biennial spoof called *The Gridiron,* featured in 1988 two lawyers portraying Gary Hart and Bill Clinton who sang, "To All the Girls We've Loved Before." (Bill and Hillary did not attend.)

A man from Texas once told me that Arkansas was good for only two things—water-skiing and sex—but in deference to his own interests he had overlooked deer hunting, duck hunting, fishing, canoeing on free-flowing natural streams, hiking, mountain climbing, country-and-western two-steppin', University of Arkansas basketball, Oaklawn Park thoroughbred racing at Hot Springs, and all-you-can-eat cholesterol buffets, which, to be candid, I found preferable to the sopping of bread and beans that qualified to many in Washington as an Ethiopian delicacy.

(In January 1994, the burial of Virginia Kelley, the president's mother, brought an all-star group to the Western Sizzlin' lunchtime buffet in Hope. There that day were the president, the First Lady, the White House chief of staff, and Barbra Streisand. The latter walked over to examine the expansive buffet containing fried meats, slow-cooked vegetables, buttery mashed potatoes, and industrial-sized coffeepots but no espresso. "Hey, Barbra," said an old boy, "I bet they don't have food like this out in Hollywood, do they?" Streisand recoiled a bit and said, "I—I don't think so.")

Arkansas also has become something of a retirement haven. The secluded hills of North Arkansas are dotted with planned retirement companies inhabited by golfing Midwestern retirees who bring up the per capita income and the deposit bases of the country banks, not to mention the reservoir of Republican thought.

Arkansas actually is a state of geographic, cultural, and economic diversity, one that has an identity problem because it is part Southern, part Texan, and part Midwestern. Its eastern region along the Mississippi River Delta is a decaying agricultural region, severely poor, predominantly black, and in the Old South style of Mississippi in appearance and attitude. Its southwestern portion is piney and hilly, ripe for paper mills and lumber mills, and shares a style and flavor that resembles eastern Texas or Oklahoma, conservative and cowboyish. Its northwestern corner in the Ozark Mountains is one of the most prosperous areas in the country, the corporate home of Wal-Mart and Tyson Foods and the J. B. Hunt transport company, with unemployment almost nonexistent, the population almost exclusively white, and the white, upper-class, churchgoing culture more in line with that of Springfield, Missouri, or Tulsa, Oklahoma, than with anything in Arkansas. Little Rock is the only real city, though a small one. It is located almost squarely in the center of the state and is the confluence of the varying landscapes and cultures, even to the point of being flat and swampy on the east side of town and hilly and tree-lined on the northwest, not to mention poor and black on the east and affluent and white on the northwest.

To paint Arkansas as a hayseed haven and bumpkin frontier where modern concepts of ethics and regulatory law hadn't been introduced—as many portrayed it in late 1993 when ethical improprieties were alleged against Bill and Hillary Clinton—is as bigoted as alleging the same thing of all New Yorkers or of Italian-Americans because questionable business practices were suggested of Geraldine Ferraro's husband in 1984. Geographic prejudice is maybe the last bastion of politically acceptable bigotry in America in the 1990s.

Actually, if the people of Arkansas have one thing in common, it is resentment of such stereotypes and a hypersensitivity to them. The hypersensitivity was born of an inferiority complex and an absence of the kind of self-assurance that would allow the people of Arkansas to understand and dismiss the fact that people make jokes based on superficial judgments about many states, many cities, and many kinds of people.

Arkansas's biggest problem through the 1980s was that no one thought about it at all. Bill Clinton's gubernatorial administration spent thousands of dollars in the early 1980s for an advertising campaign in *The Wall Street Journal* featuring a creature called "Arkie Man" whose purpose was to remind potential investors of the state's place on the map. The dollars weren't well spent. The *Journal* itself soon published a map to illustrate an article, and it had Arkansas misplaced. Campaigning in 1992, George Bush referred to the "governor of that small state between Texas and Oklahoma." There is no state between Texas and Oklahoma.

But then when Bush, in one of his debates with Clinton, called Arkansas the "lowest of the low," the resentment and hatred among Arkansas people were palpable. To no avail, I tried to explain that Bush was referring to the state's rank in such categories as per capita income and per pupil expenditure, and had done so with a typical verbal clumsiness that reflected nothing more than that he knew he stood no chance to take the state's six electoral votes. Arkansas ranks anywhere from forty-fourth to forty-eighth among the states on most scales on economic health, but that's better than forty-ninth or fiftieth, where the state had been throughout the 1960s and 1970s. But that a blue-blooded president, a Connecticut Yankee and pretend Texan, would deliberately trash one of the fifty states under his charge—well, it pierced the hearts of the people of Arkansas, who generally believed that Bush had expressed what everyone thought.

Remember that since the mid-1960s the voters of Arkansas had been favoring politicians of charisma, good appearance, and moderate image—Clinton, Bumpers, and Pryor—largely because they sought leaders who would be good ambassadors for the state and representatives of a more sophisticated, intelligent culture than the one people might know from Dogpatch cartoons or the Little Rock Central High School crisis. Actually, Arkansas was famous among political insiders for turning out two extraordinary members of Congress: J. William Fulbright, the earliest and most cerebral congressional opponent of the Vietnam War, and Wilbur Mills, who long ran the country's fiscal policies as chairman of the House Ways and Means Committee.

A prevailing view in Arkansas in 1992 was that Clinton's successful campaign for president would permanently repair the state's image, showing America that a state it had forgotten or ridiculed could produce an impressive and high-caliber leader for the country. Well, there was much disappointment in 1993: The middle class didn't get a tax cut, the Democratic Leadership Council didn't establish policy, and Arkansas got some attention all right, but not the rehabilitative kind.

The Wall Street Journal, proving if nothing else its editorial detachment from the influence of advertising dollars, referred in an editorial to "Arkansas mores," as if they were different from those of the rest of the country. *The New York Times* explained in July 1993 that Vince Foster killed himself because he came from such an out-of-the-way place that he couldn't cope with the realities of the big time. Then around Christmas, the Republicans and the press dredged up a matter that had been mentioned in the campaign. They hammered the

Clintons' sixteen-year-old investment in a failed land and vacation development company in northern Arkansas called Whitewater Development with a Democratic Party insider who subsequently ran a wheeling-dealing and eventually failed savings and loan called Madison Guaranty—and explained it in part by saying the nation's president came from a backwater culture where politicians and businesspeople didn't know an ethic from a razorback hog.

Representative Jim Leach, a moderate Rockefeller Republican from Iowa, led the assault from his perch as ranking minority member of the House Banking Committee. His reputation for thorough study and even-handedness gave the lie to White House charges that the Whitewater resurrection was nothing more than a well-timed assault from the Republican attack machine seeking to discredit the rehabilitated president. It was only partly that. Leach, liked by many Democrats and even touted to Clinton by Senator Tom Harkin of Iowa as a worthy U.N. ambassador, seemed to believe genuinely in the rightness of a public inquiry. But Bob Dole, Newt Gingrich, Alphonse D'Amato, and Phil Gramm gave him a mean, smirking, utterly partisan, and, in some cases, blatantly hypocritical supporting cast.

That wasn't all. The right-wing pit bulldog, Floyd Brown of Citizens United of Fairfax, Virginia, the chief exploiter of the Willie Horton matter in 1988 and publisher of an anti-Clinton newsletter, spent plenty of time in Arkansas in late 1993 and early 1994 digging up dirt and innuendo on Clinton and feeding it to the mainstream media. His assistant, David Bossi, even accompanied an NBC senior producer on a trip to Fayetteville for an ambush interview with the former state securities commissioner, Beverly Bassett Schaffer. NBC explained that Bossi was along for the ride as a source on a totally unrelated matter. (It wasn't so unrelated; Bossi was spreading dirt on Webb Hubbell, the NBC producer told me. Seven weeks later, Hubbell would resign as associate attorney general because of publicity about an internal billing dispute with his former partners at the Rose Law Firm.)

This curious alliance was tantamount to a network interviewer having James Carville and Paul Begala in tow as he ambushed Neil Bush, son of the former president, for an interview about the failed Silverado Savings and Loan. This unholy alliance of network producer and right-wing hit man got little to no coverage in the national media. Howard Kurtz, the seemingly fearless media critic for The Washington Post, said weeks later that he found the incident curious and worthy of his pen, but had never quite got around to delving into it. In his defense, the event coincided with Bobby Inman's withdrawal as the nominee for Secretary of Defense and his charge that Bob Dole and William Safire, a columnist for *The New York Times,* had conspired to destroy him. That subject cried out for Kurtz's analysis and commentary. By the time he was finished, the incident in Arkansas was no longer fresh.

But as the point man for the Republicans, the soft-spoken and moderate Jim Leach offset the vicious partisanship of right-wing guerrillas spreading innuendo. In an interview with *The Washington Post,* Leach tried to explain the tangled affairs of Whitewater, Madison Guaranty Savings and Loan, the Rose Law Firm, and the Arkansas governor's office by likening Bill Clinton to Ferdinand Marcos and Arkansas to the Philippines, a place of extreme wealth and extreme poverty in which the ruling elite keep down the poor masses while a kind of cultural insularity protects the leader.

These assertions were oversimplifications, stereotypes, and broad-brushings. True, Arkansas had a nasty political climate that might have better prepared Foster had he chosen to participate in it. In terms of regulation and ethics, Arkansas had come far since the 1950s when Governor Orval Faubus, in addition to disgracing the state on the issue of school desegregation, allowed illegal gambling to flourish in Hot Springs (while Bill Clinton was growing up there) and paid no attention to fly-by-night insurance scams and a corrupt loan-and-thrift. Bill Clinton, as a progressive governor for a dozen years, had improved the regulatory and ethical climate, as had Governors Pryor, Bumpers, and the late Winthrop Rockefeller, a liberal Republican, before him.

But where there's a stereotype, there's usually a truth or a pattern that has been embellished and applied too widely. These were those truths:

First, Bill Clinton, Vince Foster, and all the others from Arkansas who came to Washington in January 1993 were not familiar with a bipartisan political culture, least of all a sophisticated one. Arkansas is only now creeping out of one-party politics, nominally Democratic, owing to family heritages dating back to the Civil War, when Republicans meant Reconstruction and carpetbaggers. The historic association with the Democratic Party was reinforced in the 1930s when Republicans were blamed for the Depression and FDR was credited with ending it. Without a great influx of new blood, those attitudes perpetuated themselves from generation to generation. People called themselves Democrats because their daddies and grandpas had called themselves Democrats. Clinton was not accustomed to having a large segment of the legislative branch opposing him automatically, nor was he accustomed to organized, relentless opposition that knew how to find, exploit, exaggerate, and distort his vulnerabilities.

This single-party system created a kind of good ol' boy network that ran the state. Tyson Foods, for example, won a massive federal tax break by winning a congressional definition as a family farm. It is a food-processing conglomerate, more a manufacturer than a farm, but key Arkansas Democrats—Bumpers and Pryor in the Senate and Beryl Anthony as a member of the House Ways and Means Committee—took care of it in Washington. Don Tyson, the chairman, was a leading benefactor of Democratic candidates; reportedly he once told other businesspeople that they erred by making their bed with Republicans because the real ticket to favor in Washington was to make one's alliances among the Democrats who controlled congressional committees.

Second, we in the newspaper business in Arkansas thought we were pretty good through the 1980s, when the *Arkansas Gazette* and the *Arkansas Democrat* waged one of the last great daily newspaper wars of our time. In fact we weren't bad at all compared to the quality of comparably sized newspapers around the country. Both papers had average news holes rivaling that of *The New York Times*. But the newspapers competed mainly with widely read columnists who gave the politicians hell, by competing for mostly inconsequential "scoops," and by adding pages for what we called "scorch the earth" coverage of single news events, such as tornadoes, floods, plane crashes, or momentous court rulings affecting the public schools. The shortcoming until the latter half of the 1980s was in the coverage of business, and in turn the intersection of business and politics. Until then, business coverage in Arkansas newspapers was largely a combination of news release journalism and occasional flattering feature articles on people having success. It was boosterism. The political coverage was centered at the state Capitol, at legislative committee meetings, rather than in the outlying offices of regulatory bodies.

I covered state government for more than a decade, but can count on two hands the number of times I went to the state securities commissioner or insurance commissioner to study files. Funny, though: we went to the Public Service Commission every day to cover the regulation of utility companies. That was the populist tradition of the state: watch those utility monopolies with an eagle eye, but leave the competing private sector alone. Speaking personally, my modus operandi through the 1980s was to pursue exclusive articles by developing sources among the controlling network. Since I used that network, I was not inclined to attack its interconnectedness and inordinate power. That is not unlike the modus operandi of a Washington reporter seeking exclusive articles in the nation's capital. In both places, an outsider could see the forest while an insider busied himself with the trees.

Third, the state was initially settled by people of rugged individualism seeking cheap land and independence from government and the developing population centers. As former Governor Frank White put it once, "The people of Arkansas want a good lettin' alone." That meant that they resisted taxes, which could have provided a larger government and a stronger regulatory structure. They resisted government regulation altogether, whether it had to do with zoning or building permits or whether they could burn leaves.

Fourth, Arkansas is a small state in which a few people have most of the money. That bestows inordinate influence on the rich, and it helps explain how the politicians and the businesspeople are always running into each other. Sometimes the associations resemble a soap opera script. A ready example: Jerry Jones, the owner of the Dallas Cowboys, is a native of working-class North Little Rock who netted more than $100 million under a gas exploration contract with the Arkansas Louisiana Gas Company negotiated with his good friend who was the company president, Sheffield Nelson. In the late 1980s, Nelson resigned, already made rich through stock appreciation rights, and prepared to run as a Republican for governor against Bill Clinton. The man Nelson had handpicked as his successor at the gas company was the boyhood friend of Bill Clinton from Hope, Mack McLarty, and it was McLarty who had to settle the contract with Jones. It was McLarty who defended his boyhood friend, Clinton, against rampant charges of another friend who had picked him for a choice job, meaning Nelson. Then McLarty became chief of staff in the White House. These associations surely seem sinister or at least incredible to someone who doesn't know and understand all the players and the overlaps. To someone who knows and understands all the players, there seems to be a logical if remarkable progression.

Another example: During the 1992 presidential primary, Clinton's campaign ran short of cash as it awaited receipt of federal matching money for which it had fully qualified. The campaign came up with the idea of a bridge loan with a local bank. They went to Worthen

National Bank, one of the state's two largest, and qualified for a fully secured short-term loan. The national press—in particular *The Wall Street Journal*—found the loan questionable and parlayed it into a discussion of the facts that Worthen is partially owned by the family of Jackson T. Stephens, the patriarch of Stephens, Inc., a vast investment banking firm in Little Rock, and that Jack Stephens had been mentioned for having, at most, a detached and peripheral involvement in the BCCI matter. Actually, the Clinton campaign had gone to Worthen because Worthen's largest Little Rock competitor, First Commercial, had until very recently been chaired by a gregarious fellow named Bill Bowen. When Clinton decided to run for president, he needed to solidify his gubernatorial staff for his periods of prolonged absence. He had picked the liked and respected Bill Bowen to be his chief of staff. His campaign wanted to avoid the appearance of favoritism of a gubernatorial aide's bank. What would it have looked like for Clinton's campaign to borrow money from Clinton's chief of staff? Like Arkansas, most likely.

Fifth, ethics laws came late to Arkansas—and with a fight. Until 1987, when I began writing columns about the absence of any lobbyist disclosure law and the tendency of business lobbyists to establish cabals to help each other in the part-time citizens' legislature, the state was devoid of any regulation of lobbyists, or disclosure requirements, as well as any system of meaningful disclosure of gifts to elected officials. Clinton proposed such laws that year; the legislature blocked them. So Clinton, in 1988, led a public initiative for an ethics and lobbyist disclosure law that the voters passed overwhelmingly. But get this: it still is not illegal in Arkansas for a legislator to be a lobbyist, in effect. The most recent speaker of the House of Representatives, a job passed around in this part-time citizens' legislature at two-year intervals, is L. L. "Doc" Bryan of Russellville. For years his private sector job was "director of industrial relations" for the Arkansas Poultry Federation, the lobbying association of the state's massive chicken industry. Though the chicken lobby had other full-time lobbyists, Bryan gave it a voting seat in the House, on the Joint Budget Committee, and on the Revenue and Taxation Committee. Incredible? Certainly. The idea is that if voters want to elect and reelect a representative who is on the payroll of a special interest, then that is the voters' business. Pure democracy, one supposes.

So, Bill Clinton's Arkansas was a place without an opposing party, with a press that was strong in some ways but lax for years in coverage of the underlying financial angle of politics, with politicians and businesspeople who had overlapping and sometimes intimately curious associations, and where rugged individualists resisted taxes and government intrusion and therefore ensured that state government had understaffed and underemphasized regulatory agencies.

It was far from alone in most of those conditions, and it had improved in all regards in recent years. But its boy-wonder governor had become President of the United States, and by the end of 1993 he was threatening to be a successful one who might realign the nation's political landscape for a generation. Anyone wanting to discredit Clinton needed only to dredge up some of the old soap opera scripts from his curious little state.

Having said all of that to explain Clinton's roots, it is not enough. The central facts about what some called "Whitewatergate" had less to do with the place than with the people and the era. After all, it centered on politicians' relationships with a failed savings and loan. Arkansas hardly was alone in the abuses and failures of S&Ls in the eighties. Nor was it alone in the curious associations of politicians with some of the S&L operators.

Actually, the central character in the Whitewater affair was David Hale of Little Rock, a veteran Democratic Party operative and former municipal judge, who during the 1980s ran a lending institution that was subsidized by the Small Business Administration to make loans to women, minorities, and others with worthy business plans but little ability to borrow money conventionally because of economic or social disadvantages. When he was indicted by a federal grand jury in September 1993 for a pattern of allegedly fraudulent practices, Hale told various media that he had been pressured to make loans to such Democratic Party notables as Clinton and Clinton's successor as governor, Jim Guy Tucker. He was looking for leverage to make a deal for a grant of immunity, or partial immunity, in exchange for landing bigger fish. In September, Hale's attorney, Randy Coleman of Little Rock, called Bill Kennedy, the associate White House counsel, and told him, "If Heidi Fleiss was the madam to the stars, then David Hale was the lender to the political elite." Kennedy, by Coleman's account, was not amused.

The Whitewater matter had come up during the presidential campaign of 1992, but the story died. The Resolution Trust Corporation had turned over information about Madison Guaranty to the U.S. Attorney in Little Rock, a Republican named Chuck Banks. The prosecutor declined to move on it, questioning the propriety of Republican regulators hitting him in the middle of a presidential race with allegations that indirectly touched the Democratic nominee.

The aforementioned Sheffield Nelson—the utility executive who helped make Jerry Jones rich enough to buy the Dallas Cowboys and then selected Bill Clinton's boyhood chum, Mack McLarty, to take over Arkla—fueled much of the Whitewater affair. He had run a nasty Republican race against Clinton in 1990 and was gearing up to run against Clinton's successor, Tucker, in 1994. Reporters wanting to interview Hale sometimes went through Nelson. Nelson also had tape recordings of conversations he'd had with Jim McDougal, the central figure in Whitewater-Madison. If federal authorities would grant at least limited immunity to Hale, he would surely reveal a pattern of one-party corruption that would shock the state, Nelson said. Hale's general charge was that his and McDougal's institutions did business with each other through the mid-eighties to help what McDougal called "the Democratic family of Arkansas," up to and including the Clintons. But Sheffield Nelson himself had invested with McDougal in the early 1980s for a vacation development at Campobello, the one-time retreat of Franklin Delano Roosevelt. At that time Nelson headed Arkla and was a Democrat. (He announced for governor in 1990 without declaring his party affiliation, only later saying he had donned the Republican mantle.) The Campobello development failed, as did many of Mc-Dougal's, but not before Sheffield Nelson bailed out at a profit.

Then on March 22, 1994, Hale pleaded guilty to two of the four counts of his indictment and agreed to cooperate with a federal grand jury led by special prosecutor Robert Fiske. It wasn't an especially good deal for him, but at least Fiske had indicated a willingness to let him tell his story to the grand jury under oath. The Clintons were certain to be spattered by his allegations. The question was whether they would be more than spattered.

Wherever they happened to reside, the Clintons revealed bad business and personal judgment to invest in a faulty land development scheme with a money-chasing couple—McDougal and his wife, Susan. It was ill-advised on the face of it in 1985 for Hillary Clinton to represent legally, though only briefly and to no eventual advantage, the savings and loan run by McDougal, to the point of attaching her name to correspondence sent in Madison Guaranty Savings and Loan's behalf to the securities commissioner, Beverly Bassett Schaffer, who had been recently appointed by Hillary's husband.

One cannot blame the curious small-time culture of Arkansas for Hillary Clinton's poor judgment. She was from Chicago, then Wellesley, then Yale. She came to Arkansas only under a kind of romantic duress; she happened to be in love with a fellow who insisted on being governor of the place on his way to the White House.

That's what the Whitewater-Madison brouhaha amounted to, really: the bad personal and business judgment of the Clintons in a place where curiously overlapping political and business associations were sufficiently commonplace that they did not attract as much critical attention as they might in a larger state with a vital opposing party and newspapers more accomplished at blending political and business reporting.

(In that regard, we in the Arkansas media paid scant attention to Hillary through the 1980s because she wasn't a full-time government policy leader. She was pursuing her private career. Attacking her would get one accused of unfairness or sexism and of not understanding or accepting her right to pursue an independent career. That's what I heard in 1989, for example, when I questioned the potential conflict of her law firm's representing corporate raiders who were seeking to take over the Arkansas Best Corp. trucking company of Fort Smith, despite the opposition of her husband, who pondered for a time proposing a change in the corporate code in a special legislative session to insulate the home company. Where Hillary and a professional woman's independence were concerned, backwoods Arkansas often seemed more progressive and enlightened through the 1980s than the nation appeared in 1993.)

At its core, the story of Whitewater-Madison was not worthy of the name "Whitewatergate" because it encompassed no potential criminality by the Clintons inside the current White House, or, by nearly all objective accounts, outside the current White House. Bill Clinton was not motivated by money. If he was, he could have parlayed his impeccable credentials into prosperity in the private sector. His validation was provided electorally, not financially. Hillary was motivated, too, by the achievement of political power; she sacrificed for her husband, but she benefited mightily in return—to the point that I never considered her a feminist or an inspiring role model for working women. What's the model? Marry a brilliant politician, endure his philandering, and take over the health care industry when he goes to the White House? I think not.

Her business endeavors were for the purpose of providing long-term family security in the absence of her husband's help. That's not to say she was as uninterested in money as he. She came from a more affluent background than her husband. A campaign aide driving her to an engagement asked her in the early eighties, "Have you and Bill ever thought about getting out of politics and making a lot of money?" She replied, "I have. He hasn't." Actually, as *The New York Times* would uncover in March 1994, Hillary had made a quick $100,000 in 1978, before Clinton was governor, trading commodities on the advice of her and Bill's friend, Jim Blair, who was counsel for Tyson Foods.

For his part, Clinton's chief fear of Whitewater was that he couldn't be sure what would come out because he had never made it a priority and had no earthly idea what might have transpired over more than a decade. He could tell you the number of votes he received in a rural precinct of Arkansas in 1978, but he couldn't tell you much if anything about the intricacies of the land development business he went into that year.

Of all the pronouncements by Jim McDougal, the one that rang truest was, "Bill's eyes just glazed over," whenever business subjects were raised.

The resistance to public disclosure of Whitewater was based mostly on Hillary's adamant and lawyerly belief in a "zone of privacy" and concern that public disclosure would embarrass her personally and professionally while providing fodder for a media frenzy and partisan exploitation, thus distracting attention from the policy initiatives she and her husband lived for. That would be health care reform, primarily.

Hillary has long been inclined toward a bunker mentality. She tolerates criticism much less graciously than her husband, who might blow up at a critic one day and hug him the next. Clinton is accustomed to public embarrassment; Hillary isn't. She defines morality on the legacy of the issues of her youth—Vietnam, civil rights, Watergate—and assigns partisan evil to most detraction. Together, the Clintons were fully capable of a Nixonian stonewall to protect personal privacy or to protect themselves from exploitation or embarrassment, but not of an active cover-up or obstruction of justice. They could be counted on to stop short of that.

At its core Whitewater was a story of bad judgment, embarrassment, ethical lapses, and relatively minor financial loss for the Clintons covering a time from the late 1970s to the mid-1980s when they were young and free and powerful in a backwoods state, and thought they were invincible and invisible. Bill Clinton was notoriously reckless and indiscreet in his personal associations. That was nothing new. Hillary's job sometimes was to watch him, but as I've explained, she'd never made baby-sitting her full-time responsibility.

Her husband was the one who, in 1978, before he was governor, got her into Whitewater with McDougal, his witty, big-talking pal from Senator Fulbright's staff, and she had been steamed at her husband for years about the loss of money and the personal embarrassment.

Hillary was relatively new to Arkansas and McDougal when Clinton put her in business with him; she had a right to blame her husband for the initial association. But Clinton had reason to be steamed at his wife, too. In time she had assumed control of the Whitewater matter, and it was more her fault than his that records were missing, that she crossed an ethical line, and that McDougal made dubious dealings under the name of Whitewater that the Clintons knew nothing about.

So it was Hillary, not Bill, who most staunchly resisted a full public release of the Whitewater documents and acquiescence to a special counsel to investigate McDougal, Whitewater, and any peripheral allegations. And it was Hillary who could not be challenged comfortably by White House staffers. Her iciness and toughness made her unapproachable; Bill could be talked to, but she couldn't.

There was lingering mythology through 1993 that Hillary was smarter than the president and the better person. He had more glaring flaws and she had more glaring backbone. But she could be tyrannically self-absorbed, cold, and quite impolitic. (Remember that once she asserted control of my travel arrangements, dictating that I be hauled from Fort Smith to Fayetteville by a state trooper, and that it was Clinton who went behind her back to make sure I understood the impropriety of that.) It was nearly unanimous among Clinton insiders in Arkansas that while Hillary was more organized and better able to focus than her husband, she was merely smart, while his brainpower could seem spectacular in the breadth of knowledge and the speed of study.

As a young political phenom, Bill Clinton had been a sucker for someone like Jim McDougal, who was bright—though not as bright as he wanted you to think—as well as fairly urbane, funny, irreverent, and a traditional Democrat who adored FDR to the point of imitating him in speech and mannerisms. Clinton had many of those qualities, but he had to temper them with the realities of political viability. He sometimes drew his sense of humor and healthy irreverence through others, like McDougal. Hillary, on the other hand, had much less need for such vicarious pleasures. She does not suffer fools gladly; her husband suffers them exuberantly.

Clinton was a collegian working part time on Fulbright's staff when he befriended McDougal, who was six years older than he. The friendship flourished when Clinton was in his twenties and the business partnership began when Clinton was barely thirty. Youth and immaturity are not excuses, but they are constant factors with Clinton. Remember, he had grown up in public in Arkansas as a work-in-progress, erring and recovering, blundering and rallying.

McDougal, who always talked of business schemes and making money, sensed the land development opportunities of northern Arkansas, where retirees and vacationers are coming with increasing frequency, and in 1978 he cut his thirty-two-year-old buddy, the governor-elect, in on the Whitewater Development Corporation to develop lots and homes along the White River. Their signature on bank notes bought the Clintons a half-interest in McDougal's dream. Then McDougal joined Clinton's first and ill-fated gubernatorial term, 1979–80, as an economic development adviser, leaving that position early to go into small-town banking. Clinton made countless errors in his appointees in that disastrous first term, and McDougal wasn't the best example. Clinton tapped a small-town police chief named Tommy Robinson to be his director of public safety. The status and high profile enabled Robinson to become elected sheriff of Pulaski County, the state's largest county, containing Little Rock. Robinson chained county prisoners to the fence of the state prison, arrested political opponents, falsely accused a prominent criminal defense lawyer of conspiring to kill his wife, and then got elected to Congress, where he distinguished himself by writing more hot checks at the House Bank than anyone else.

Then, in 1982, when Clinton was making his first political comeback, McDougal ran a quixotic campaign against the entrenched Republican congressman from northwest Arkansas—John Paul Hammerschmidt, a close friend of George Bush who quietly perpetuated his tenure in Congress by remaining invisible on policy and issues while tending with unparalleled efficiency to constituent services on matters such as veterans' affairs and Social Security disability. I suspected that McDougal's candidacy was an attempt to keep Hammerschmidt preoccupied so that he wouldn't bother Clinton's gubernatorial campaign, though it could have been a simple McDougal lark. With his young and attractive wife, Susan, McDougal drove from campaign rally to campaign rally to orate on the rich Rooseveltian heritage of the Democratic Party and berate Hammerschmidt—this in a conservative Republican district where Hammerschmidt was a god and FDR was blamed for nearly every modern problem. McDougal was having fun. Over coffee one morning, he joked that if at any point in his impending speech he accused Reagan of the cliché of "trying to balance the budget on the backs of the poor," he hoped someone would pull him off the stage. McDougal got 35 percent of the vote. Afterward he assessed his loss cleverly: he said that when a person campaigns for office, he is heartened when one in three people he encounters offers him support; but then, on election day, it becomes dishearteningly obvious that one in three equals 33 percent.

After that, McDougal decided to apply his talents to banking. He had bought the tiny Madison Bank in Kingston in the secluded hills of northern Arkansas, which had all of seven hundred depositors, with Steve Smith, a native of Kingston and witty academic who had been one of Clinton's top bearded liberal aides in the ill-fated first gubernatorial term. Smith had a wry irreverence and intellect that left McDougal's in the shade. As a delegate to a state constitutional convention, Smith had proposed for his own amusement an interest-rate ceiling for the proposed new state constitution: "passbook plus one," which meant banks could charge on loans an interest rate one percentage point higher than what they paid on standard savings accounts.

Later Smith would get a $69,000 loan from David Hale's SBA-backed lender, then use the money to pay off another debt at Worthen Bank. An original shareholder in the bank with McDougal and Smith was Jim Guy Tucker, Clinton's successor as governor of Arkansas. Tucker's wife borrowed extensively from Hale's firm for various enterprises. Such were the overlapping associations of bright young Democrats in Arkansas through the 1980s, especially around a man like McDougal who described himself as a "political businessman."

They ended up selling the bank at a loss after making bad loans. In their zeal to prosper, they had lent a major employer in the area three times the bank's loan maximum—making loans to the man, his wife, and his company. Then the man went out of business, and it turned out that the bank had made fatal errors in describing the real estate pledged as security for the loan.

But in the meantime McDougal had realized the real potential of the 1980s: It was in the deregulated savings and loan business. There was no reason, he told friends, for Republicans to have exclusive rights to these deregulated riches. An extraordinarily partisan person, McDougal told friends he wanted to help Democrats make money. With borrowed funds he bought a small thrift in eastern Arkansas, relocated it to Little Rock, and named it Madison Guaranty Savings and Loan. Whitewater meanwhile was a bust as the land business went sour in a recession, and the only time it came up in Arkansas was when Bill Clinton filed a personal financial statement listing an interest exceeding $1,000 in it.

"What is that?" one reporter would ask another as the two of them perused Clinton's personal financial disclosure form.

"Oh, it's that deal with Jim McDougal."

"Oh, yeah."

Such was the interest Whitewater generated in Arkansas over a decade.

Clinton remained cozy with McDougal, much too cozy for a governor and a regulated businessman. The state housing development agency, which issued tax-free bonds for low-interest housing loans, and which Clinton later expanded into a full-fledged finance authority issuing tax-free bonds for capital projects and entrepreneurial financing, was housed through much of the 1980s in McDougal's Madison building in downtown Little Rock. Leasing of private office space by state agencies is handled by an agency called State Building Services; its director and board members are appointed by the governor. It is not uncommon in Arkansas for friends of the governor to lease office space to state agencies. Throughout the 1980s Little Rock was overbuilt in office space; whether an office development profited depended sometimes on whether state government agencies could be secured as tenants.

Whitewater came to nothing. The Clintons occasionally wrote checks to make loan payments. Meanwhile Clinton established himself as a national-class education reformer with a tax program he pushed through the legislature in 1983 with the considerable help of his wife. Madison Guaranty grew rapidly. It had $10 million in assets when McDougal bought it with borrowed money in 1982. But deregulation allowed S&Ls to lend heavily for commercial real estate development; by 1983, McDougal had reappointed himself head of Madison's real estate development operation, turning over the leadership of the S&L

itself to someone else. But he remained majority owner. By the end of 1984, the S&L showed assets of $45 million.

McDougal was seen around Little Rock driving a Bentley; his wife drove a Jaguar. It was about that time that he got the idea to develop Campobello, the FDR retreat, which turned out to be another of his ill-conceived and ill-fated projects.

Arkansas still had two-year gubernatorial terms at the time, and Clinton faced reelection in the fall of 1984. He was opposed by a Republican businessman named Woody Freeman who was underfunded and not a particularly talented politician, and Clinton won easily.

But he'd been a bit lax in his fund-raising, and at one point in that race he did something quite common in Arkansas politics. Since campaigns cannot borrow money, he went to the Bank of Cherry Valley, owned in part by his crusty old executive secretary and father figure, Maurice Smith, and personally borrowed $50,000, then put the money into his campaign. It is customary in Arkansas that politicians come around after campaigns seeking fund-raisers and donations to retire their campaign debts, which actually are personal debts.

There was hardly a more secure short-term loan in Arkansas in 1984 than one for $50,000 to Bill Clinton, who was a cinch to be reelected in a walk and then, as sitting governor, raise the money with dispatch.

Early in 1985 Clinton began to put together fund-raisers to retire that debt. Historically one of the principal sources of campaign money in Arkansas was Stephens, Inc., the investment banking giant and an intensely private and politically eclectic company. The colorful founder and patriarch was W. R. "Witt" Stephens, now deceased, who in the 1940s won the approval of the Securities and Exchange Commission to buy a gas company in Fort Smith by responding as follows when the hearing examiner asked whether he had collateral: "Yeah, I brung it with me." He had his collateral in cash in his pocket. He'd been selling bonds since 1933. Mr. Witt, as he was known, was a staunch Democrat. He'd backed everyone from Orval Faubus to Walter Mondale.

But the modern-day patriarch of the firm was Jackson T. Stephens, the much younger brother of Mr. Witt, and a less colorful Naval Academy graduate, who by 1985 was becoming a bona fide Reagan Republican. He was particularly angry at Clinton for proposing in the legislature that year the establishment of a central state agency to be the clearinghouse for tax-free bond issues in the state. Stephens, Inc., had made some of its money by handling municipal bond issues for Arkansas towns. Clinton's plan sounded like socialism to him, Jack Stephens told me that year.

Clinton's relationship with the Stephenses was always volatile, and the point was that Clinton couldn't rely on money from that source in 1985. But with the savings and loan and investment banking explosions, there were brash new kids on the town's financial block: McDougal, for example. Also growing was an investment banking firm called Collins, Locke & Lasater. By 1986, the Stephenses would underwrite former Governor Frank White's bitter challenge to Clinton, and White would make an issue of Clinton's personal association with some of the principals of Collins, Locke & Lasater who eventually went to prison for recreational distribution of cocaine.

Clinton asked McDougal to have a fund-raiser for him, which, quite audaciously, was held in the thrift's offices. About $35,000 was raised.

It was shortly after that when Hillary, for a $2,000-a-month retainer paid to her Rose Law Firm, briefly represented Madison. The bottom was falling out of the firm through bad investments and strange and failed deals among interlocking McDougal corporations, among them Whitewater and other failing real estate ventures. Hillary put her name on a letter to Securities Commissioner Beverly Bassett Schaffer. The regulator was an appointee of Bill Clinton (and, incidentally, wife of Tyson Foods' public relations man, who also was the nephew of Senator Dale Bumpers), asking whether an unconventional $3 million preferred stock plan for recapitalization was permissible under Arkansas law for an S&L. Schaffer said that it was, or that no law seemed to prohibit it. But she would have been required to formally approve any actual stock issuance, and Madison never came forward with a proposal. Many published reports falsely stated that Schaffer had approved the plan; she hadn't.

Susan McDougal, meanwhile, was consuming conspicuously. She also went out and got a $300,000 loan guaranteed through David Hale's SBA-backed lender. It was for a firm she headed called Master Marketing.

In 1986 the Madison board, under pressure from regulators, removed McDougal from the firm. Later he was tried and acquitted on federal bank fraud charges after seeking to have himself declared unfit for trial on the assertion that he had suffered an emotional breakdown. He was diagnosed as manic-depressive and prescribed medication.

In 1989, regulators closed Madison at a cost to taxpayers exceeding $50 million, which was minuscule in the S&L scheme of things in the eighties. Investigators with the Resolution Trust Corporation, surveying the wreckage, found curious dealings, some involving apparent shell companies bearing names like "McDougal-Smith-Tucker," and others involving at least on the periphery the names of Bill and Hillary Clinton.

For example, more than a third of that $300,000 SBA-guaranteed loan to Susan McDougal's Master Marketing went instead to Whitewater Development Corp., and was not repaid. The Clintons professed to know nothing of that, and Jim McDougal backed them up in an interview with *The Washington Post* in the fall of 1993: he said the Clintons "were the last goddamn people" you would consult on a business deal.

Investigators also were curious about that Clinton fund-raiser at Madison, especially the use of cashier's checks drawn straight from the S&L and given to the campaign. When at least one of the cashier's checks began to appear dubious, the Clintons explained that it was not their reponsibility to authenticate every check they received, which was true.

In Arkansas the newspapers routinely tracked campaign contribution reports closely, usually listing all individual contributions of $500 or more, but they did that only during campaigns. The report containing itemized contributions from the Madison fund-raiser would have been in a supplemental, post-election report—filed during a time in 1985 when reporters weren't making regular checks of the election services office in the Secretary of State's office. Apparently that report never got any publicity in either statewide daily newspaper; no clipping could be found. By 1993 it also had been destroyed by the Secretary of State, and Betsey Wright, the chief source of Clinton campaign materials, said she had no copy in her personal possession.

The other more serious matter was that Hillary's firm represented Madison at one point and then turned around later in the decade and represented the FDIC in a suit against Madison's certified public accounting firm. Webb Hubbell handled part of the case for the FDIC despite the fact that his father-in-law, Seth Ward, a prominent Little Rock businessman, had done extensive business with Madison.

Vince Foster, it turned out, had solicited the FDIC business in a letter in February 1989 which asserted that there were no existing conflicts of interest and failed to mention the previous representation of Madison. Most legal ethics experts said no actual conflict existed and that disclosure, while advisable in retrospect, was not necessary.

The FDIC decreed in early 1994 that no conflict had existed, but Republicans cried cover-up to the point that the FDIC agreed to reopen the question. Foster sought the FDIC business because he, Hillary, Hubbell, and Bill Kennedy had forced out the firm's "rainmaker," Joe Giroir, in a dispute about Giroir's banking activities, and Giroir had taken big business, such as Tyson Foods, with him.

The role of the Rose Law Firm, specifically of Associate Attorney General Hubbell, a former partner there with Hillary Clinton and Vince Foster, should have been enough to convince Attorney General Janet Reno to appoint an independent counsel to take over the investigation of Madison that three career Justice Department criminal lawyers had undertaken in Little Rock on the referral of the Resolution Trust Corporation. But Reno and the White House resisted until the pressure became too great. When both *The New York Times* and *The Washington Post* called on their editorial pages for an independent counsel, the Clinton White House lost its two best press friends. Then, when a smattering of Democratic members of Congress called for an independent counsel, it was inevitable.

The Clintons had resisted calls for a special prosecutor for reasons beyond personal privacy. They were so leery of right-wing investigations, attacks, and exploitations that they feared that if they gave in on Whitewater, they might set a precedent that would have them agreeing to special prosecors every time Floyd Brown, the pit bull, dug up an accusation back in Arkansas. "We're just not as mean as they are; we don't even think of the things they do," Betsey Wright said.

But in the case of a special prosecutor for Whitewater, the problem wasn't Floyd Brown; it was *The New York Times, The Washington Post,* Senator Daniel Patrick Moynihan, Senator Bill Bradley, and a half dozen other Democrats, all of whom publicly decreed that the matter was serious enough—politically, not legally—to warrant special investigation.

But what about a simple public release of the Clintons' Whitewater documents? Wouldn't that have been wise? Shouldn't the First Couple simply have taken their lumps for horrible judgment and ethical lapses dating back to those zany youthful days in Arkansas? Key advisers to Clinton would nearly have him convinced of the wisdom of that, but then Hillary would say no.

The more she said no, the more people began to wonder if she was doing more than protecting herself from personal embarrassment and her husband's administration and policy initiatives from whatever dirt the Republican attack machine might dig up or distort from the documents. Remember, she was a lawyer and a former senior partner of a prominent law firm that cared not a whit for the negative national media attention heaped on it.

Vince Foster had arranged in late 1992 for the Clintons' long-overdue dissolution of their Whitewater relationship with McDougal. (Clinton once explained that the partnership was never dissolved because it would have been improper for McDougal to bail him out of losses.) Foster had handled the late payment of taxes related to Whitewater, another breakdown in Hillary's handling of the matter.

Foster's role, his suicide, and the removal of the Whitewater files from his office by Bernie Nussbaum, when combined with Webb Hubbell's role in the matter and Hillary's stubborn refusal to agree to a public release, led to plenty of questions and theories about what if anything she might be protecting.

When the Clintons agreed on December 23 to turn over Whitewater documents to Justice Department investigators, they asked for and received a broadened subpoena to protect the confidentiality of those and other documents. And the Clintons' lawyer sought and failed to get a vow from the Justice Department not to give the documents to another section where the matter of Foster's suicide was being investigated.

That might have been only a question of trying to head off selective leaking by investigators and Republicans who didn't wish the president well. It may also have had to do with trying to protect the memory and grieving family of a departed friend from partisan exploitation. But at year's end the matter was growing into one with overtones of John Grisham–style intrigue, all centered on Foster's suicide, and the Clintons attempted the one thing that always will arouse curiosities and never succeed in Washington: stonewalling.

That considerable cloud aside, the Clintons seemed on the periphery, the very close periphery, of the more serious financial allegations, or to have been oblivious stooges. But on clear matters of ethical indiscretions and unwise associations, they had made plenty of serious blunders, Hillary more than Bill.

And it was not fair to define these as the typical cultural blunders of a backwater state. They were the personal past blunders of the President and First Lady of the United States, the former chronically indiscreet in his personal associations and the latter not at all sensitive to political implications.

The central question, then, was this: What of these blunders?

Failing criminality, which hardly anyone other than Republican attack artists was willing to suggest, their public worthiness was to help define the First Couple as imperfect, capable of judgmental error, hypocritical in their decrying of the greed of the Reagan era, poor businesspeople, and grudgingly unwilling to accept the fact that the President of the United States, unlike the governor of Arkansas, has no "zone of privacy." It was conceivable that the Clintons might owe yet more taxes and be subject to penalties because of improperly claimed Whitewater-related deductions. The myth of Hillary Clinton as "Saint Hillary" preaching the "politics of meaning" was deflated.

But Watergate and Iran-contra were credible allegations of legal or ethical improprieties against White House officials stemming from the performance of their duties in the White House. "Whitewatergate" was sixteen years old; if Clinton violated a public trust, its relevance would be historical reference. It might be a factor for voters in 1996 in contributing to the portrait of their president. It was fair to bring it up; it was important to bring it up. But as a compelling scandal, it paled in comparison with some of its presidential predecessors.

Clinton himself seemed about a step-and-a-half removed from the principal allegations: his securities commissioner, Beverly Bassett Schaffer, was a tough regulator who extended no irregular favors to Madison and insisted Clinton never said one word to her about Jim McDougal. Clinton was guilty of accepting a campaign fund-raiser from an old friend who turned out to be an unwise association, but if there was irregularity in the sources of money, he seemed to be oblivious to it and legally detached from complicity. When confronted initially with Whitewater-related allegations in the campaign of 1992, he said he thought he had lost about $25,000, and that, yes, he probably should have gotten out of the partnership long before. There was a kind of reassurance to that answer, suggesting as it did that he didn't know enough about the situation to be aware of his losses and that he readily accepted the improprieties of the arrangement.

Again, the more intricate questions concerned Hillary, who spent much of 1993 in a frenzied public relations campaign to build a strong public image that would define her as part Bobby Kennedy, right hand to the president and policy powerhouse; part Barbara Bush, warm First Spouse and First Mom; and part Princess Diana, royal family fashion plate, posing with semi-sensuousness in *Vogue* magazine. She had the closer relationship with Vince Foster, and while Webb Hubbell was the president's good buddy, it was Hillary who was professionally tied to him from their days as senior partners at the Rose Law Firm. It was Hillary who had sought power of attorney for Whitewater matters; it was Hillary who inappropriately represented McDougal for a short time; and it was Hillary's law firm that was enmeshed in the legal battles between the Resolution Trust Corporation and Madison.

She had long prided herself on professional independence from her husband's political career, and it appeared that she might sustain the most damage from Whitewater because of that professional independence. But that might insulate her husband from the more serious implications, though Mrs. Clinton obviously was not interested in taking any falls for her husband. She had sacrificed for him aplenty already.

Even so, even if the Whitewater affair turned out to provide severe embarrassment for Hillary, Hubbell, and the Rose Law Firm, and if speculation grew that the trigger for Vince Foster's torment and suicide was related to what he saw as the inevitable problems for his friends and his firm stemming from that matter, there appeared in early 1994 to be nothing that would directly implicate the President of the United States in anything criminal or be otherwise expository beyond what already was known.

But at the very least it perpetuated the image that the new president was not quite trustworthy. That image was reinforced in early 1994 when the press learned that federal regulators had met three times in late 1993 with top White House officials to give them a "heads up" on the Madison investigation.

Bernie Nussbaum, blundering again as chief White House counsel by participating in inappropriate meetings that he should have legally advised against, was fired at last by Clinton on March 4, 1994. Mack McLarty, George Stephanopoulos, and Harold Ickes—who finally joined the White House in January 1994 as deputy chief of staff—pleaded with the president to do it. The problem was Hillary, who had been chiefly responsible for his hiring. She had known and trusted Nussbaum for decades. As a lawyer, she respected Nussbaum's loyalty to his clients and his tendency to see issues not in terms of political appearances, but only in a strict legal sense. It was a view of the world that had served him well as a corporate lawyer in New York. But it had made him an uninterrupted disaster in the White House, and Hillary accepted grudgingly, even bitterly, that he had to go.

A few weeks later Webb Hubbell would resign as associate attorney general. A few of his former partners at the Rose Law Firm—most likely those who had never cared for the "Famous Four" (Hillary, Foster, Hubbell, and Bill Kennedy)—leaked to the press that they suspected Hubbell of leaving them with at least $100,000 in unrecoverable expenses incurred wastefully in a failed lawsuit he handled on a contingency basis for his brother-in-law's parking-meter business. Hubbell simply could not lead the federal Justice Department while accused of unethical behavior by his former law partners. The Clintons did not object to his resignation, though it hurt them. Hubbell "is the person whose company the President enjoys most in the world," Mack McLarty had told me.

Clinton's reputation for not telling the whole truth, for having a basic character flaw, was mostly deserved. Reporters who had heard him chop the truth into tiny parcels, or dissemble or evade with artful lawyer-speak, were compelled to pursue Whitewater because, based on their experience with him, they saw no reason to accept his explanations at face value. They thought that Whitewater might bear resemblance to the tortured matter of his military avoidance, meaning the truth would come out only through persistent reporting that would force Clinton to parcel out a little more truth when confronted with it. For example, after Clinton had asserted that he had told the entire story of his draft history, he confirmed casually a new report: Oh, yes, he did get a draft notice.

As he entered 1994, Clinton appeared to have firm control of the job of president. He was performing it well. The economy was solid. The White House appeared to be running more efficiently. The only problem was the old problem: Bill Clinton's character.

As one who had studied him for years, I comfortably declared him to be no crook. But would I vouch for the truth of everything he had said? No, I couldn't do that. Were the questions about his truthfulness unfair? No, I couldn't say that. Did the American people want a capable president or did they want a great role model? If they wanted both, Clinton had some work to do in the latter regard.

The Whitewater affair served mainly to sap his already limited presidential stature. As a youthful minority president who had avoided the draft and admitted euphemistically to marital infidelity, he could command respect as a politician, but not as a man.

Near the end of 1993, David Gergen spoke in downtown Washington to a mostly conservative group of businesspeople at the Cosmos Club. He said two questions confronted the Clinton administration for the new year: How would it deal with the major issues, which he listed as education, health reform, and violence? And who was Bill Clinton?

It was Gergen's answer to the second question that seemed to cross the line from spin to revelation and candor.

"He was a product of the sixties," Gergen said of his boss, "with its best and its worst. It was a time when everything went in private life so long as one was straight in public life. It has taken a lot of time to grow up since then."

That's Bill Clinton, growing up in public, a product of a time when JFK was revered and the press protected the charming, debonair president's legendary indiscretions on the argument that they weren't relevant to his public responsibility, and of a time when young people were preaching a public morality about race and war while breaking drug laws and copulating with random liberty.

From that time and culture came a young and brilliant politician who believed morality and character were defined by public policy initiatives—by how you felt about the war and civil rights and health care—and who thought it clever and sophisticated to pursue a private life that was a kind of inside joke among the brightest and best.

In 1986 I asked Clinton about taking a drug test, which he had just done to preempt a challenge he knew to be coming from his Republican opponent. He said with laughter that first he checked to see how long evidence of controlled substances remained in one's system, and that then he checked the statute of limitations. Being of Clinton's generation, I laughed as heartily as did he. Weren't we clever, joking privately about such things? I felt like Ben Bradlee to his JFK.

I remember a small dinner party in 1982, during which Clinton telephoned the host after having made a campaign appearance at a meeting of Parents Without Partners. He was invited over; Hillary, not unusually, was not with him on this Saturday night. He showed up, had a couple of beers that eventually put him to sleep in his chair, but not before a comical performance that had me doubled in laughter. He was opposed in the Democratic primary that year by the current Arkansas governor, Jim Guy Tucker, and both were trying to out-demagogue the other on the question of which of them was a nasty liberal. Clinton slipped into self-caricature. He said he would accuse Tucker of being friendly with the American Civil Liberties Union, which at the time was threatening a lawsuit against the traditional Nativity scene at Christmastime on the state Capitol steps. "Why," roared Clinton, intoning as a holy-roller preacher, "this man is a member of the A, C, L, and U, and he wants to take baby Jeeee-sus off the Capitol grounds."

I thought of that when two state troopers with an idea for a book deal granted their infamous interview to the ultra-right *American Spectator,* accusing Clinton, on the basis of mostly circumstantial evidence, of up-to-date sexual sins and innumerable other indiscretions. The article's allegations, made with partisan glee by a writer named David Brock, "were maybe 20 percent truth," as one Clinton insider assessed. The troopers accused Clinton, among other things, of having sinisterly declared that he "never met a tax I didn't like." That, for goodness sakes, was a private joke, a self-caricature, the kind of thing I'd heard Clinton say countless times over the years. He'd met plenty of taxes he didn't like; essentially he didn't like any that might impair his political career.

So, from the sixties generation and culture came the first baby-boom president, growing up in public, ascending to the national stage *after,* not before, Watergate, and *after,* not before, Gary Hart. Bill Clinton moved into the White House at a time when the press was stronger, more diverse, and more determined to penetrate a "zone of privacy" than ever before, extending its interest carte blanche. After Watergate, no business indiscretion or claim of privacy would be tolerated. After Hart, sexual peccadilloes were bound to show up in print somewhere, even if they showed up first in a supermarket tabloid or an ultra-right rag. Any reporter cutting Clinton slack would be ridiculed, not made editor of *The Washington Post.*

America's new president ended his first year in office much as he began it: full of promise, talent, and accomplishment, but undefined, distrusted, and a subject of the reserved judgment of the American people.

Joe Klein, the writer for *Newsweek* who had embraced Clinton's candidacy, wrote in early January 1994 that the people of America still didn't know what to make of their president. He wrote that Clinton was so elusive in style and substance, so complex, that comic impersonators couldn't quite capture him. He wrote that Clinton could make a great speech and the American people would applaud, but then immediately become suspicious that Clinton was a politician who might not have meant what he said.

As one with about a fifteen-year head start in Clinton-watching, I knew that sometimes it seemed that the more you knew about him, the less you understood. But I had finally reached some conclusions.

CHAPTER 12

Taking Stock

In 1992, I filled the ears of a television reporter with accounts of Clinton's dissembling, expediency, overoptimism, and over-compromise in a dozen years as governor of Arkansas. America needed to know such things about the man who would be president. Then the reporter asked if Arkansas was better off for Clinton's having been governor, and in spite of everything I had said before, I could only answer that it was. Everything I had said until then was essentially irrelevant to the general worthiness of Clinton's governorship.

The schools were improved. The tax system was a bit fairer, though not fair enough. The economy had grown. There was a new public ethics law, lax though it be. There was a new initiative in early child-hood intervention to identify underprivileged children in their pre-school years and attend to their needs in learning, socialization, and health care. One limited but successful program, borrowed by Hillary Clinton from Israel, taught single parents to teach their pre-school children in the home. Race relations were volatile, owing to the state's heritage and modern complications, but Clinton's record was solidly progressive, and black voters embraced him throughout his term, as solidly at the end as in the beginning. "The man relates," Richard Mays, a black Little Rock lawyer, explained. A financial settlement to end a smothering, long-running lawsuit over the resegregration of the Little Rock public schools had been achieved partly as a result of his leadership, which helped persuade the legislature to approve an extraor-dinary appropriation of tens of millions of dollars to the state's largest school system. The government and business community had worked together to modernize the state's system of vocational education with a self-imposed tax on business.

Clintonism in Arkansas had leaned more heavily toward well-intended pilot programs based on study and theory than toward broad and proven results, partly because he was better at sales than service; but on the whole, Arkansas had crept forward under Clinton.

It was true that the Medicaid system was a mess, left nearly bankrupt because of Clinton's inattention to administrative detail, reliance on funding gimmicks that didn't pan out, and preoccupation with running for president. He had concocted a tax that Medicaid providers would impose on themselves, thus generating more federal matching money on a 3-to-1 ratio. He told me one day in 1991, "The only thing that'll queer this deal is if the federal government stops us from doing it." Within eighteen months, the federal government had queered the deal. Environmental standards had been waived to create jobs, but Arkansas remained underdeveloped and, for the moment, relatively pristine.

All things considered, Arkansas could have done a lot worse for a governor, to borrow a phrase. We could have had a governor more forthright, less slick, and, in the latter years, more engaged. But we probably couldn't have found one brighter, more politically clever, or more pragmatically progressive.

The state had a history of susceptibility to the wiles of populist demagogues who railed against government, the newspapers, and big business; maybe the greatest benefit of Clinton's governorship was that he was slick enough to keep the populist demagogues at bay while he fashioned progress that was smartly packaged to make it palatable. It seemed that the key to Clinton's political success was that in every race he ever ran, in Arkansas or nationally, his motto could have been, "You may not quite trust me, but I'm better than the alternative." In Arkansas I found it hard to believe he was the Democrats' best hope in 1992; in Washington in 1993, I came to understand that in his combination of political talent and policy command, he probably had been.

I've said that with Clinton's arrival at the White House, a little dramatic production from Arkansas had opened to standing-room-only on Pennsylvania Avenue. I could not have imagined how accurate that statement would turn out to be. By year's end the Republicans and media fixated on a curious land deal involving 200 acres along the White River in northern Arkansas, and the nation was introduced to a cast of Arkansas characters more extensive and colorful than I had expected to rise from the backwoods to fame or notoriety.

Jim McDougal, Clinton's old friend and erstwhile business partner, taking medication to control manic depression, appeared on national television saying things sometimes curious, sometimes irreverent, sometimes funny. His much younger wife, Susan, was shown in newspapers across the land in a police mug shot: she had departed for California and been charged with embezzlement. David Hale, a minor-league political figure in Arkansas, was charged and convicted of fraudulent activities in a lending company he operated with subsidies for the economically disadvantaged through the Small Business Administration. He tried to take the president down with him, and, at this writing, had turned state's evidence as a special federal prosecutor honed in on the political and business culture of Arkansas.

Dare I say it again? Clinton is not a crook. He is, in my estimation, an occasional corner-cutter afflicted with bad personal judgment about people and possessed of no head for business. But he knows when and where to draw lines and is entirely too obsessed with political advancement to risk violating laws. Clinton, as a consummate party politician, might well have conveniently turned his back on abuses or inappropriateness in the cozy business and political relationships in a one-party state. That seemed to be the most serious personal charge even his harshest detractors would level as he began the second year of his presidency.

But this much should be said: I have described Clinton as a synthesis—mostly self-styled—of many modern presidents, but I haven't mentioned Richard Nixon. By year's end it was time to add Nixon to the blend. Alas, it should have been done in the beginning. Nixon was a savvy, keenly intelligent, and adaptable politician who fashioned incremental progress as a moderate president branching beyond his own party, but who behaved with a bunker mentality. Ditto Clinton. Nixon also was a resilient politician who rose from near death with the "Checkers" speech and mounted a dramatic personal comeback. Again, ditto Clinton. Nixon was "Tricky Dick," a first cousin, maybe once removed, of "Slick Willie."

What I had meant by the analogy of an Arkansas drama was that the nation would be introduced to the schizophrenia of Bill Clinton and probably confront its own schizophrenia in determining what to make of him.

On one hand he is a spectacularly talented and well-meaning politician with an extraordinary ability to communicate and connect, using his considerable brainpower and tendency toward compromise to fashion slow, steady progress—a worthy product after a messy process—while serving the nation best by moving it away from the trends and practices of the Reagan-Bush years and protecting it from populist demagogues like Ross Perot. The nation could have done worse for a president.

On the other hand, as a friend of his once told him colorfully, there is something about Clinton that people find irksome, something beyond the natural dislike of conservatives for a mostly liberal president. He seems to have an almost pathological inability to tell the whole truth. Something was missing in his personal development; it seemed to be the self-imposed discipline and personal ethic that one shouldn't make promises one can't or won't keep.

"But he *wants* to keep his promises, and he thinks at the time that he can," Betsey Wright, his longtime aide in Arkansas, insisted.

Her job in Arkansas, expertly performed for years, had been to discipline Clinton and keep him from saying and promising too much. On the very rare occasion when she took a vacation, staff members complained that they couldn't get any work done because Clinton kept showing up at their desks wanting to talk policy, or something else. Otherwise they complained that everything had to go through Betsey's desk.

Mack McLarty, George Stephanopoulos, David Gergen, and Bruce Lindsey between them couldn't quite do the work in the White House that Betsey Wright had done alone in Arkansas. Once Wright was out of his hair, Clinton was burned out on her kind of obsessive control and wouldn't tolerate it. None of those men was quite the obsessive personality that Wright was.

There were other things that troubled Americans about Clinton. As a professed devout Christian with a history of marital infidelity and clever finesse of full truth, he struck many as the Jimmy Swaggart of the secular left. But it wasn't just that; Clinton was hardly the first modern American political figure to preach a public morality and behave privately in a way that could be called hypocrisy. Clinton simply struck many people as phony; it was because of his look and his style, sometimes smug, sometimes pandering. As an extraordinary salesman, he charmed Americans at the moment of sale—in a personal meeting demonstrating empathy, in a State of the Union speech, at a televised town meeting, or at a news conference dominated by questions about his curious associations in Arkansas. But then Americans were left to wonder if they had been duped by the fast talker who just drove away.

Clinton is next to impossible to dislike in a personal meeting, but hard to like over a long period of acquaintance. It's hard to resist his rhetoric at the moment of hearing, but for much of America, it appeared to be easy to dismiss it shortly thereafter.

So, did he have enough credibility as a man and as a 43 percent president to lead? Of the four questions that would decide his presidency, that was the one that held the success of his presidency in the balance.

"The way to judge Bill is by what he accomplishes," Betsey Wright said.

Yes, that was one way to judge him, and it was a convenient one for Clinton supporters who believed morality should be judged by policy positions and public performance.

To be sure, Clinton's first year as president was a very good one substantively. For the first time, the White House and Congress had worked together to reduce the spiraling federal budget deficit; by year's end, it appeared that a deficit that otherwise might have exceeded $300 billion would in fact drop to $180 billion or below. Interest rates remained low, though they surely would have to inch upward. Inflation was controlled. There was job growth, though the nature of the modern American economy was that the jobs weren't necessarily good or secure ones. Clinton had a plan for repairing that: better schools, coordinated and improved lifetime job retraining; and new investment in infrastructure and high technology. Some might disagree philosophically, but that was the least of Clinton's problems. His leadership deserved a large measure of the credit for ratification of the North American Free Trade Agreement and for advancement on the General Agreement on Tariffs and Trade (GATT), forward-thinking strategies for competing in the world economy. He had declared war on crime, an issue ripe for demagoguery, which he managed to keep reasonably in check. America's system of health care needed improvement, if not full overhaul, and already he had used the power of the bully pulpit to focus attention on the problem and push the medical care industry toward self-imposed reforms. A working group was toiling diligently to propose a credible, workable means of reforming welfare, hanging up on an ugly truth: the cheapest way to deal with welfare was to continue the current system.

Giving a good speech was the easiest part of the job for Clinton, and usually it seemed the least consequential. But any assessment of his first year in the White House would be incomplete without considering the speech he gave late in the evening of November 13, 1993, in Memphis, Tennessee.

He gave the kind of speech and made the kind of connection that perhaps he alone among contemporary American politicians could perform and achieve. As a white Southerner and professed "new Democrat" with an extraordinary ability to relate to blacks, Clinton delivered a speech so compelling, candid, and seemingly heartfelt that even his top aides were surprised by the intensity with which he gave it and the punch it contained. They were surprised, too, by what he said: as usual when he is at his best, he had veered liberally from the text.

The speech was delivered to an audience of black ministers at the eighty-sixth annual Holy Convocation of the Church of God in Christ at the Mason Temple Church of God in Christ, the venue for Dr. Martin Luther King, Jr.'s, famous "I have been to the mountaintop" speech the night before his assassination.

After a typical litany of his accomplishments and programs, Clinton turned his attention to the issues of black-on-black crime, teenage pregnancy, and the decline of the traditional family, especially in the black community. It was Bill Clinton at his very best, addressing deep social and cultural problems in a way that showed sensitivity and enough chutzpah to tell a black audience that it had deep responsibilities of its own. It was only a speech, worth little alone, but it represented Clinton's potential in one area of moral leadership, and it distinguished him from his immediate predecessors, none of whom could be imagined connecting as well or speaking as directly or comfortably to that audience about those subjects.

Here is part of what he said:

". . . I guess what I really want to say to you today, my fellow Americans, is that we can do all of this and still fail unless we meet the great crisis of spirit that is gripping America today. . . .

"If Martin Luther King, who said, 'Like Moses, I am on the mountaintop and I can see the promised land, but I'm not going to be able to be there with you, but we will get there'—if he were to reappear by my side today and give us a report card on the last twenty-five years, what would he say? He would say . . . you did a good job in opening opportunity.

"But he would say, I did not live and die to see the American family destroyed. I did not live and die to see thirteen-year-old boys get automatic weapons and gun down nine-year-olds just for the kick of it. I did not live and die to see young people destroy their own lives with drugs and then build fortunes destroying the lives of others. That is not what I came here to do.

"I fought for freedom, he would say, but not for the freedom of people to kill each other with reckless abandon; not for the freedom of children to have children and the fathers of the children walk away from them and abandon them as if they don't amount to anything. I fought for people to have the right to work, but not to have whole communities and people abandoned. This is not what I lived and died for.

"My fellow Americans, he would say, I fought to stop white people from being so filled with hate that they would wreak violence on black people. I did not fight for the right of black people to murder other black people with reckless abandon. . . .

"The freedom to do that kind of thing is not what Martin Luther King lived and died for. It's not what people gathered in this hallowed church for the night before he was assassinated in April of 1968. If you had told anybody who was here in that church on that night that we would abuse our freedom in that way, they would have found it hard to believe. And I tell you it is our moral duty to turn it around. . . .

"And there is something for each of us to do. There are changes we can make from the outside in—that's the job of the president and the Congress and the governors and the mayors and the social service agencies. Then there's some changes we're going to have to make from the inside out, or the others won't matter. That's what that magnificent song was about, wasn't it? Sometimes there are no answers from the outside in; sometimes all the answers have to come from values and stirrings and the voices that speak to us from within. . . .

"So I say to you, we have to make a partnership—all the government agencies, all the business folks—but where there are no families, where there is no order, where there is no hope, where we are reducing the size of our armed services because we have won the Cold War—who will be there to give structure, discipline, and love to these children? You must do that. And we must help you.

"Scripture says, 'You are the salt of the earth and the light of the world.' That if your light shines before men they will give glory to the Father in heaven. That is what we must do. How would we explain it to Martin Luther King if he showed up today and said: Yes, we won the Cold War. Yes, the biggest threat that all of us grew up under, communism and nuclear war—communism gone; nuclear war receding. Yes, we developed all these miraculous technologies. Yes, we all have got a VCR in our home. It's interesting. Yes, we get fifty channels on the cable. Yes, without regard to race, if you work hard and play by the rules, you can get into a service academy or a good college, you'll do just great.

"How could we explain to him all these kids getting killed and killing each other? How would we justify the things that we permit that no other country in the world would permit? How could we explain that we gave people the freedom to succeed and we created conditions in which millions abuse that freedom to destroy the things that make life worth living and life itself? We cannot.

"And so I say to you today, my fellow Americans, you gave me this job. And we're making progress on the things you hired me to do. But unless we deal with the ravages of crime and drugs and violence and unless we recognize that it's due to the breakdown of the family, the community and the disappearance of jobs, and unless we say some of this cannot be done by government because we have to reach deep inside to the values, the spirit, the soul and the truth of human nature, none of the other things we seek to do will ever take us where we need to go."

This wasn't the Gettysburg Address. It wasn't particularly eloquent, at least in its transcribed form. But it was gritty and honest, dramatic in delivery. It was the President of the United States speaking from the spot where Dr. Martin Luther King, Jr., had spoken. It was delivered with passion to a group not accustomed to rapport with a president of the United States. It confronted real issues with an effective combination of personal connection and lecture, and it was applauded enthusiastically.

Bill Clinton had a first year in the White House that looked awful along the way—miscalculations and blunders abounding—but ended with a record of solid accomplishment and reasonably inspiring rhetoric that addressed vital issues. The problem was that all he had done and said was diluted by lingering uncertainty about who and what he was.

In fifteen years spent studying Bill Clinton, I had identified seven of him. I liked and respected four of him.

These were the Bill Clintons I liked:

- The talented, well-meaning, and accomplished public servant who believed with charmingly boyish enthusiasm and optimism in the nobility of public service and the morality of his public policies. "Don't let it get you down; you've got to keep the faith," he told me at the end of a telephone conversation in 1981, when he was out of office, after I had expressed my despair over Reaganism.

- The traditional liberal, a civil libertarian who believed a better life could come from government activism and social engineering.

- The pragmatic centrist, the "new Democrat," which, I finally became convinced, was more a result of his innovative and original thinking than an exercise in electoral tactics, though, naturally, it was partly tactical.

- The private person demonstrating compassion, emotionalism, and an uncanny ability to connect and empathize with all kinds of people, especially blacks.

But there were three other Bill Clintons:

- An insecure, overgrown boy, who seemed to lack grounding or certainty about who or what he was.

- A man utterly devoid of personal discipline, who acted impulsively and self-indulgently, eating too much, pursuing women, cutting corners, disregarding the basic courtesy to others of staying on a schedule, and waking up each day without regard for whatever commitments he may have made the day before.

- Finally there was a self-absorbed, hot-tempered, calculating, manipulative politician who gained personal validation by winning votes and adulation and could all too easily tell less than the truth to protect himself in the only arena that seemed to matter to him in the end, the political one. This Clinton was inexcusably abusive to the people around him. He could allow his campaign to play a dirty trick on Paul Tsongas in Florida, with last-minute pamphlets and radio commercials misrepresenting Tsongas's views on Israel and Society Security, then speak privately about his great admiration for the honor and integrity of the man he had wronged.

If he was essentially admitting that he had less honor and integrity, he never let on.

Was he ever introspective about such things? Once on the campaign trail Clinton instigated a conversation about whether it was ever permissible to lie, but it turned into mostly an intellectual exercise about what he had read and heard on the subject. His good friend from high school, David Leopoulos, says Clinton asked him during the heat of the 1992 primary campaign, "Am I too slick?" Leopoulos said no. One hopes that wasn't the end of it. Once Clinton became engaged in conversation with a man named Tom McRae, who he had vanquished in a governor's race. Clinton intellectually analyzed the race blow-by-blow, finally detailing one of his tactics and pronouncing it the crowning blow. "Yeah, but that wasn't true," said McRae, introducing a fact to the conversation that Clinton dismissed with a wave of the hand as if to say, "So what?"

What one thinks of Bill Clinton depends on which version one finds most defining, most endearing, most distressing, or most disgusting. I know conservatives who despise him for his liberalism. I know liberals who despise him for his expedient centrism. I know lifelong friends who swear by his goodness and greatness. I know lifelong acquaintances who say he was self-absorbed in kindergarten and never changed. I know people who find him the most inspiring person they know. I know others who eschew my use of euphemism and call him a character-flawed hollow man—a liar.

As I began to write this last chapter, a friend of Clinton's told me, "You're down to the hard part now. Who is he? It's not like a newspaper column you can change the next day. I don't envy you." Yes, this man was Clinton's friend. He liked the president, but he, too, found him hard to figure.

Two points should be made.

First, for reasons beyond his control, Clinton endured a level of public scrutiny and personal critique not applied to previous presidents. He endured it largely because of the era in which he happened to ascend to the White House. America had other presidents who shaded the truth and were flawed in character, but most of them were judged by a standard based on public performance and public behavior. It was true that presidents since George Washington had been attacked and subjected to rumor, but no other president was beset as was Clinton

by the immediacy, saturation, and viciousness of the Information Age—
by home computer news services, by Rush Limbaugh and other radio
talk shows, by 24-hour news operations, and by a mainstream media
that decided in the post-Nixon, post-Hart age to search the depths of
a president's soul, looking for darkness and sin. Clinton was the second
president to come along in the post-Hart era as it evolved into the era
of information saturation. But he was the first interesting presidential
subject to come along in that era.

Second, criticizing the president is an American pastime, but Clinton
offered an especially juicy target because of his age and eagerness to
please. His age made him the first presidential contemporary of leading
mainstream journalists. Over the years in Arkansas I had criticized
Clinton with a frequency and fervor that I did not apply to older
Democratic politicians in the state, such as Senators Bumpers and Pryor,
though they sometimes behaved as expediently or disingenuously. Part
of it had to do with the fact that Clinton was the local story while
Bumpers and Pryor were in Washington. But, yes, Clinton's age had
something to do with it. I didn't quite respect him as much as I respected
more mature figures. Clinton's eagerness to please compounded the
image of one not worthy of respect. It served to make critics feel
powerful. A self-assured politician who never responded to journalistic
criticism was much less fun to pick on than one who had a translucent
need for approval and would let you get under his skin. It was as if
Clinton, like an unpopular schoolchild, wore a sign on his backside
that read: "Kick me."

And kick him we did.

That said, who is he?

In fifteen years of close observation I concluded that Bill Clinton
was a special politician, the best of his generation, who was motivated
by the need for ego gratification that drives many to electoral politics,
afflicted a bit more severely than was politically normal to convenient
disregard for the whole truth, a public work-in-progress who learned
and matured in full view of voters; but a decent person committed to
the idea that he could do good works in public office, uncommonly
talented in public policy, and a man whose glaring foibles, while exasperating and making him not at all likable, were neither dark nor
malignant.

His budget bill was credible. His trade policies were credible. His ability to identify, articulate, and address the nation's problems was credible. His presidency deserved credibility, even if he didn't, quite.

What he needed as he entered his second year was to be granted enough credibility to be allowed to apply his political and policy skills to an assignment for which he was fully capable: leading the country through changing times toward the twenty-first century. What he also needed was to follow his practical instinct to adhere to the political center and behave as a "new Democrat," because that worked. What he also needed was to grow into a more certain man, less susceptible to the breeze, more quietly assured when things went wrong, less cocky when things went right. Surely the personal trials of the presidency could help with that.

The other thing Clinton needed was a staff that served him more effectively—handled him better—than was the case in his first presidential year. That meant he needed to resubmit to personal control, to baby-sitting, if you will.

The "collegial" White House wasn't effective; no one seemed in charge. Someone around Clinton should have had the power and good sense to veto a runway haircut; someone should have had the constant access and good sense to stop Clinton before he telephoned state troopers in Arkansas to talk even indirectly about jobs for some of their colleagues rumored to be going public with charges about his personal life; someone should have had the access and control to convince him— and Hillary, too—that the appearance of stonewalling on Whitewater would only exacerbate his problems. (David Gergen reportedly gave that very advice, but by the end of Clinton's first year, Gergen's value had been pretty much used up and his star was in decline.)

Among Hillary, Al Gore, George Stephanopoulos, Mack McLarty, Bruce Lindsey, and Gergen, there were too many "handlers" and not enough handling. Clinton had an uncommonly powerful wife, an uncommonly powerful vice president, a chief of staff, two senior advisers, and a "counselor to the president." The idea was that with his extraordinary mental ability, he would synthesize brilliantly by borrowing parts from all. It could work intellectually. It could work in developing policy, as it did from mid-year onward through a troika of Gergen, McLarty, and Stephanopoulos: Gergen and McLarty pushed Clinton to go all-out on NAFTA; Stephanopoulos balked; Clinton embraced the majority position and rehabilitated himself and his presidency temporarily. But it couldn't work in developing strategy and tactics; one of the advisers giving smart counsel on what McLarty called the "intersection of policy and politics" ran the risk of being overridden by another giving bad counsel. And it couldn't work in doing the job most vital in the White House, "managing up," as McLarty called it, to keep the president on schedule, in focus, and out of trouble.

The job I am describing, baby-sitting the president, was performed for most of the year by George Stephanopoulos, who had a special rapport with Clinton. But his political advice tended to be to the left, which didn't serve well Clinton's political need to be a "new Democrat." And at this writing Stephanopoulos was under fire for making an indiscreet call to a friend at the Treasury Department to complain about the hiring of a former Republican prosecutor, which served as a reminder that, at thirty-three, Stephanopoulos was rather young to be the president's baby-sitter.

Stephanopoulos was joined in the handling role late in the year by Clinton's longtime friend and Little Rock confidant, Bruce Lindsey. But Lindsey spent too much of his time leading the defense against Whitewater allegations, and the fact was that he was traveling with Clinton on the day the president sat for a politically devastating haircut on the runway of Los Angeles International Airport. A Clinton staffer in Arkansas said a few days after that incident: "I told Bruce he wouldn't be tough enough."

The most comforting addition to the White House staff came in March 1994: the wise, Washington-seasoned Lloyd Cutler was named chief counsel to replace the disastrous Bernie Nussbaum. But Cutler took the job only on a temporary basis. Someone like him would be needed on a longer-term basis if this presidency was to succeed.

Around April, as the Whitewater affair raged in the press, Clinton began to accept the need for stronger control both of himself and his White House. For a time White House officials told the press that Mack McLarty had assumed a more autocratic role in directing the White House staff and operation. But by June, with health care in big trouble, the president's boyhood friend from Hope began wondering whether he was the right man to be chief of staff. He had hesitated about taking the job in the first place and was genuinely surprised when Clinton offered it. The thinking in Arkansas had been that he might become energy secretary, tapping his experience in the natural gas industry.

McLarty had a strong ego and a burning desire to succeed; "he has spent his life building a solid reputation," his top aide, Bill Burton, said. But he didn't seem to need the typical high profile or the protected turf of the modern-day chief of staff. His management style was predicated on getting the right people in the right job, and that extended to himself. He also had an extraordinary loyalty to the well-being of Clinton, about whom he would make only the mildest constructive criticisms. He also remembered that James Baker, chief of staff to both Reagan and Bush, and the only successful presidential chief of staff in a decade, had advised him that two years was long enough for anyone in the job.

McLarty's White House, open and collegial by design, appeared unsuitable for the culture of Washington, where events could spin out of control unless there was a single dominant finger on the pulse, if not the dike. (And they would spin out of control even then.) That was especially true with a president at the hub who loved nothing more than intellectual byplay, tried to make too many decisions himself, and was agonizingly indecisive. For his part, McLarty was neither a commanding figure nor an incisive political thinker. His strengths were cautious efficiency and simple decency.

McLarty had told friends that the job of the White House chief of staff was an improbable mix: to "manage up," meaning to the president himself, and "manage down," meaning to the staff. In early June he mentioned to Clinton that perhaps a change was needed to separate those tasks. Leon Panetta, the affable but combative director of the Office of Management and Budget, had more than two decades of Beltway experience, both as a Nixon Republican and then a leading Democratic congressman. He knew the city and its culture; he knew Capitol Hill; he was a confirmed moderate and deficit hawk, like McLarty, and he had an extraordinary ability to be gregarious and firm at the same time. His only public flaw as director of OMB had been speaking too candidly about the Clinton administration's congressional prospects to a group of Washington journalists. Clinton quickly forgave him. Panetta was an interesting possibility for chief of staff, McLarty said.

Clinton was receptive, perhaps a bit more receptive than McLarty might have preferred. It is impossible to imagine Clinton firing or reassigning McLarty; it was up to McLarty to recommend it.

On Saturday, June 25, 1994, McLarty telephoned me for what appeared to be a courtesy chat. He said health care reform was dangling by a thread. Then he began talking about Clinton, describing him as "melancholy lately" and regretful that he and McLarty hadn't spent as much time together as they had expected. McLarty said he suspected that Clinton wanted him around more often as a security blanket, as "someone to look to and ask, 'Do you think he's duping me here?' "

"So I'm going to find a way to spend more time with him," McLarty said.

That was his euphemistic way of intimating what was about to happen. It also was his way of putting his own advance spin on impending events.

Two days later, Clinton named Leon Panetta his new chief of staff. McLarty became counselor to the president, replacing the used-up David Gergen, who simply could not get along with Hillary Clinton and who was shipped out to a State Department job for the remainder of 1994.

Washington reacted as expected, portraying McLarty as failed and exiled. But Washington had made the same assessment the year before when George Stephanopoulos was reassigned, only to be shown wrong. Stephanopoulos was promoted to a more valuable spot. McLarty wasn't in any way promoted, but he was in a more valuable spot if he would "manage up" to the president and tug him toward the political center while Panetta tried his hand at running the Clinton White House.

Finally, a word about Whitewater. Assuming Clinton survives it without being indicted or damaged irreparably, the central question will be how he reacts. His arrogance may lead him to deem himself invincible, in which case he will have learned nothing and will plunge forward into the same mistakes. Or, as a public work-in-progress, he could take lessons from the experience. He could and should learn that attempted secrecy never works in Washington; that spin-control should be a mere element of governing, not an obsession; that hyper-critical or overstated rhetoric about morality extracts a price; and that Americans seek truth and strength in their president—and expect him to find it in himself as well.

If Bill Clinton is incapable of sustained error, as some say, and as I tend to agree, he will learn the lessons. The presidency may make a better man of him yet.

EPILOGUE

Credibility Is Like Beauty

My manuscript deadline passed without a second interview with Bill Clinton, much less the "two or three" additional visits he had suggested without solicitation. I went home to Little Rock, which Robert Fiske, the special counsel investigating the matters known as Whitewater, had called "the center of gravity." At least one staff member had encouraged Clinton to ring me up when he was in Hot Springs in March to visit his late mother's husband, Dick Kelley. Clinton had nodded, and I had waited near a telephone for a weekend, though I knew that in Clinton's body language, a nod could mean no, as indeed it had.

The absence of a second visit suited my theme, actually. I had no right to expect even one exclusive interview with a President of the United States whose campaign and career I had criticized and who had far more pressing matters on his agenda. But he was the one who had suggested two or three more sessions, typically aiming to please or placate without sufficient regard for the need not to make hollow statements. I had no right to be angry or even disappointed. But I did have the right to illustrate a central point about Bill Clinton. Nothing could more clearly explain his defining foible, which is the seemingly incurable tendency to try to please at the moment without sufficient regard for commitments later.

Then, on April 14, two weeks after the manuscript deadline, Nancy Hernreich, the Oval Office gatekeeper and a longtime acquaintance from Fort Smith, telephoned. The president wondered if I would still like a second interview. Did I mention that he's always late?

Certainly I could work the president into my schedule and make arrangements to amend or amplify the text.

What had come over him? I could only wonder. It was possible, one person close to him said, that he simply woke up that morning in a new world in which he remembered having promised me another interview. It was conceivable that in that new world, he thought of the good things I had written about him instead of the bad. There was plenty of both. Or it was possible that he had a purpose—that there were things he wanted to say, and a book such as this offered a suitable forum. Or maybe Mack McLarty shamed him into it. There was always that.

At any rate, when I received a telephone call from the Oval Office eighteen days later, on May 2, I thanked the president and told him that I understood that he had no obligation. He responded not with "you're quite welcome" but by asking about the weather in Little Rock.

This was not an especially pleasant time for Clinton, though the specific issues known as Whitewater seemed to be abating and speculation grew that Clinton had no strictly legal problem in those matters of horrible judgment. He was under wide attack for foreign policy vacillation and weakness. Demonstrators in Washington protested his Haitian policy, declaring his refusal to accept refugees racist. He had reprised his pattern of tough talk and hollow delivery in regard to the Bosnian Serbs. Joe Klein, a writer for *Newsweek* who had adored Clinton during the campaign and differed with me when I criticized Clinton's tendency toward expediency, had written an article in the latest issue assailing Clinton's "politics of promiscuity" and declaring that the president's basic character flaws affected the credibility not only of the man, but of the president. (Klein seemed afflicted by my old pattern: adore, detest, adore, detest.) A twenty-seven-year-old woman named Paula Corbin Jones, who once worked as a clerk in the Arkansas Industrial Development Commission, was preparing to file a lawsuit alleging that in May 1991, Clinton, with his face "red as a beet," sexually harassed her in a hotel room in Little Rock, dropping his pants without invitation and asking her to perform oral sex. Clinton denied it all and explained her emergence as the handiwork of the well-funded right-wing attack machine.

These were strange and unsettling times. We were hearing things about this president of a nature that we had never heard about past presidents, at least not while they were in office trying to lead the country. The president and I would get around to discussing that.

But first I told him that I had used the word "coast" to refer to his first-year desire in foreign policy; that is, that he had hoped to coast through foreign policy while pressing his touted domestic agenda, not unlike Ronald Reagan's desire in 1981. I suspected he would differ with the choice of verb. He suggested "contain" as a better choice than "coast."

"Yeah—let me try to characterize how I saw it," he said. "I wanted to be able to devote most of the first year to dealing with the domestic problems of the country that I thought were necessary to strengthen us so that we could formulate and carry out a successful foreign policy in the post–Cold War world, and so that it would be consistent with what we were doing here at home.

"And I knew that that would require a whole series of struggles in the Congress that would take a lot of my intense personal effort and a lot of my personal involvement in the development of policy like health care and welfare reform and other things. So I had hoped that in the first year there would be no unmanageable crises.

"Now, that does not mean that I wanted to coast in the sense of not being involved, because I had basically the following things that I hoped would happen the first year.

"Number one, I wanted to put our relationship with Russia on a very strong footing and continue the work of denuclearizing the former Soviet Union. And even though things have changed in Russia, I think that was the right policy and it's been largely successful.

"Number two, I wanted to pass a new and streamlined defense program that would still meet our defense needs, and, therefore, would be adequately funded.

"And number three, I wanted to try to take some of the problems that I have been bequeathed and at least make them better. I wanted to successfully terminate our involvement in Somalia, and it was more costly than I had hoped it would be. But, still, I think it's hard to quarrel with the proposition that we shouldn't have been there forever, and that there had to come a time when the U.N. would take over for the U.S. And the thing has not fallen apart completely yet, so it may not. So I think that we did our job there. I wanted to try to involve the United States more in partnership with Europe to try to contain the war in Bosnia, to Bosnia, first of all; and then secondly, hopefully to get a fair and decent peace negotiation. So I think we've been successful in containing it. We got—two of the parties agreed with one another, and we're nowhere near home on the other one, although we've made maybe some progress. And then the third thing I wanted to do was to try to restore democracy in Haiti, which I have not been able to do. I just—I have failed to do it. It was a difficult thing. And there was no consensus when the Governors Island agreement was breached [to reinstate Aristide]—no consensus within this country or within our allies in the Caribbean and Latin America that the United States should unilaterally try to change the outcome there. So we've been on a different course, which has basically not succeeded. And I'm reexamining that now.

"But I wanted to be able to do that in a way that I wouldn't say coasted through foreign policy but contained it, so I could put more than half my energies and intensity into these other things. As we came forward toward the end of the year, and, you know, after Mother died, you know, then I had that trip to Europe for NATO and to Russia, stopping in Prague and Kiev and then going on to Geneva to meet with Assad. It's obvious to anybody that this year we're going to have to do more. So this year, I've spent a lot more time on foreign policy."

Otherwise, my interests were more of a personal than a policy nature. What was it about Clinton that, as a friend of his once put it, "pisses people off"? What was it about the 1990s, or about Clinton, or both, that led to his personal life being laid bare? And, toughest of all, just what about his credibility?

In his responses he assigned all of that to a loss of civility and an alarming tendency toward character assassination—"moral annihilation," E. J. Dionne had called it—in modern-day partisan politics by right-wing hate groups, the effect of which was exacerbated in the era of instant saturation of information. He sounded partly paranoid, but mostly insightful. As the old saying goes, "Just because you're paranoid doesn't mean someone is not out to get you." Despite my prodding, he declined to engage in much personal psychoanalysis, saying he would leave that to me. And he said his fight for survival was a fight for the very future of decency and decorum in American politics.

Here are some of the relevant discussions:

Q: "I make the point in this book that there's something about you that causes people—that bugs people. I read or saw an interview with Richard Nixon, and he said some politicians are destined to be widely disliked and others just naturally get a great deal of affection. Do you think that's true? And do you think my observation is fair or correct?"

Clinton: "I think both of them are true of me. I mean, I've always had fanatic supporters and strong opponents, always—even when I started out. I think the quality of public discourse has deteriorated pretty significantly in the last few years. But if you remember when I ran for Congress in '74, I had all these strong supporters who became the bedrock of every campaign I ran thereafter. But I also had all these people who spread that tree story on me. You remember that?"

[As the study went, Clinton sat in a tree on the campus of the University of Arkansas at Fayetteville in 1969 to protest the Vietnam War. Clinton was at Oxford at the time, and the press eventually identified the young man who actually sat in the tree. It wasn't Clinton. In 1986, the old warrior, former Governor Orval Faubus, made one last-ditch attempt at a political comeback, challenging Clinton and losing overwhelmingly. In his campaign, Faubus put the tree story in this perspective: "I never said he sat in a tree. I don't know if the boy can climb a tree."]

Clinton: "And they just thought it would have been the end of life as we know it if I had been elected to Congress. So I just—there's always been that."

Q: "Why do you think that is?"

Clinton: "Oh, I don't know. I really don't know. Part of it is nobody likes everybody, and part of it is, I think, nearly anybody who's got a lot of strong supporters has people that don't like him. It's almost like a law of physics. And I think that I sometimes get the worst of both worlds. I lay out real ambitious agendas and I try to get them done. And the people that don't agree with me are threatened by it and really don't like me. And the people that do agree with me sometimes hold it against me if I don't get it all done or if I have to compromise or make the democratic system work to get it done.

"And I think part of it is, you know—I mean, there may

be other reasons, too. There may be a lot of reasons. Your judgment would be better than mine on that."

Q: "I remember you told me once there were things about being governor you can only learn by doing it. That's got to be exponentially true of the presidency."

Clinton: "Absolutely true. And I think a lot of it is you don't—you know, for example, a lot of this about me not seeming to be candid and not anticipating what people want to know, and all that kind of stuff on this Whitewater stuff was plainly a case of that. If you remember back in 1990 when I released ten years of my tax returns—I think I was the first governor to do that. I always thought I was going above and beyond the call. So by the time I got here, I'd released thirteen years of tax returns. I think I just missed a lot of the cultural cues and the sort of deep-seated cynicism that had kind of gotten into the atmosphere up here."

To ease into the difficult subject of personal credibility, I related to Clinton the four questions that would decide the political and policy success of his presidency: the state of the economy, whether he ended gridlock, whether he proved to be a "new Democrat," and whether he had enough credibility, as a president and a man, to lead.

On the economy: "We've got stable and strong growth and the fundamentals to continue it. . . . You've got twice as much private sector job growth in this first fifteen months of this administration than in the previous four years. I think last year's low interest rates and deficit-reduction triggered that. I also think there's a lot of other good things that will have huge long-term benefits: changes in the tax system giving roughly one-sixth of the working families in the country a tax credit through the earned income tax credit. . . . So we're doing very well on that, I think. You know, you still have two big problems with the economy, and one is that there's still a lot of regional and, within regions, other differences between cities and rural areas, for example. There's still some places that haven't felt any recovery. And the second you've got is the income inequality problem, which has been developing over twenty years, which will be partly alleviated by the earned income tax credit, but over the long run has to be changed by a dramatic increase in education and training of the entire American workforce. So on that score I think we're doing fine."

On ending gridlock: "We've got a very good batting average. Depending on how you count, we did better than any first year since either Johnson or Eisenhower, and I think you could argue that our issues were harder than either one of them in the first year. It's been sixty years since a president went a year without vetoing a bill."

On whether he is a "new Democrat": "I think we have been successful, but not as successful as I would like. Last year at the DLC meeting I read a list of all the things that they asked me to do that we've done, and it's a very long list. I mean, favoring work over welfare: that's what the earned income tax credit was all about. National service was one of the biggest things that the Democratic Leadership Council was for. It's government empowering people instead of just doing something. We passed the empowerment zone legislation. The crime bill has the community policing in it and a lot of other things that I think are very good. And we took on NAFTA and GATT. We passed the GATT thing at the end of the year. So I think far more of that new Democrat than not [had been implemented]. We've had two problems with making the new Democrat theme go all the way—one is political and one is financial. We could have had a better new Democrat record if the Republicans hadn't decided on the front end to boycott the budget. And to boycott some other things that we've done. And, secondly, to finish the new Democrat agenda you're got to pass welfare reform, and the problem there is that under our budget rules, it's hard to pay for that and the GATT thing and everything else at one time."

I mentioned that his health plan was more liberal than that of the DLC, and he replied: "We got the managed competition that they favor. But like the DLC advocated, having coverage for everybody, and understanding that you could never control costs and stop it from bankrupting the budget unless you had coverage, they never came to grips with how to get it [paid for]. If there were easy decisions, they would have been done a long time ago. And I think that by trying to address it all in a big, comprehensive bill, we held ourselves open to looking like it was too much government. I think that's the big rap on the health care thing. But I think we can fix it as we go along."

In the "new Democrat" context, he added that he still wanted to fashion some kind of middle-class tax cut, perhaps based on child care costs, before the end of his term. Irresponsible though it be, Americans should look for such a sop to the middle class as election time nears. They also should demand that he pay for it elsewhere to keep from raising the deficit.

That left the question of credibility, both as a minority president and as a man who bore the nickname "Slick Willie." We were back where we began, in a real-life psychodrama with judgment reserved.

"On the credibility thing, I think it just depends on—it's almost like beauty—it's more or less in the eyes of the beholder," he said.

"I think if you define it in terms of having a clear vision about where we ought to go and trying to get it done and fighting for it and getting a high percentage of it done, then I ought to have high credibility. If you define it in terms of mistakes that were made operationally, or trying to do things that didn't work out, like not getting the Europeans to go along with not lifting the arms embargo, or what happened with Lani Guinier and Zoe Baird where we had vetting mix-ups, or the gays in the military—it just depends on whether you think I should have signed an executive order and had it overridden. I think again, it just depends on how you view it.

"And on the personal credibility thing, I mean, certainly, I've done what I said I'd do. I've worked hard and tried to get done what I said I'd get done. We haven't solved some of the thorniest problems of foreign policy and I have continued to be under the most relentless assault, probably, of any president ever, in highly personal ways. But that's obviously part of their strategy. Someday when we've got time to talk about it, I'll tell you the whole story. You can make another whole book on that."

By saying "their" strategy, did he mean the Republicans?

"Yes," he answered. "And the right. And the extreme right. You can go back to the campaign and realize that one of the things that they realized was that I had a record and a message and a vision for this country very different from what had been offered before, and that one of the ways to deal with it was just try to assault me personally. And it's been reckless and intense. It started in the campaign, and for the first time, I guess ever, there was no cessation when I took office. If anything it just stepped up. *The Wall Street Journal* basically said they're just sort of determined to try to act as if the election hadn't occurred, as if I was some usurper, that there was no legitimacy to the outcome of the vote. And never mind the electoral vote victory or what all the polls showed would have happened if Perot hadn't been in there. They were just mad that I won. And I think that the relentless assault that they have made, and the fact that some of that breathes back into the regular press, has obviously taken its toll.

"And I think I've had a few bad breaks, too. For example, you and Greenberg [the editorial page editor of the *Arkansas Democrat-Gazette*] might call me 'Slick Willie,' but that huge majority of newspaper editors in Arkansas endorsed me every time I ran for office; most of them liked me. But the *Arkansas Gazette* [a liberal newspaper] is out of business now. So when all the Washington press corps goes down there trying to do an assessment, they don't really have a picture of the people that shaped, or at least expressed the opinions of the voters during most of the time I was governor."

I felt a need to defend the *Democrat-Gazette* and did so by saying it was not nearly as transparently partisan as the *Washington Times,* which, actually, wasn't an especially strong line of defense.

"Oh, no," Clinton responded. "That's because the *Washington Times* is part of the national right-wing movement. It was a Moonie paper. No, you've got the editorial page of *The Journal,* the *Washington Times,* Rush Limbaugh, Pat Robertson, Jerry Falwell, the Christian Radio Network, the *American Spectator,* and the Floyd Brown operation. They are all part of a national thing which has access to unlimited money, and has basically poured it into Arkansas as part of their sort of national strategy. It's a spooky thing, really. The Democrats have nothing to contend with it. Nothing."

I suggested to him that perhaps political pragmatism demanded that his opponents hit him on the issue of credibility. I said that of the four questions I raised, he was potentially vulnerable only on that one.

"On what?" he asked.

"On credibility," I replied.

"But it's interesting because the people who knew me for twelve years—nobody ever accused me of being dishonest," he said.

(The statement simply was not true, though I hardly wished to contest it directly over the telephone. The one charge heard in Arkansas more than any other was that he wouldn't tell the truth, and it's eerie that Clinton would say or see otherwise. My best explanation, or hypothesis, is that he equates "dishonest" with "crooked," but that he doesn't use "dishonest" in regard to clever, evasive, or misleading political rhetoric, which he dismisses as the simple business of politics. It was quite true that over a dozen years in Arkansas no one ever seriously charged that he was on the take or in any way crooked.)

On the other hand, Clinton quite correctly said: "A lot of the folks who have come out against me have been covered with sleaze. Their motives, their evidence, and their information are suspect. But it doesn't matter. They just figure that on a personal deal, if they hit you hard enough, you can just take a certain number of people away.

"Other presidents have been subject to this, but never in an environment in which information was drenched across the country. People said terrible things about Thomas Jefferson and Franklin Roosevelt. One newspaper editor suggested in an editorial it would be better if Lincoln was assassinated rather than re-elected. They had hard stuff. What they said about Franklin and Eleanor Roosevelt would curl the back of your hair. But it was never subject to mass distribution, and certainly highly personal attacks never found their way from the right wing back into the mainstream media. So I think that's the difference in the time in which we live.

"I'll tell you one thing: If it works on me, then the Democrats will take it up and then nobody will ever have a restful moment again. I mean, you know, in a way, I feel like by surviving and continuing to do my job, I'm fighting for a decent political order in America. Because if this sort of thing prevails, then you're just going to have a mud fight from now on. I mean, really, the implications of it are pretty troubling when you consider what the government ought to be doing and what the president ought to be thinking about.

"I'm going to try to endure it: get up and show up for work every day."

We were truly back where we began, with a young minority president who is a public work-in-progress. The pure political talent of this young president frightened his opponents and led them to venomous assaults to try to destroy him lest he rearrange the American political landscape as the country embarked on the twenty-first century.

Clinton had told staff intimates and friends that he saw "character" not as a permanent condition, but as a struggle and a progression. Of course it is that. But some people certainly aimed for an earlier permanence. Surely Americans would feel more at ease if their president had been less beset by fluidity of character by the time he moved into the White House to lead the country through a changing world. One gets the idea that Abraham Lincoln, Teddy Roosevelt, Harry Truman— even Jimmy Carter—had a pretty good idea who and what they were by the time they took their positions.

Alas, the rest of us grow up in private without the weight of the world on our shoulders. Bill Clinton grows up in front of us as he tries to lead us.

So it is with the forty-second President of the United States. In time perhaps he can use the Whitewater experience to take personal stock rather than strike out at the campaign of moral annihilation being waged against him.

I must close, then, as I closed before. The presidency might make a better man of him yet. And if the little Arkansas drama plays out fully on Pennsylvania Avenue, defeating him in 1996 wouldn't get rid of him. At the youthful age of fifty, with his character a matter of continuing progression, he'd surely come back à la Nixon for us to kick around some more.

A postscript, late June 1994:

Ending on the personal note, the matter of Clinton's character, might be appropriate, since that seemed to be the source of America's fascination. But it seems fairer and more responsible to conclude with policy.

Remember the five priorities listed in February 1993 by Mack McLarty: The economy and deficit reduction, health care, campaign finance reform, welfare reform, and national service. Let's take a look.

Clinton's economic plan was by most objective assessments a success, although interest rates were climbing. Campaign finance reform was tied up in a House-Senate conference committee, perhaps never to be heard from again in a culture in which incumbents simply wouldn't severely limit their extensive political advantages. Clinton was parading to soft-money fund-raisers, which he had vowed to end, explaining that the Democrats needn't disarm unilaterally. Welfare reform finally had been introduced but couldn't be pushed for months because budget constraints required that the Clinton administration first find a way to fund the provisions of the General Agreement on Tariffs and Trade. National service had been passed, and Clinton, in our May interview, was encouraged at the prospect that participation would exceed in numbers the early stages of participation in the Peace Corps.

That left health care reform, the defining issue for the First Couple and one that, at this writing, was perilously close to being lost. The highwire act of the first year's budget battle was being revisited on health care. "It's like a car perched on a cliff," Mack McLarty said. He complained that the plan had been demonized unfairly as leftist by Republican rhetoric, a reprise of what happened to the budget. Even as a leading White House moderate, McLarty insisted that the only credible way to extend health care coverage to the uninsured was to pay for it, and that the only credible way to pay for it was to require a combination of employer and personal contributions for every American. That's universal coverage. He feared it wouldn't happen. It might even be that Congress would send Clinton an incrementally progressive health care reform bill he would have to veto, first on the principle that it wasn't fiscally sound and second because he had boxed himself in by vowing a veto for any legislation that failed to provide health insurance to all Americans. That dramatic vow of a veto was a political mistake, one encouraged by Mrs. Clinton, again strong on policy while weak on politics.

Losing health care would be a severe blow. Clinton would appear anemic against the old forces of gridlock. He could cite accomplishments in other areas—trade, gun control, and crime, primarily. But if he could not hold a Rose Garden ceremony to sign a health care reform bill, his political fortunes for the remainder of his term would be left to hinge exclusively on matters sometimes beyond his control: the unpredictability of the economy as interest rates rose, foreign affairs troubles, and public assessments of his character and credibility. He would be down, but, as always, not out.

INDEX